AF661598

HISTORY
OF
AMERICAN LITERATURE

HISTORY OF AMERICAN LITERATURE

P. K. Sinha
Jagdish K. Ghosh

Commonwealth

History of American Literature

© Reserved

Edition : 2023

ISBN 978-81-311-0321-0

Published by :
COMMONWEALTH PUBLISHERS PVT. LTD.
4831/24, Prahlad Street,
Ansari Road, Darya Ganj,
New Delhi - 110002
Ph. : 23275511, 23257835
Fax : 91- 011- 23257835
e-mail : commonwealthbooks@gmail.com

Laser Typesetting by :
Arnav Computers
Delhi

Printed at :
Roshan Offset Printers
Delhi

Preface

American literature is the written or literary work produced in the area of the United States and its preceding colonies. During its early history, America was a series of British colonies on the eastern coast of the present-day United States. Therefore, its literary tradition begins as linked to the broader tradition of English literature. However, unique American characteristics and the breadth of its production usually now cause it to be considered a separate path and tradition.

Some of the earliest forms of American literature were pamphlets and writings extolling the benefits of the colonies to both a European and colonist audience. Captain John Smith could be considered the first American author. Other writers of this manner included Daniel Denton, Thomas Ashe, William Penn, George Percy, William Strachey, Daniel Coxe, Gabriel Thomas, and John Lawson.

The present book comprehensively explains the historical development of American literature. It aims to provide education, entertainment and enlightenment to the readers. It is intended for advanced level students of literature, who are taking exams or modules in this field. It may also be suitable for teachers, researchers and the general reader who is interested in the history of literature.

Authors

Contents

1

Introduction

American literature is the written or literary work produced in the area of the United States and Colonial America. For more specific discussions of poetry and theater. During its early history, America was a series of British colonies on the eastern coast of the present-day United States. Therefore, its literary tradition begins as linked to the broader tradition of English literature. However, unique American characteristics and the breadth of its production usually now cause it to be considered a separate path and tradition.

Colonial Literature

Some of the earliest forms of American literature were pamphlets and writings extolling the benefits of the colonies to both a European and colonist audience. Captain John Smith could be considered the first American author with his works: *A True Relation of ... Virginia ...* (1608) and *The General Historie of Virginia, New England, and the Summer Isles* (1624). Other writers of this manner included Daniel Denton, Thomas Ashe, William Penn, George Percy, William Strachey, Daniel Coxe, Gabriel Thomas, and John Lawson.

The religious disputes that prompted settlement in America were also topics of early writing. A journal written by John Winthrop discussed the religious foundations of the Massachusetts Bay Colony. Edward Winslow also recorded a diary of the first years after the *Mayflower's* arrival. Other religiously influenced writers included Increase Mather and William Bradford, author of the journal published as a History of Plymouth Plantation, 1620–47. Others like Roger Williams and Nathaniel Ward more fiercely argued state and church separation.

Some poetry also existed. Anne Bradstreet and Edward Taylor are especially noted. Michael Wiggles worth wrote a best-selling poem, *The Day of Doom,* describing the time of judgment. Nicholas Noyes was also known for his doggerel verse.

Other late writings described conflicts and interaction with the Indians, as seen in writings by Daniel Gookin, Alexander Whitaker, John Mason, Benjamin Church, and Mary Rowlandson. John Eliot translated the Bible into the Algonquin language.

Jonathan Edwards and George Whitefield represented the Great Awakening, a religious revival in the early 18th century that asserted strict Calvinism. Other Puritan and religious writers include Thomas Hooker, Thomas Shepard, John Wise, and Samuel Willard. Less strict and serious writers included Samuel Sewall, Sarah Kemble Knight, and William Byrd.

The revolutionary period also contained political writings, including those by colonists Samuel Adams, Josiah Quincy, John Dickinson, and Joseph Galloway, a loyalist to the crown. Two key figures were Benjamin Franklin and Thomas Paine. Franklin's *Poor Richard's*

Almanac and *The Autobiography of Benjamin Franklin* are esteemed works with their wit and influence toward the formation of a budding American identity. Paine's pamphlet *Common Sense* and *The American Crisis* writings are seen as playing a key role in influencing the political tone of the period.

During the revolution itself, poems and songs such as "Yankee Doodle" and "Nathan Hale" were popular. Major satirists included John Trumbull and Francis Hopkinson. Philip Morin Freneau also wrote poems about the war's course.

Post-Independence

In the post-war period, Thomas Jefferson's United States Declaration of Independence, his influence on the American Constitution, his autobiography, the Notes on the State of Virginia, and his many letters solidify his spot as one of the most talented early American writers. The Federalist essays by Alexander Hamilton, James Madison, and John Jay presented a significant historical discussion of American government organization and republican values. Fisher Ames, James Otis, and Patrick Henry are also valued for their political writings and orations.

Much of the early literature of the new nation struggled to find a uniquely American voice in existing literary genre, and this tendency was also reflected in novels. European forms and styles were often transferred to new locales and critics often saw them as inferior.

American Style of Writing

With the War of 1812 and an increasing desire to produce uniquely American literature and culture, a number of key new literary figures emerged, perhaps most prominently Washington Irving, William Cullen Bryant, James Fenimore Cooper, and Edgar Allan Poe. Irving, often considered the first writer to develop a unique American style (although this has been debated) wrote humorous works in *Salmagundi* and the well-known satire *A History of New York, by Diedrich Knickerbocker* (1809). Bryant wrote early romantic and nature-inspired poetry, which evolved away from their European origins. In 1832, Poe began writing short stories – including "The Masque of the Red Death," "The Pit and the Pendulum," "The Fall of the House of Usher," and "The Murders in the Rue Morgue" – that explore previously hidden levels of human psychology and push the boundaries of fiction toward mystery and fantasy. Cooper's *Leatherstocking Tales* about Natty Bumppo (which includes *The Last of the Mohicans*) were popular both in the new country and abroad.

Humorous writers were also popular and included Seba Smith and Benjamin P. Shillaber in New England and Davy Crockett, Augustus Baldwin Longstreet, Johnson J. Hooper, Thomas Bangs Thorpe, and George Washington Harris writing about the American frontier.

The New England Brahmins were a group of writers connected to Harvard University and its seat in Cambridge, Massachusetts. The core included James Russell Lowell, Henry Wadsworth Longfellow, and Oliver Wendell Holmes, Sr.

In 1836, Ralph Waldo Emerson (1803-1882), an ex-minister, published a startling nonfiction work called *Nature,* in which he claimed it was possible to dispense with organized religion and reach a lofty spiritual state by studying and responding to the natural world. His work influenced not only the writers who gathered around him, forming a movement known as Transcendentalism, but also the public, who heard him lecture.

Emerson's most gifted fellow-thinker was perhaps Henry David Thoreau (1817-1862), a resolute nonconformist. After living mostly by himself for two years in a cabin by a wooded pond, Thoreau wrote *Walden*, a book-length memoir that urges resistance to the meddlesome dictates of organized society. His radical writings express a deep-rooted tendency toward individualism in the American character. Other writers influenced by Transcendentalism were Bronson Alcott, Margaret Fuller, George Ripley, Orestes Brownson, and Jones Very.

The political conflict surrounding Abolitionism inspired the writings of William Lloyd Garrison and his paper *The Liberator*, along with poet John Greenleaf Whittier and Harriet Beecher Stowe in her world-famous *Uncle Tom's Cabin*.

In 1837, the young Nathaniel Hawthorne (1804-1864) collected some of his stories as *Twice-Told Tales*, a volume rich in symbolism and occult incidents. Hawthorne went on to write full-length "romances," quasi-allegorical novels that explore such themes as guilt, pride, and emotional repression in his native New England. His masterpiece, *The Scarlet Letter*, is the stark drama of a woman cast out of her community for committing adultery.

Hawthorne's fiction had a profound impact on his friend Herman Melville (1819-1891), who first made a name for himself by turning material from his seafaring days into exotic and sensational sea narrative novels. Inspired by Hawthorne's focus on allegories and dark psychology, Melville went on to write romances replete with philosophical speculation. In *Moby-Dick,* an adventurous whaling voyage becomes the vehicle for examining such themes as obsession, the nature of evil, and human struggle against the elements. In another fine work, the short novel *Billy Budd,* Melville dramatizes the conflicting claims of duty and compassion on board a ship in time of war. His more profound books sold poorly, and he had been long forgotten by the time of his death. He was rediscovered in the early decades of the 20th century.

Anti-transcendental works from Melville, Hawthorne, and Poe all comprise the Dark Romanticism subgenre of literature popular during this time.

American Poetry

America's two greatest 19th-century poets could hardly have been more different in temperament and style. Walt Whitman (1819-1892) was a working man, a traveler, a self-appointed nurse during the American Civil War (1861-1865), and a poetic innovator. His magnum opus was *Leaves of Grass,* in which he uses a free-flowing verse and lines of irregular length to depict the all-inclusiveness of American democracy. Taking that motif one step further, the poet equates the vast range of American experience with himself without being egotistical. For example, in *Song of Myself,* the long, central poem in *Leaves of Grass,* Whitman writes: "These are really the thoughts of all men in all ages and lands, they are not original with me ..."

Whitman was also a poet of the body – "the body electric," as he called it. In *Studies in Classic American*

Literature, the English novelist D. H. Lawrence wrote that Whitman "was the first to smash the old moral conception that the soul of man is something 'superior' and 'above' the flesh."

Emily Dickinson (1830-1886), on the other hand, lived the sheltered life of a genteel unmarried woman in small-town Amherst, Massachusetts. Within its formal structure, her poetry is ingenious, witty, exquisitely wrought, and psychologically penetrating. Her work was unconventional for its day, and little of it was published during her lifetime.

Many of her poems dwell on death, often with a mischievous twist. One, "Because I could not stop for Death," begins, "He kindly stopped for me." The opening of another Dickinson poem toys with her position as a woman in a male-dominated society and an unrecognized poet: "I'm nobody! Who are you? / Are you nobody too?"

American poetry arguably reached its peak in the early to mid 20th century, with such noted writers as Wallace Stevens, Sylvia Plath, Anne Sexton, Ezra Pound, T. S. Eliot, William Carlos Williams, Stephen Vincent Benet, Robert Frost, Carl Sandburg, Robinson Jeffers, Hart Crane, E. E. Cummings, John Berryman, Allen Ginsberg, Robert Lowell, Edna St. Vincent Millay, and many others.

Realism, Twain and James

Mark Twain (the pen name of Samuel Langhorne Clemens, 1835-1910) was the first major American writer to be born away from the East Coast – in the border state of Missouri. His regional masterpieces were the memoir *Life on the Mississippi* and the novel *Adventures of Huckleberry Finn.* Twain's style –

influenced by journalism, wedded to the vernacular, direct and unadorned but also highly evocative and irreverently humorous – changed the way Americans write their language. His characters speak like real people and sound distinctively American, using local dialects, newly invented words, and regional accents. Other writers interested in regional differences and dialect were George W. Cable, Thomas Nelson Page, Joel Chandler Harris, Mary Noailles Murfree (Charles Egbert Craddock), Sarah Orne Jewett, Mary E. Wilkins Freeman, Henry Cuyler Bunner, and William Sydney Porter (O. Henry).

William Dean Howells also represented the realist tradition through his novels, including *The Rise of Silas Lapham* and his work as editor of the *Atlantic Monthly*.

Henry James (1843-1916) confronted the Old World-New World dilemma by writing directly about it. Although born in New York City, he spent most of his adult years in England. Many of his novels center on Americans who live in or travel to Europe. With its intricate, highly qualified sentences and dissection of emotional and psychological nuance, James's fiction can be daunting. Among his more accessible works are the novellas *Daisy Miller*, about an enchanting American girl in Europe, and *The Turn of the Screw*, an enigmatic ghost story.

Turn of the Century

At the beginning of the 20th century, American novelists were expanding fiction's social spectrum to encompass both high and low life and sometimes connected to the naturalist school of realism. In her stories and novels, Edith Wharton (1862-1937) scrutinized the upper-class, Eastern-seaboard society in which she had grown up. One of her finest books, *The Age of Innocence,* centers on a man who chooses to marry a conventional, socially acceptable woman rather than a fascinating outsider. At about the same time, Stephen Crane (1871-1900), best known for his Civil War novel *The Red Badge of Courage,* depicted the life of New York City prostitutes in *Maggie: A Girl of the Streets.* And in *Sister Carrie,* Theodore Dreiser (1871-1945) portrayed a country girl who moves to Chicago and becomes a kept woman. Hamlin Garland and Frank Norris wrote about the problems of American farmers and other social issues from a naturalist perspective.

More directly political writings discussed social issues and power of corporations. Some like Edward Bellamy in *Looking Backward* outlined other possible political and social frameworks. Upton Sinclair, most famous for his meat-packing novel *The Jungle,* advocated socialism. Other political writers of the period included Edwin Markham, William Vaughn Moody. Journalistic critics, including Ida M. Tarbell and Lincoln Steffens were labeled The Muckrakers. Henry Brooks Adams' literate autobiography, *The Education of Henry Adams* also depicted a stinging description of the education system and modern life.

Experimentation in style and form soon joined the new freedom in subject matter. In 1909, Gertrude Stein (1874-1946), by then an expatriate in Paris, published *Three Lives,* an innovative work of fiction influenced by her familiarity with cubism, jazz, and other movements in contemporary art and music. Stein labeled a group of American literary notables who lived in Paris in the 1920s and 1930s as the "Lost Generation."

The poet Ezra Pound (1885-1972) was born in Idaho but spent much of his adult life in Europe. His work is complex, sometimes obscure, with multiple references to other art forms and to a vast range of literature, both Western and Eastern. He influenced many other poets, notably T.S. Eliot (1888-1965), another expatriate. Eliot wrote spare, cerebral poetry, carried by a dense structure of symbols. In *The Waste Land*, he embodied a jaundiced vision of post-World War I society in fragmented, haunted images. Like Pound's, Eliot's poetry could be highly allusive, and some editions of *The Waste Land* come with footnotes supplied by the poet. In 1948, Eliot won the Nobel Prize in Literature.

American writers also expressed the disillusionment following upon the war. The stories and novels of F. Scott Fitzgerald (1896-1940) capture the restless, pleasure-hungry, defiant mood of the 1920s. Fitzgerald's characteristic theme, expressed poignantly in *The Great Gatsby*, is the tendency of youth's golden dreams to dissolve in failure and disappointment. Fitzgerald also elucidates the collapse of some key American Ideals, set out in the Declaration of Independence, such as liberty, social unity, good governance and peace, features which were severely threatened by the pressures of modern early 20th century society. Sinclair Lewis and Sherwood Anderson also wrote novels with critical depictions of American life. John Dos Passos wrote about the war and also the U.S.A. trilogy which extended into the Depression.

Ernest Hemingway (1899-1961) saw violence and death first-hand as an ambulance driver in World War I, and the carnage persuaded him that abstract language was mostly empty and misleading. He cut out unnecessary words from his writing, simplified the sentence structure, and concentrated on concrete objects and actions. He adhered to a moral code that emphasized grace under pressure, and his protagonists were strong, silent men who often dealt awkwardly with women. *The Sun Also Rises* and *A Farewell to Arms* are generally considered his best novels; in 1954, he won the Nobel Prize in Literature.

Five years before Hemingway, another American novelist had won the Nobel Prize: William Faulkner (1897-1962). Faulkner managed to encompass an enormous range of humanity in Yoknapatawpha County, a Mississippian region of his own invention. He recorded his characters' seemingly unedited ramblings in order to represent their inner states, a technique called "stream of consciousness." (In fact, these passages are carefully crafted, and their seemingly chaotic structure conceals multiple layers of meaning.) He also jumbled time sequences to show how the past – especially the slave-holding era of the Deep South – endures in the present. Among his great works are *The Sound and the Fury, Absalom, Absalom!, Go Down, Moses,* and *The Unvanquished.*

Depression-era Literature

Depression era literature was blunt and direct in its social criticism. John Steinbeck (1902-1968) was born in Salinas, California, where he set many of his stories. His style was simple and evocative, winning him the favor of the readers but not of the critics. Steinbeck often wrote about poor, working-class people and their struggle to lead a decent and honest life. *The Grapes of Wrath,* considered his masterpiece, is a strong, socially-oriented novel that tells the story of the Joads, a poor family from Oklahoma and their journey to California in search of a better life. Other popular novels include *Tortilla Flat, Of Mice and Men, Cannery Row,* and *East of Eden.* He was awarded the Nobel Prize in Literature in 1962. Steinbeck's contemporary, Nathanael West's two most famous short novels, *Miss Lonelyhearts,* which plumbs the life of its eponymous antihero, a reluctant (and, to comic effect, male) advice columnist, and the effects the tragic letters exert on it, and *The Day of the Locust,* about the unconscious struggle of American society to conform to the mold held up by Hollywood, have come to be avowed classics of American literature. Other writers sometimes considered part of the proletarian school include Olive Tilford Dargan, Tom Kromer, Robert Cantwell, and Edward Anderson.

Henry Miller assumed a unique place in American Literature in the 1930s when his semi-autobiographical novels, written and published in Paris, were banned from the US. Although his major works, which include *Tropic of Cancer* and *Black Spring,* would not be cleared for American sale and publication until 1962, their themes and stylistic innovations had already exerted a major influence on succeeding generations of American writers.

Literature of Post-World War II

The period in time from the end of World War II up until roughly, the late 1960s and early 1970s saw the publication of some of the most popular works in American history. The last few of the more realistic modernists along with the wildly Romantic beatniks largely dominated the period, while the direct respondents to America's involvement in World War II contributed in their notable influence. Though born in Canada, Chicago-raised Saul Bellow would become one of the most influential novelists in America in the decades directly following World War II. In works like *The Adventures of Augie March* and *Herzog*, Bellow painted vivid portraits of the American city and the distinctive characters that peopled it. Bellow went on to win the Nobel Prize for Literature in 1976.

From J.D. Salinger's *Nine Stories* and *The Catcher in the Rye* to Sylvia Plath's *The Bell Jar*, the perceived madness of the state of affairs in America was brought to the forefront of the nation's literary expression. Émigré authors such as Vladimir Nabokov, with *Lolita*, forged on with the theme, and, at almost the same time, the beatniks took a concerted step away from their Lost Generation predecessors, developing a style and tone of their own by drawing on Eastern theology and experimenting with recreational drugs.

The poetry and fiction of the "Beat Generation," largely born of a circle of intellects formed in New York City around Columbia University and established more officially some time later in San Francisco, came of age. The term *Beat* referred, all at the same time, to the countercultural rhythm of the Jazz scene, to a sense of rebellion regarding the conservative stress of post-war society, and to an interest in new forms of spiritual experience through drugs, alcohol, philosophy, and religion, and specifically through Zen Buddhism. Allen Ginsberg set the tone of the movement in his poem *Howl*, a Whitmanesque work that began: "I saw the best minds of my generation destroyed by madness ..." At the same time, his good friend Jack Kerouac (1922-1969) celebrated the Beats' rollicking, spontaneous, and vagrant life-style in, among many other works, his masterful and most popular novel *On the Road.*

Regarding the war novel specifically, there was a literary explosion in America during the post-World War II era. Some of the best known of the works produced included Norman Mailer's *The Naked and the Dead* (1948), Joseph Heller's *Catch-22* (1961) and Kurt Vonnegut Jr.'s *Slaughterhouse-Five* (1969). *MacBird,* written by Barbara Garson, was another well-received work exposing the absurdity of war. *The Moviegoer* (1962), by Southern author Walker Percy, winner of the National Book Award, was his attempt at exploring "the dislocation of man in the modern age."

In contrast, John Updike approached American life from a more reflective but no less subversive perspective. His 1960 novel *Rabbit, Run,* the first of four chronicling the rising and falling fortunes of Harry "Rabbit" Angstrom over the course of four decades against the backdrop of the major events of the second half of the twentieth century, broke new ground on its release in its characterization and detail of the American middle class and frank discussion of taboo topics such as adultery. Notable among Updike's characteristic innovations was his use of present-tense narration, his rich, stylized language, and his attention to sensual detail. His work is also deeply imbued with Christian themes. The two final installments of the Rabbit series, *Rabbit is Rich* (1981) and *Rabbit at Rest* (1990), were both awarded the Pulitzer Prize for Fiction. Other notable works include the Henry Bech novels (1970-98), *The Witches of Eastwick* (1984), *Roger's Version* (1986) and *In the Beauty of the Lilies* (1996), which literary critic Michiko Kakutani called "arguably his finest."

Frequently linked with Updike is the novelist Philip Roth. Roth vigorously explores Jewish identity in American society, especially in the postwar era and the early 21st century. Frequently set in Newark, New Jersey, Roth's work is known to be highly autobiographical, and many of Roth's main characters, most famously the Jewish novelist Nathan Zuckerman, are thought to be alter egos of Roth. With these techniques, and armed with his articulate and fast-paced style, Roth explores the distinction between reality and fiction in literature while provocatively examining American culture. His most famous work includes the Zuckerman novels, the controversial *Portnoy's Complaint* (1969), and *Goodbye, Columbus* (1959). Among the most decorated American writers of his generation, he has won every major American literary award, including the Pulitzer Prize for his major novel *American Pastoral* (1997).

Ralph Ellison's 1953 novel *Invisible Man* was instantly recognized as among the most powerful and sensational works of the immediate post-war years. The story of a black man in the urban north, the novel laid bare the often repressed racial tension still prevailing in the nation while also succeeding as an existential character study.

Flannery O'Connor (b. March 25, 1925 in Georgia – d. August 3, 1964 in Georgia) also explored and developed the theme of 'the South' in American literature that was dear to Mark Twain and other leading authors of American literary history (*Wise Blood* 1952; *The Violent Bear It Away* 1960; *Everything That Rises Must Converge*, her best-known short story, and an eponymous collection published posthumously in 1965).

1970 - 2000

Though its exact parameters remain debatable, from the early 1970s to the present day the most salient literary movement has been postmodernism. Thomas Pynchon, a seminal practitioner of the postmodern style, drawing on modernist fixtures such as temporal distortion, unreliable narrators and internal monologue and coupling them with distinctly postmodern techniques such as metafiction, absurdist humor and a subversive commingling of high and low culture, in 1973 published one of the seminal works of postmodernism, *Gravity's Rainbow*. His other important works include *The Crying of Lot 49* (1966) and *Mason & Dixon* (1997).

Toni Morrison, the most recent American recipient of the Nobel Prize for Literature, writing in the realist tradition in a distinctive poetic and deeply evocative prose style, published her controversial debut novel, *The Bluest Eye*, to widespread critical acclaim in 1970. Coming on the heels of the signing of the Civil Rights Act of 1965, the novel includes a description of incestuous rape and explores the conventions of beauty established by a historically racist society, painting a portrait of a self-immolating black family in search of beauty in whiteness. Among her best-known novels are *Sula* (1974), *Song of Solomon* (1977), and *Beloved* (1987). The latter was chosen in a 2006 survey conducted by the *New York Times* as the most important work of fiction of the last 25 years.

Writing in a lyrical, flowing style that eschews excessive use of the comma and semicolon and recalls William Faulkner and Ernest Hemingway in equal measure, rich with metaphor and polysyndeton, Cormac McCarthy is an author whose oeuvre seizes on the literary traditions of several regions in the United States and spans multiple genres. He writes in the Southern Gothic aesthetic in his distinctly Faulknerian 1965 debut, *The Orchard Keeper*; in the western tradition in *Blood Meridian* (1985), which critic Harold Bloom likened to *Moby-Dick*; in a much more pastoral tone in his celebrated Border Trilogy (1992-98), including *All the Pretty Horses* (1992), winner of the National Book Award; and in the post-apocalyptic genre in the Pulitzer Prize-winning *The Road* (2007). His novels are noted for achieving both commercial and literary success, several of his works having been adapted to film.

Don DeLillo, who rose to literary prominence with the publication of his 1985 novel, *White Noise*, a work broaching the subjects of death and consumerism and doubling as a piece of social criticism, began his writing career in 1971 with *Americana*. He is listed by Harold Bloom as being among the preeminent contemporary American writers, in the company of such giants as Philip Roth, Cormac McCarthy, and Thomas Pynchon. His 1997 novel *Underworld*, a gargantuan work chronicling American life through and immediately after the Cold War and examining with equal depth subjects as various as baseball and nuclear weapons, is generally agreed upon to be his masterpiece and was the runner-up in a survey asking writers to identify the most important work of fiction of the last 25 years. Among his other important novels are *Libra* (1988), *Mao II* (1991) and *Falling Man* (2007).

Among the younger generation of contemporary American writers, Paul Auster, like Thomas Pynchon an acolyte of postmodernism, stands out. Known for his experimentation with fragmented narratives, unreliable narrators, metafiction, intertextuality and multiple points of view, Auster marries absurdism with elements of crime fiction. A former translator of French literature, he brings to American letters a distinct pool of influences, among them those of Albert Camus, Jacques Derrida and Jean-Paul Sartre on the one hand and pulp fiction writer Dashiell Hammett on the other.

Millennial and Immigrant Literature

At the turn of the twenty-first century, several new writers surfaced, drawing on immigrant experiences in an ever more culturally diverse American landscape. Indian-American author Jhumpa Lahiri won the Pulitzer Prize for Fiction for her debut collection of short stories, *Interpreter of Maladies* (1999), and went on to write a well-received novel, *The Namesake* (2003), which was shortly adapted to film in 2007. In her second collection of stories, *Unaccustomed Earth*, released to widespread commercial and critical success, Lahiri shifts focus and treats the experiences of the second and third generation.

Chinese-American author Ha Jin in 1999 won the National Book Award for his second novel, *Waiting*, about a Chinese soldier in the Revolutionary Army who has to wait 18 years to divorce his wife for another woman, all the while having to worry about persecution for his protracted affair, and twice won the PEN/Faulkner Award, in 2000 for *Waiting* and in 2005 for *War Trash*. Other notable Asian-American novelists include Amy Tan, best known for her novel, *The Joy Luck Club* (1989), tracing the lives of four immigrant families brought together by the game of Mahjong; and Maxine Hong Kingston, best known for her memoir, *The Woman Warrior* (1976), and debut novel, *China Men*

(1980). Dominican-American author Junot Díaz, spurred to writing by Mexican-American author Sandra_Cisneros, an icon of an emerging Chicano literature whose 1984 bildungsroman *The House on Mango Street* is taught in schools across the United States, was awarded the Pulitzer Prize for Fiction for his 2007 novel *The Brief Wondrous Life of Oscar Wao,* which tells the story of an overweight Dominican boy growing up as a social outcast in Paterson, New Jersey. Both authors are members of a growing community of Latin American writers and artists.

Other notable writers of the turn of the century include David Foster Wallace, whose 1996 novel *Infinite Jest,* a futuristic portrait of America and a withering critique of the media-saturated nature of American existence, has been consistently ranked among the most important works of the twentieth century; Michael Chabon, whose Pulitzer Prize-winning *The Amazing Adventures of Kavalier & Clay* (2000) tells the story of two friends, Joe Kavalier and Sam Clay, as they rise through the ranks of the comics industry in its heyday; Jonathan Franzen, whose 2001 novel *The Corrections,* a tragicomedy about the disintegrating Lambert family, won the National Book Award; Richard Russo, author of the Pulitzer Prize-winning *Empire Falls* (2002), a novel laying bare the mysteries and legacies of the flagging logging and textile industries in the fictional Maine town of Empire Falls; and Marilynne Robinson, whose 2004 novel *Gilead,* a family saga centered around religion and set during the Civil War, was awarded the Pulitzer Prize for Fiction.

2

Southern Literature

Southern literature is defined as American literature about the Southern United States or by writers from this region. Characteristics of Southern literature include a focus on a common Southern history, the significance of family, a sense of community and one's role within it, the region's dominant religion and the burdens/rewards religion often brings, issues of racial tension, land and the promise it brings, a sense of social class and place, and the use of the Southern dialect.

Southern literature consists of writing about the American South, with the South being defined for historical as well as geographical reasons as the states of South Carolina, Georgia, Florida, Alabama, North Carolina, Virginia, Tennessee, Mississippi, Louisiana, Texas, Oklahoma, Missouri, Maryland, Delaware, Kentucky, West Virginia and Arkansas.

In addition to the geographical component of Southern literature, certain themes have appeared because of the similar histories of the Southern states in regard to slavery, the American Civil War, and Reconstruction. The conservative culture in the South has also produced a strong focus within Southern literature on the significance of family, religion, community in one's personal and social life, the use of the Southern dialect, and a strong sense of "place." The South's troubled history with racial issues also continually appears in its literature.

Despite these common themes, what makes writers and their literature Southern is often debated. For example, Mark Twain, arguably the father of Southern literature, defined the characteristics that many people associate with Southern writing in his novel *The Adventures of Huckleberry Finn*. He even referred to himself as a "Southern writer." In addition, many famous Southern writers headed to the Northern U.S. as soon as they were old enough to make it on their own. So while geography is a factor, the geographical birth of the author is not *the* defining factor in Southern writing.

Early and Antebellum Literature

During the 17th and 18th centuries, English colonists in the Southern part of the American colonies produced a number of notable works. Two of the most famous were early memoirs of Virginia: Captain John Smith's account of the founding of Jamestown in the 1610s and 1620s, and William Byrd II's secret plantation diary, kept in the early 18th century. Both sets of recollections are critical documents in early Southern history.

After American independence, in the early 19th century, the expansion of cotton planting and slavery began to distinguish Southern society and culture more clearly from the rest of the young republic. During this antebellum period, South Carolina, and particularly the city of Charleston, rivaled and perhaps surpassed

Virginia as a literary community. Writing in Charleston, the lawyer and essayist Hugh Swinton Legare, the poets Paul Hamilton Hayne and Henry Timrod, and the novelist William Gilmore Simms composed some of the most important works in antebellum Southern literature.

Simms was a particularly significant figure, perhaps the most prominent Southern author before the American Civil War. His novels of frontier life and the American revolution celebrated the history of South Carolina. Like James Fenimore Cooper, Simms was strongly influenced by Walter Scott, and his works bore the imprint of Scott's heroic romanticism. In *The Yemassee, The Kinsmen,* and the anti-*Uncle Tom's Cabin* novel The Sword and the Distaff, Simms presented idealized portraits of slavery and Southern life. While popular and well-regarded in South Carolina—and highly praised by such critics as Edgar Allan Poe—Simms never gained a large national audience.

Some critics regard Poe himself as a Southern author—he was raised in Richmond, attended the University of Virginia, and edited the *Southern Literary Messenger* from 1835 to 1837. Yet in his poetry and fiction Poe rarely took up distinctively Southern themes or subjects; his status as a "Southern" writer remains ambiguous.

In the Chesapeake region, meanwhile, antebellum authors of enduring interest include John Pendleton Kennedy, whose novel *Swallow Barn* offered a colorful sketch of Virginia plantation life; and Nathaniel Beverley Tucker, whose 1836 work *The Partisan Leader* foretold the secession of the Southern states, and imagined a guerrilla war in Virginia between federal and secessionist armies.

Not all noteworthy Southern authors during this period were white. Frederick Douglass's *Narrative* is perhaps the most famous first-person account of black slavery in the antebellum South. Harriet Jacobs, meanwhile, recounted her experiences in bondage in North Carolina in Incidents in the Life of a Slave Girl. And another Southern-born ex-slave, William Wells Brown, wrote *Clotel; or, The President's Daughter* – widely believed to be the first novel ever published by an African-American. The book depicts the life of its title character, a daughter of Thomas Jefferson and his black mistress, and her struggles under slavery.

"Lost Cause" Years

In the second half of the 19th century, the South lost the Civil War and suffered through what many white southerners considered a harsh occupation (called Reconstruction). In place of the Anti-Tom literature came poetry and novels about the "Lost Cause of the Confederacy." These writers idealized the defeated South and its lost culture. Prominent writers with this point of view included poets Henry Timrod, Daniel B. Lucas and Sidney Lanier and fiction writer Thomas Nelson Page. Others, like African American writer Charles W. Chesnutt, dismissed this nostalgia by pointing out the racism and exploitation of blacks that happened during this time period in the South.

In 1884, Samuel Langhorne Clemens, better known by his pen name Mark Twain, published what is arguably the most influential southern novel of the 19th century, *The Adventures of Huckleberry Finn*. Ernest Hemingway said of the novel, "All modern American literature comes from one book by Mark Twain called *Huckleberry Finn*." This statement applies even more to southern literature because of the novel's frank dealings with issues such as race and violence.

Kate Chopin was another central figure in post-Civil War Southern literature. Focusing her writing largely on the Acadian/Cajun communities of Louisiana, Chopin established her literary reputation with the short story collections *Bayou Folk* (1894) and *A Night in Acadie* (1897). These stories offered not only a sociological portrait of a specific Southern culture but also furthered the legacy of the American short story as a uniquely vital and complex narrative genre. But it was with the publication of her second and final novel *The Awakening* (1899) that she gained notoriety of a different sort. The novel not only shocked audiences with its frank and unsentimental portrayal of female sexuality and psychology. It paved the way for the Southern novel as both a serious genre (based in the realism that had dominated the western novel since Balzac) and one that tackled the complex and untidy emotional lives of its characters. Today she is widely regarded as not only one of the most important female writers in American literature, but one of the most important chroniclers of the post-Civil War South and one of the first writers to treat the female experience complexity and without condescension.

During the first half of the 20th Century, the lawyer, politician, minister, orator, actor, and author Thomas Dixon, Jr. wrote a number of novels, plays, sermons, and non-fiction pieces which were quite popular with the general public all over the USA. Today Dixon is perhaps best known for writing a trilogy of novels about Reconstruction, one of which was entitled *The Clansman* (1905), a book which would eventually become the inspiration for D. W. Griffith's infamous 1915 film *The Birth of a Nation*. Overall Dixon wrote 22 novels, numerous plays and film scripts, Christian sermons, and some non-fiction works during his lifetime.

Southern Renaissance

In the 1920s and '30s, a renaissance in Southern literature began with the appearance of writers such as William Faulkner, Caroline Gordon, Tennessee Williams, Katherine Anne Porter, Allen Tate, Thomas Wolfe, and Robert Penn Warren, among others. Because of the distance the Southern Renaissance authors had from the American Civil War and slavery, they were more objective in their writings about the South. During the 1920s, Southern poetry thrived under the Vanderbilt University "Fugitives." In nonfiction, H.L. Mencken's popularity increased nationwide as he continued to shock and astound readers with his satiric writing that highlighted the deficiencies of the South to produce anything of cultural value. In reaction to Mencken's essay, "The Sahara of the Bozart," the Southern Agrarians (also based mostly around Vanderbilt) called for a return to the South's agrarian past and bemoaned the rise of Southern industrialism and urbanization. They noted that creativity and industrialism weren't compatible and desired the return to the lifestyle that would afford the Southerner leisure (a quality the Agrarians most felt conducive to creativity). Writers like Faulkner, who won the Nobel Prize in Literature in 1949, also brought new techniques such as stream of consciousness and complex narrative techniques to their writings. For instance, his novel *As I Lay Dying* is told by changing narrators ranging from the deceased Addie to her young son.

The late 1930s also saw the publication of one of the most well-known Southern novels, *Gone with the Wind* by Margaret Mitchell. The novel, published in 1936, quickly became a bestseller. It won the 1937 Pulitzer Prize, and in 1939 an equally famous movie of the novel premiered. Southern literature became popular across genres; children's books like *Ezekiel*, published in 1937 by writer/illustrators like Elvira Garner, drew audiences outside the South.

From the 1940s onward, Southern literature grew thematically as it embraced the social and cultural changes in the South resulting from the American Civil Rights Movement. In addition, more female and African American writers began to be accepted as part of Southern literature, including African Americans such as Zora Neale Hurston, Sterling Allen Brown, and Dori Sanders, along with women such as Eudora Welty, Flannery O'Connor, Ellen Glasgow, Carson McCullers, and Shirley Ann Grau, among many others. Other well-known Southern writers of this period include Reynolds Price, James Dickey, William Price Fox, Davis Grubb and Walker Percy. One of the most highly praised Southern novels of the 20th century, *To Kill a Mockingbird* by Harper Lee, won the Pulitzer Prize when it was published in 1960. Another famous novel of the 1960s is *A Confederacy of Dunces*, written by New Orleans native John Kennedy Toole in the 1960s but not published until 1980 – won the Pulitzer Prize in 1981 and has since become a cult classic.

Southern Literature Today

Today the American South is undergoing a number of cultural and social changes, including rapid industrialization and an influx of immigrants to the region. As a result, the exact definition of what constitutes southern literature is changing. Some critics specify that the previous definitions of southern literature still hold, with some of them suggesting, only somewhat in jest, that all southern literature must still contain a dead mule within its pages. Still, the successful crime novels of James Lee Burke are not ashamed of making a point of their own southernness and their nationwide popularity has been attributed to their southern appeal.

Others, though, say that the very fabric of the South has changed so much that the old assumptions about southern literature no longer hold. For example, Truman Capote, born and raised in the Deep South, is best known for his novel *In Cold Blood,* a piece with absolutely none of the characteristics associated with "southern writing." Other southern writers, such as popular author John Grisham, rarely write about traditional southern literary issues at all. John Berendt, who wrote the popular Midnight in the Garden of Good and Evil, is not a Southerner.

Among the prominent southern writers today are Tim Gautreaux, Barry Hannah, William Gay, Padgett Powell, Pat Conroy, Fannie Flagg, Randall Kenan, Ernest Gaines, Erskine Caldwell, John Grisham, Mary Hood, Lee Smith, Tom Robbins, Tom Wolfe, Wendell Berry, Cormac McCarthy, Ron Rash, Anne Rice, Edward P. Jones, Barbara Kingsolver, Willie Morris, R.B. Morris, Anne Tyler, Larry Brown, Allan Gurganus, Clyde Edgerton, Daniel Wallace, Kaye Gibbons, Nicholas Sparks, Winston Groom, Lewis Nordan, and Richard Ford.

3

African-American Literature

African-American literature is the body of literature produced in the United States by writers of African descent. The genre traces its origins to the works of such late 18th century writers as Phillis Wheatley and Olaudah Equiano, reaching early high points with slave narratives and the Harlem Renaissance, and continuing today with authors such as Toni Morrison, Maya Angelou and Walter Mosley being ranked among the top writers in the United States. Among the themes and issues explored in African American literature are the role of African Americans within the larger American society, African-American culture, racism, slavery, and equality. African American writing has also tended to incorporate within itself oral forms such as spirituals, sermons, gospel music, blues and rap.

As African Americans' place in American society has changed over the centuries, so, too, have the foci of African American literature. Before the American Civil War, African American literature primarily focused on the issue of slavery, as indicated by the subgenre of slave narratives. At the turn of the 20th century, books by authors such as W. E. B. Du Bois and Booker T. Washington debated whether to confront or appease racist attitudes in the United States. During the American Civil Rights movement, authors such as Richard Wright and Gwendolyn Brooks wrote about issues of racial segregation and black nationalism. Today, African American literature has become accepted as an integral part of American literature, with books such as *Roots: The Saga of an American Family* by Alex Haley, *The Color Purple* by Alice Walker, and *Beloved* by Toni Morrison achieving both best-selling and award-winning status.

Characteristics and Themes

In broad terms, African American literature can be defined as writings by people of African descent living in the United States of America. However, just as African American history and life is extremely varied, so too is African American literature. That said, African American literature has generally focused on themes of particular interest to Blacks in the United States, such as the role of African Americans within the larger American society and what it means to be an American.

As Princeton University professor Albert J. Raboteau has said, all African-American studies, including African American literature, "speaks to the deeper meaning of the African-American presence in this nation. This presence has always been a test case of the nation's claims to freedom, democracy, equality, the inclusiveness of all." As such, it can be said that African American Literature explores the very issues of freedom and equality which were long denied to Blacks in the United States, along with further themes such as African American culture, racism, religion, slavery, a sense of home and more.

African American literature constitutes a vital branch of the literature of the African diaspora, with African American literature both being influenced by the great African diasporic heritage and in turn influencing African diasporic writings in many countries. In addition, African American literature exists within the larger realm of post-colonial literature, even though scholars draw a distinctive line between the two by stating that "African American literature differs from most post-colonial literature in that it is written by members of a minority community who reside within a nation of vast wealth and economic power."

African American oral culture is rich in poetry, including spirituals, African American gospel music, blues and rap. This oral poetry also appears in the African American tradition of Christian sermons, which make use of deliberate repetition, cadence and alliteration. African American literature—especially written poetry, but also prose—has a strong tradition of incorporating all of these forms of oral poetry.

However, while these characteristics and themes exist on many levels of African American literature, they are not the exclusive definition of the genre and do not exist within all works within the genre. In addition, there is resistance to using Western literary theory to analyze African American literature. As Henry Louis Gates, Jr., one of the most important African American literary scholars, once said, "My desire has been to allow the black tradition to speak for itself about its nature and various functions, rather than to read it, or analyze it, in terms of literary theories borrowed whole from other traditions, appropriated from without."

Early African American Literature

Just as African American history predates the emergence of the United States as an independent country, so too does African American literature have similarly deep roots.

Lucy Terry is the author of the oldest known piece of African American literature: "Bars Fight". Although written in 1746, the poem was not published until 1855, when it was included in Josiah Holland's "History of Western Massachusetts". Poet Phillis Wheatley (1753–84), who published her book *Poems on Various Subjects* in 1773, three years before American independence. Born in Senegal, Africa, Wheatley was captured and sold into slavery at the age of seven. Brought to America, she was owned by a Boston merchant. Even though she initially spoke no English, by the time she was sixteen she had mastered the language. Her poetry was praised by many of the leading figures of the American Revolution, including George Washington, who personally thanked her for a poem she wrote in his honor. Despite this, many white people found it hard to believe that a Black woman could be so intelligent as to write poetry. As a result, Wheatley had to defend herself in court by proving she wrote her own poetry. Some critics cite Wheatley's successful defense as the first recognition of African American literature.

Another early African American author was Jupiter Hammon (1711–1806?). Hammon, considered the first published Black writer in America, published his poem "An Evening Thought: Salvation by Christ with Penitential Cries" as a broadside in early 1761. In 1778 he wrote an ode to Phillis Wheatley, in which he discussed their shared humanity and common bonds.

In 1786, Hammon gave his well-known Address to the Negroes of the State of New York. Hammon wrote the speech at age seventy-six after a lifetime of slavery and it contains his famous quote, "If we should ever get to Heaven, we shall find nobody to reproach us for being black, or for being slaves." Hammon's speech also promoted the idea of a gradual emancipation as a way of ending slavery. It is thought that Hammon stated this plan because he knew that slavery was so entrenched in American society that an immediate emancipation of all slaves would be difficult to achieve. Hammon apparently remained a slave until his death. His speech was later reprinted by several groups opposed to slavery.

William Wells Brown (1814–84) and Victor Sejour (1817–74) produced the earliest works of fiction by African American writers. Sejour was born free in New Orleans and moved to France at the age of 19. There he published his short story "Le Mulâtre" ("The Mulatto") in 1837; the story represents the first known fiction by an African American, but written in French and published in a French journal, it had apparently no influence on later American literature. Sejour never returned to African American themes in his subsequent works. Brown, on the other hand, was a prominent abolitionist, lecturer, novelist, playwright, and historian.

Born into slavery in the Southern United States, Brown escaped to the North, where he worked for abolitionist causes and was a prolific writer. Brown wrote what is considered to be the first novel by an African American, *Clotel; or, The President's Daughter* (1853). The novel is based on what was at that time considered to be a rumor about Thomas Jefferson fathering a daughter with his slave, Sally Hemings. However, because the novel was published in England, the book is not considered the first African American novel published in the United States. This honor instead goes to Harriet Wilson, whose novel *Our Nig* (1859) details the difficult lives of Northern free Blacks

Slave Narratives

A subgenre of African American literature which began in the middle of the 19th century is the slave narrative. At the time, the controversy over slavery led to impassioned literature on both sides of the issue, with books like Uncle Tom's Cabin (1852) representing the abolitionist view of the evils of slavery, while the so-called Anti-Tom literature by white, southern writers like William Gilmore Simms represented the pro-slavery viewpoint.

To present the true reality of slavery, a number of former slaves such as Harriet Jacobs and Frederick Douglass wrote slave narratives, which soon became a mainstay of African American literature. Some six thousand former slaves from North America and the Caribbean wrote accounts of their lives, with about 150 of these published as separate books or pamphlets

Slave narratives can be broadly categorized into three distinct forms: tales of religious redemption, tales to inspire the abolitionist struggle, and tales of progress. The tales written to inspire the abolitionist struggle are the most famous because they tend to have a strong autobiographical motif. Many of them are now recognized as the most literary of all 19th-century writings by African Americans, with two of the best-known being Frederick Douglass's autobiography and *Incidents in the Life of a Slave Girl* by Harriet Jacobs (1861).

Frederick Douglass

While Frederick Douglass (c. 1818–95) first came to public attention as an orator and as the author of his autobiographical slave narrative, he eventually became the most prominent African American of his time and one of the most influential lecturers and authors in American history.

Born into slavery in Maryland, Douglass eventually escaped and worked for numerous abolitionist causes. He also edited a number of newspapers. Douglass' best-known work is his autobiography, *Narrative of the Life of Frederick Douglass, an American Slave*, which was published in 1845. At the time some critics attacked the book, not believing that a black man could have written such an eloquent work. Despite this, the book was an immediate bestseller.

Douglas later revised and expanded his autobiography, which was republished as *My Bondage and My Freedom* (1855). In addition to serving in a number of political posts during his life, he also wrote numerous influential articles and essays.

Post-slavery era

After the end of slavery and the American Civil War, a number of African American authors continued to write nonfiction works about the condition of African Americans in the country.

Among the most prominent of these writers is W. E. B. Du Bois (1868–1963), one of the original founders of the NAACP. At the turn of the century, Du Bois published a highly influential collection of essays titled *The Souls of Black Folk*. The book's essays on race were groundbreaking and drew from Du Bois's personal experiences to describe how African Americans lived in American society. The book contains Du Bois's famous quote: "The problem of the twentieth century is the problem of the color-line." Du Bois believed that African Americans should, because of their common interests, work together to battle prejudice and inequity.

Another prominent author of this time period is Booker T. Washington (1856–1915), who in many ways represented opposite views from Du Bois. Washington was an educator and the founder of the Tuskegee Institute, a Black college in Alabama. Among his published works are *Up From Slavery* (1901), *The Future of the American Negro* (1899), *Tuskegee and Its People* (1905), and *My Larger Education* (1911). In contrast to Du Bois, who adopted a more confrontational attitude toward ending racial strife in America, Washington believed that Blacks should first lift themselves up and prove themselves the equal of whites before asking for an end to racism. While this viewpoint was popular among some Blacks (and many whites) at the time, Washington's political views would later fall out of fashion.

A third writer who gained attention during this period in the US, though not a US citizen, was the Jamaican Marcus Garvey (1887–1940), a newspaper publisher, journalist, and crusader for Pan Africanism through his organization the UNIA. He encouraged people of African ancestry to look favorably upon their ancestral homeland. He wrote a number of essays published as editorials in the UNIA house organ the *Negro World* newspaper. Some of his lecture material and other writings were compiled and published as nonfiction books by his second wife Amy Jacques

Garvey as the *Philosophy and Opinions of Marcus Garvey or, Africa for the Africans* (1924) and *More Philosophy and Opinions of Marcus Garvey* (1977).

Paul Laurence Dunbar, who often wrote in the rural, black dialect of the day, was the first African American poet to gain national prominence. His first book of poetry, *Oak and Ivy*, was published in 1893. Much of Dunbar's work, such as *When Malindy Sings* (1906), which includes photographs taken by the Hampton Institute Camera Club, and *Joggin' Erlong* (1906) provide revealing glimpses into the lives of rural African-Americans of the day. Though Dunbar died young, he was a prolific poet, essayist, novelist (among them *The Uncalled*, 1898 and *The Fanatics*, 1901) and short story writer.

Even though Du Bois, Washington, and Garvey were the leading African American intellectuals and authors of their time, other African American writers also rose to prominence. Among these is Charles W. Chesnutt, a well-known short story writer and essayist.

Harlem Renaissance

The Harlem Renaissance from 1920 to 1940 brought new attention to African American literature. While the Harlem Renaissance, based in the African American community in Harlem in New York City, existed as a larger flowering of social thought and culture—with numerous Black artists, musicians, and others producing classic works in fields from jazz to theater—the renaissance is perhaps best known for the literature that came out of it.

Among the most famous writers of the renaissance is poet Langston Hughes. Hughes first received attention in the 1922 poetry collection, *The*

Book of American Negro Poetry. This book, edited by James Weldon Johnson, featured the work of the period's most talented poets (including, among others, Claude McKay, who also published three novels, *Home to Harlem, Banjo* and *Banana Bottom* and a collection of short stories). In 1926, Hughes published a collection of poetry, *The Weary Blues*, and in 1930 a novel, *Not Without Laughter*. Perhaps, Hughes' most famous poem is "The Negro Speaks of Rivers," which he wrote as a young teen. His single, most recognized character is Jesse B. Simple, a plainspoken, pragmatic Harlemite whose comedic observations appeared in Hughes's columns for the *Chicago Defender* and the *New York Post*. *Simple Speaks His Mind* (1950) is, perhaps, the best-known collection of Simple stories published in book form. Until his death in 1967, Hughes published nine volumes of poetry, eight books of short stories, two novels, and a number of plays, children's books, and translations.

Another famous writer of the renaissance is novelist Zora Neale Hurston, author of the classic novel *Their Eyes Were Watching God* (1937). Altogether, Hurston wrote 14 books which ranged from anthropology to short stories to novel-length fiction. Because of Hurston's gender and the fact that her work was not seen as socially or politically relevant, her writings fell into obscurity for decades. Hurston's work was rediscovered in the 1970s in a famous essay by Alice Walker, who found in Hurston a role model for all female African American writers.

While Hurston and Hughes are the two most influential writers to come out of the Harlem Renaissance, a number of other writers also became well known during this period. They include Jean Toomer, who wrote *Cane*, a famous collection of stories, poems, and sketches about rural and urban Black life, and Dorothy West, author of the novel *The Living is Easy*, which examined the life of an upper-class Black family. Another popular renaissance writer is Countee Cullen, who described everyday black life in his poems (such as a trip he made to Baltimore, which was ruined by a racial insult). Cullen's books include the poetry collections *Color* (1925), *Copper Sun* (1927), and *The Ballad of the Brown Girl* (1927). Frank Marshall Davis's poetry collections *Black Man's Verse* (1935) and *I am the American Negro* (1937), published by Black Cat Press, earned him critical acclaim. Author Wallace Thurman also made an impact with his novel *The Blacker the Berry: A Novel of Negro Life* (1929), which focused on intraracial prejudice between lighter-skinned and darker-skinned African Americans.

The Harlem Renaissance marked a turning point for African American literature. Prior to this time, books by African Americans were primarily read by other Black people. With the renaissance, though, African American literature—as well as black fine art and performance art—began to be absorbed into mainstream American culture.

Civil Rights Movement era

A large migration of African Americans began during World War I, hitting its high point during World War II. During this Great Migration, Black people left the racism and lack of opportunities in the American South and settled in northern cities like Chicago, where they found work in factories and other sectors of the economy.

This migration produced a new sense of independence in the Black community and contributed to the vibrant Black urban culture seen during the Harlem Renaissance. The migration also empowered the growing American Civil Rights movement, which made a powerful impression on Black writers during the 1940s, '50s and '60s. Just as Black activists were pushing to end segregation and racism and create a new sense of Black nationalism, so too were Black authors attempting to address these issues with their writings.

One of the first writers to do so was James Baldwin, whose work addressed issues of race and sexuality. Baldwin, who is best known for his novel *Go Tell It on the Mountain*, wrote deeply personal stories and essays while examining what it was like to be both Black and homosexual at a time when neither of these identities was accepted by American culture. In all, Baldwin wrote nearly 20 books, including such classics as *Another Country* and *The Fire Next Time*.

Baldwin's idol and friend was author Richard Wright, whom Baldwin called "the greatest Black writer in the world for me". Wright is best known for his novel *Native Son* (1940), which tells the story of Bigger Thomas, a Black man struggling for acceptance in Chicago. Baldwin was so impressed by the novel that he titled a collection of his own essays *Notes of a Native Son*, in reference to Wright's novel. However, their friendship fell apart due to one of the book's essays, "Everybody's Protest Novel," which criticized *Native Son* for lacking credible characters and psychological complexity. Among Wright's other books are the autobiographical novel *Black Boy* (1945), *The Outsider* (1953), and *White Man, Listen!* (1957).

The other great novelist of this period is Ralph Ellison, best known for his novel *Invisible Man* (1952), which won the National Book Award in 1953. Even though Ellison did not complete another novel during his lifetime, *Invisible Man* was so influential that it secured his place in literary history. After Ellison's death in 1994, a second novel, *Juneteenth* (1999), was pieced together from the 2,000-plus pages he had written over 40 years. A fuller version of the manuscript will be published as *Three Days Before the Shooting* (2008). Jones, Edward "The Known World", 2003 Carter Stephen, "New England White" 2007 Wright W.D. "Crisis of the Black Intellectual",2007

The Civil Rights time period also saw the rise of female Black poets, most notably Gwendolyn Brooks, who became the first African American to win the Pulitzer Prize when it was awarded for her 1949 book of poetry, *Annie Allen.* Along with Brooks, other female poets who became well known during the 1950s and '60s are Nikki Giovanni and Sonia Sanchez.

During this time, a number of playwrights also came to national attention, notably Lorraine Hansberry, whose play *A Raisin in the Sun* focuses on a poor Black family living in Chicago. The play won the 1959 New York Drama Critics' Circle Award. Another playwright who gained attention was Amiri Baraka, who wrote controversial off-Broadway plays. In more recent years, Baraka has become known for his poetry and music criticism.

Recent History

Beginning in the 1970s, African American literature reached the mainstream as books by Black writers continually achieved best-selling and award-winning status. This was also the time when the work of African American writers began to be accepted by academia as a legitimate genre of American literature.

As part of the larger Black Arts Movement, which was inspired by the Civil Rights and Black Power Movements, African American literature began to be defined and analyzed. A number of scholars and writers are generally credited with helping to promote and define African American literature as a genre during this time period, including fiction writers Toni Morrison and Alice Walker and poet James Emanuel.

James Emanuel took a major step toward defining African American literature when he edited (with Theodore Gross) *Dark Symphony: Negro Literature in America,* the first collection of black writings released by a major publisher. This anthology, and Emanuel's work as an educator at the City College of New York (where he is credited with introducing the study of African-American poetry), heavily influenced the birth of the genre. Other influential African American anthologies of this time included *Black Fire: An Anthology of Afro-American Writing,* edited by LeRoi Jones (now known as Amiri Baraka) and Larry Neal in 1968 and *The Negro Caravan,* co-edited by Sterling Brown, Arthur P. Davis and Ulysses Lee in 1969.

Toni Morrison, meanwhile, helped promote Black literature and authors when she worked as an editor for Random House in the 1960s and 70s, where she edited books by such authors as Toni Cade Bambara and Gayl Jones. Morrison herself would later emerge as one of the most important African American writers of the 20th century. Her first novel, *The Bluest Eye,* was published in 1970. Among her most famous novels is *Beloved,* which won the Pulitzer Prize for Fiction in 1988. This story describes a slave who found freedom but killed her infant daughter to save her from a life of slavery. Another important novel is *Song of Solomon,* a tale about materialism and brotherhood. Morrison is the first African American woman to win the Nobel Prize in Literature.

In the 1970s novelist and poet Alice Walker wrote a famous essay that brought Zora Neale Hurston and her classic novel *Their Eyes Were Watching God* back to the attention of the literary world. In 1982, Walker won both the Pulitzer Prize and the American Book Award for her novel *The Color Purple.* An epistolary novel (a book written in the form of letters), *The Color Purple* tells the story of Celie, a young woman who is sexually abused by her stepfather and then is forced to marry a man who physically abuses her. The novel was later made into a film by Steven Spielberg.

The 1970s also saw African American books topping the bestseller lists. Among the first books to do so was *Roots: The Saga of an American Family* by Alex Haley. The book, a fictionalized account of Haley's family history—beginning with the kidnapping of Haley's ancestor Kunta Kinte in Gambia through his life as a slave in the United States—won the Pulitzer Prize and became a popular television miniseries. Haley also wrote *The Autobiography of Malcolm X* in 1965.

Other important writers in recent years include literary fiction writers Gayl Jones, Rasheed Clark, Ishmael Reed, Jamaica Kincaid, Randall Kenan, and John Edgar Wideman. African American poets have also garnered attention. Maya Angelou read a poem at Bill Clinton's inauguration, Rita Dove won a Pulitzer Prize and served as Poet Laureate of the United States from 1993 to 1995, and Cyrus Cassells's *Soul Make a Path through Shouting* was nominated for a Pulitzer Prize in 1994. Cassells is a recipient of the William Carlos Williams Award. Lesser-known poets like

Thylias Moss, and Natasha Trethewey also have been praised for their innovative work. Notable black playwrights include Ntozake Shange, who wrote *For Colored Girls Who Have Considered Suicide When the Rainbow Is Enuf*; Ed Bullins; Suzan-Lori Parks; and the prolific August Wilson, who won two Pulitzer Prizes for his plays. Most recently, Edward P. Jones won the 2004 Pulitzer Prize for Fiction for *The Known World*, his novel about a black slaveholder in the antebellum South.

Young African American novelists include Edwidge Danticat, David Anthony Durham, Tayari Jones, Kalisha Buckhanon, Mat Johnson, ZZ Packer and Colson Whitehead, just to name a few. African American literature has also crossed over to genre fiction. A pioneer in this area is Chester Himes, who in the 1950s and '60s wrote a series of pulp fiction detective novels featuring "Coffin" Ed Johnson and "Gravedigger" Jones, two New York City police detectives. Himes paved the way for the later crime novels of Walter Mosley and Hugh Holton. African Americans are also represented in the genres of science fiction, fantasy and horror, with Samuel R. Delany, Octavia E. Butler, Steven Barnes, Tananarive Due, Robert Fleming, Brandon Massey, Charles R. Saunders, John Ridley, John M. Faucette, Sheree Thomas and Nalo Hopkinson being just a few of the well-known authors.

Finally, African American literature has gained added attention through the work of talk show host Oprah Winfrey, who repeatedly has leveraged her fame to promote literature through the medium of her Oprah's Book Club. At times, she has brought African American writers a far broader audience than they otherwise might have received.

Critiques

While African American literature is well accepted in the United States, there are numerous views on its significance, traditions, and theories. To the genre's supporters, African American literature arose out of the experience of Blacks in the United States, especially with regards to historic racism and discrimination, and is an attempt to refute the dominant culture's literature and power. In addition, supporters see the literature existing both within and outside American literature and as helping to revitalize the country's writing. To critics, African American literature is part of a Balkanization of American literature. In addition, there are some within the African American community who do not like how their own literature sometimes showcases Black people.

Dominant Literary Culture

Throughout American history, African Americans have been discriminated against and subject to racist attitudes. This experience inspired some Black writers, at least during the early years of African American literature, to prove they were the equals of European American authors. As Henry Louis Gates, Jr, has said, "it is fair to describe the subtext of the history of black letters as this urge to refute the claim that because blacks had no written traditions they were bearers of an inferior culture."

However, by refuting the claims of the dominant culture, African American writers weren't simply "proving their worth"—they were also attempting to subvert the literary and power traditions of the United States. Scholars expressing this view assert that writing has traditionally been seen as "something defined by the dominant culture as a white male activity." This means that, in American society, literary acceptance has traditionally been intimately tied in with the very power dynamics which perpetrated such evils as racial discrimination. By borrowing from and incorporating the non-written oral traditions and folk life of the African diaspora, African American literature thereby broke "the mystique of connection between literary authority and patriarchal power." This view of African American literature as a tool in the struggle for Black political and cultural liberation has been stated for decades, perhaps most famously by W. E. B. Du Bois.

According to James Madison University English professor Joanne Gabbin, African American literature exists both inside and outside American literature. "Somehow African American literature has been relegated to a different level, outside American literature, yet it is an integral part," she says.

This view of African American literature is grounded in the experience of Black people in the United States. Even though African Americans have long claimed an American identity, during most of United States history they were not accepted as full citizens and were actively discriminated against. As a result, they were part of America while also outside it.

The same can be said for African American literature. While it exists fully within the framework of a larger American literature, it also exists as its own entity. As a result, new styles of storytelling and unique voices are created in isolation. The benefit of this is that these new styles and voices can leave their isolation and help revitalize the larger literary world. This artistic pattern has held true with many aspects of African American culture over the last century, with jazz and hip hop being just two artistic examples that developed in isolation within the Black community before reaching a larger audience and eventually revitalizing American culture.

Whether African American literature will keep to this pattern in the coming years remains to be seen. Since the genre is already popular with mainstream audiences, it is possible that its ability to develop new styles and voices—or to remain "authentic," in the words of some critics—may be a thing of the past.

Balkanization of American Literature

Despite these views, some conservative academics and intellectuals argue that African American literature only exists as part of a balkanization of literature over the last few decades or as an extension of the culture wars into the field of literature. According to these critics, literature is splitting into distinct and separate groupings because of the rise of identity politics in the United States and other parts of the world. These critics reject bringing identity politics into literature because this would mean that "only women could write about women for women, and only Blacks about Blacks for Blacks."

People opposed to this group-based approach to writing say that it limits the ability of literature to explore the overall human condition and, more importantly, judges ethnic writers merely on the basis of their race. These critics reject this judgment and say it defies the meaning of works like Ralph Ellison's *Invisible Man*, in which Ellison's main character is invisible because people see him as nothing more than a Black man. Others criticize special treatment of any ethnic-based genre of literature. For example, Robert

Hayden, the first African-American Poet Laureate Consultant in Poetry to the Library of Congress, once said (paraphrasing the comment by the black composer Duke Ellington about jazz and music), "There is no such thing as Black literature. There's good literature and bad. And that's all."

Proponents counter that the exploration of group and ethnic dynamics through writing actually deepens human understanding and that, previously, entire groups of people were ignored or neglected by American literature.

The general consensus view appears to be that American literature is not breaking apart because of new genres like African American literature. Instead, American literature is simply reflecting the increasing diversity of the United States and showing more signs of diversity than ever before in its history. This view is supported by the fact that many African American authors—and writers representing other minority groups—consistently reach the tops of the best-seller lists. If their literature only appealed to their individual ethnic groups, this would not be possible.

African American Criticism

Some of the criticism of African American literature over the years has come from within the African American community; some argue that Black literature sometimes does not portray Black people in a positive light.This clash of aesthetics and racial politics has its beginnings in comments made by W. E. B. Du Bois in the NAACP publication *The Crisis*. For example, in 1921 he wrote, "We want everything that is said about us to tell of the best and highest and noblest in us. We insist that our Art and Propaganda be one." He added to this in 1926 by saying, "All Art is propaganda and ever must be, despite the wailing of the purists." Du Bois and the editors of *The Crisis* consistently stated that literature was a tool in the struggle for African American political liberation.

Du Bois's belief in the propaganda value of art showed most clearly when he clashed in 1928 with African American author Claude McKay over McKay's best-selling novel *Home to Harlem*. To Du Bois, the novel's frank depictions of sexuality and the nightlife in Harlem only appealed to the "prurient demand[s]" of white readers and publishers looking for portrayals of Black "licentiousness." Du Bois also said, "*Home to Harlem* ... for the most part nauseates me, and after the dirtier parts of its filth I feel distinctly like taking a bath." This criticism was repeated by others in the Black community when author Wallace Thurman published his novel *The Blacker the Berry* in 1929. This novel, which focused on intraracial prejudice between lighter-skinned and darker-skinned Blacks, infuriated many African Americans, who did not like such a public airing of their culture's "dirty laundry."

Naturally, many African American writers did not agree with the viewpoint that all Black literature should be propaganda, and instead stated that literature should present the truth about life and people. Langston Hughes articulated this view in his essay "The Negro Artist and the Racial Mountain", when he said that Black artists intended to express themselves freely no matter what the Black public or white public thought.

A more recent occurrence of this Black-on-Black criticism arose in charges by some critics that Alice Walker's novel *The Color Purple* unfairly attacked Black men. In addition, African American author Charles R. Johnson, in the updated 1995 introduction to his novel *Oxherding Tale,* criticized Walker's novel for its negative portrayal of African-American males, adding "I leave it to readers to decide which book pushes harder at the boundaries of convention, and inhabits most confidently the space where fiction and philosophy meet." Walker responded to these charges in her book *The Same River Twice: Honoring the Difficult.*

4

Chinese-American Literature

Chinese American literature is the body of literature produced in the United States by writers of Chinese descent. The genre began in the 19th century and flowered in the 20th with such authors as Sui Sin Far, Frank Chin, Maxine Hong Kingston, and Amy Tan.

Chinese American literature deals with many topics and themes. A common topic is the challenges, both inner and outer, of assimilation in mainstream, white American society by Chinese Americans. Another common theme is that of interaction between generations, particularly older, Chinese-born and younger, American-born generations. Questions of identity and gender are often dealt with as well.

Historical Development

19th century Chinese American literature has only recently come to be studied, as much of it was written in Chinese. These Chinese-language writings of Chinese Americans immigrants have only recently been made available.

19th century Chinese American writers were primarily workers and students. These early Chinese

American authors produced autobiographies as well as novels and poems, mostly in Cantonese. Many wrote in both English and Chinese, sometimes exploring similar themes in each language, sometimes translating their own works from language into the other. Tone as well as content differed, as Chinese American writers in English dealt with rampant stereotypes of the Yellow Peril. Among these early writers are Lin Yutang, novelist Yu Lihua, and Yung Wing, the first Chinese student to graduate from an American University (Yale, in 1854), whose autobiography, *My Life in China and America,* was published in 1909.

Chinese American literature written of the 20th century is written almost exclusively in English. Edith Maude Eaton, writing as Sui Sin Far, was one of the first Chinese American authors to publish fiction in English, although her works, first published in the teens, were not re-discovered and re-printed until 1995.

Chinese American authors became more prolific and accepted after the lifting of the Chinese Exclusion Act. Authors who achieved success in the 1950s included C.Y. Lee (author), whose *Flower Drum Song* was made into a Rodgers and Hammerstein musical, and Jade Snow Wong, author of Fifth Chinese Daughter.

The 1970s saw further progress. Playwright Frank Chin's play "The Chickencoop Chinaman" (1971) became the first play by an Asian American to be produced as a major New York production. Maxine Hong Kingston won the National Book Critics Circle Award in 1976 for The Woman Warrior.

In the 1980s, David Henry Hwang won the Obie award for his play, FOB, as well as a Tony Award for

Best Play for his M. Butterfly. Amy Tan's The Joy Luck Club was published to immediate popularity and wide, though not universal, acclaim. The book stayed on the New York Times bestseller list for over forty weeks, and won the National Book Award, the L.A. Times Book Award, and the Commonwealth Gold Award. *The Joy Luck Club* was produced as a major motion picture in 1993 and was nominated for Best Picture.

The 1990s saw further growth, as David Wong Louie received acclaim for his short story collection, *Pangs of Love.* Chang-Rae-Lee received the Hemingway Foundation/PEN Award for his novel *Native Speaker,* published in 1995. Chang-rae Lee is Korean American, and not Chinese American.

Chinese American Criticism

Frank Chin and others have been vocal critics of popular Chinese American authors, particularly Chinese American women authors, such as Maxine Hong Kingston and Amy Tan. Chin argues that Tan and others paint a world in which Chinese Americans must repudiate "the icky-gooey evil of Chinese culture". Others have criticized Chinese American women authors for criticizing sexism in Chinese culture; in so doing, critics argue, these women are participating in the "racial castration" of Chinese and Asian American men, who are already "materially and psychically feminized" by mainstream, white American culture.

Some of these criticisms are fueled by anger over the way in which female Chinese American authors have portrayed the sexism and patriarchy of Imperial

China, ways which male critics feel are sometimes unfair. For example, Maxine Hong Kingston has been criticized for her claim in The Woman Warrior that, in Chinese, the character for "woman" is also the character for "slave." Critics of Kingston claim that while (slave) contains (woman), it is only as a radical to indicate the pronunciation of the character; however, this, while true, does not address the questions of why the spoken words for slave and woman should sound so similar, and if that similarity could have its origins in a patriarchal society.

5

American Detective Fiction

Detective fiction is a branch of crime fiction in which a detective, either professional or amateur, investigates a crime, often murder.

The earliest known example of a detective story was "The Three Apples", one of the tales narrated by Scheherazade in the *One Thousand and One Nights* (*Arabian Nights*). In this tale, a fisherman discovers a heavy locked chest along the Tigris river and he sells it to the Abbasid Caliph, Harun al-Rashid, who then has the chest broken open only to find inside it the dead body of a young woman who was cut into pieces. Harun orders his vizier, Ja'far ibn Yahya, to solve the crime and find the murderer within three days, or be executed if he fails his assignment. Suspense is generated through multiple plot twists that occur as the story progresses. This may thus be considered an archetype for detective fiction.

The main difference between Ja'far in "The Three Apples" and later fictional detectives such as Sherlock Holmes and Hercule Poirot, however, is that Ja'far has no actual desire to solve the case. The whodunit mystery is solved by the murderer himself confessing his crime, which in turn leads to another assignment in which Ja'far has to find the culprit who instigated the murder within three days or else be executed. Ja'far again fails to find the culprit before the deadline, but due to his chance discovery of a key item, he eventually manages to solve the case through reasoning, in order to prevent his own execution.

Another strand of detective fiction is the Ming Dynasty Chinese detective fiction such as *Bao Gong An* and the 18th century novel *Di Gong An*. The latter was translated into English as *Dee Goong An* (*Celebrated Cases of Judge Dee*) by Dutch sinologist Robert Van Gulik, who then used the style and characters to write an original Judge Dee series.

The hero of these novels is typically a traditional judge or similar official based on historical personages such as Judge Bao (Bao Qingtian) or Judge Dee (Di Renjie). Although the historical characters may have lived in an earlier period (such as the Song or Tang dynasty) the novels are often set in the later Ming or Manchu period.

These novels differ from the Western tradition in several points as described by van Gulik:

1) The detective is the local magistrate who is usually involved in several unrelated cases simultaneously;
2) The criminal is introduced at the very start of the story and his crime and reasons are carefully explained, thus constituting an inverted detective story rather than a "puzzle";
3) The stories have a supernatural element with ghosts telling people about their death and even accusing the criminal;

4) The stories were filled with digressions into philosophy, the complete texts of official documents, and much more, making for very long books;
5) The novels tended to have a huge cast of characters, typically in the hundreds, all described as to their relation to the various main actors in the story;

One of the earliest examples of detective fiction is Voltaire's *Zadig* (1748), which features a main character who performs feats of analysis. The Danish crime story The Rector of Veilbye by Steen Steensen Blicher was written in 1829, and the Norwegian crime novel "Mordet på Maskinbygger Rolfsen" ("The Murder of Engine Maker Rolfsen") by Maurits Hansen was published in 1839.

Das Fräulein von Scuderi, by E.T.A. Hoffmann 1819, in which Mlle de Scudery, a kind of 18th century Miss Marple, establishes the innocence of the police's favorite suspect in the murder of a jeweller, is sometimes cited as the first detective story and a direct influence on Edgar Allan Poe's "The Murders in the Rue Morgue". However, detective fiction is more often considered in the English-speaking world to have begun in 1841 with the publication of "The Murders in the Rue Morgue" itself, featuring "the first fictional detective, the eccentric and brilliant C. Auguste Dupin". Poe set up a plot formula that's been successful ever since, give or take a few shifting variables." Poe followed with further Auguste Dupin tales: "The Mystery of Marie Roget" in 1843, and "The Purloined Letter" in 1844. Poe referred to his stories as "tales of ratiocination". In stories such as these, the primary concern of the plot is ascertaining truth, and the usual means of obtaining the truth is through a complex and mysterious process combining intuitive logic, astute observation, and perspicacious inference. "Early detective stories tended to follow an investigating protagonist from the first scene to the last, making the unraveling a practical rather than emotional matter."

"The Mystery of Marie Roget" is particularly interesting because it is a barely fictionalized account based on Poe's theory of what happened to the real-life Mary Cecilia Rogers. The style of the analysis, with its attention to forensic detail, makes it a precursor and perhaps inspiration for the stories about the most famous of all fictional detectives, Arthur Conan Doyle's Sherlock Holmes. Indeed, Holmes mentions the Poe story in the first Conan Doyle novel.

Emile Gaboriau, was a pioneer of the detective fiction genre in France. In *Monsieur Lecoq* the eponymous detective is adept at disguise, a key characteristic of detectives. Gaboriau's writing is also considered to be the first example of a detective minutely examining a crime scene for clues.

Another early example of a whodunit is a sub-plot in the vast novel *Bleak House* (1853) by Charles Dickens. The conniving lawyer Tulkinghorn is killed in his office late one night, and the crime is investigated by Inspector Bucket of the Metropolitan police force. Numerous characters appeared on the staircase leading to Tulkinghorn's office that night, some of them in disguise, and Inspector Bucket must penetrate these mysteries to identify the murderer.

Dickens's protege, Wilkie Collins (1824–1889) — sometimes referred to as the "grandfather of English detective fiction" — is credited with the first great mystery novel, *The Woman in White*. His novel *The Moonstone* (1868) was described by T. S. Eliot as "the first and greatest of English detective novels" and by Dorothy L. Sayers as "probably the very finest detective story ever written". Although technically preceded by Charles Felix's *The Notting Hill Mystery* (1865), *The Moonstone* can claim to have established the genre with several classic features of the twentieth-century detective story:

a) A country house robbery

b) An "inside job"

c) A celebrated investigator

d) Bungling local constabulary

e) Detective enquiries

f) False suspects

g) The "least likely suspect"

h) A rudimentary "locked room" murder

i) A reconstruction of the crime

j) A final twist in the plot

Some readers have suggested much earlier prototypes for the whodunnit, most notably the Old Testament story of Susanna and the Elders; *Oedipus Rex*, Sophocles' dramatic masterpiece, in which the young Oedipus tries to find out what happened to his murdered father and to his mother; the story of the dog and the horse related in the third chapter of Voltaire's *Zadig*.

Golden Age Detective Novels

Many English and some North American readers, in what became known as the Golden Age of Detective

Fiction between the wars, generally preferred a type of detective story in which an outsider – sometimes a salaried investigator or a police officer, but often a gifted amateur – investigates a murder committed in a closed environment by one of a limited number of suspects. The most widespread subgenre of the detective novel became the whodunit (or *whodunnit*), where great ingenuity may be exercised in narrating the events of the crime, usually a homicide, and of the subsequent investigation in such a manner as to conceal the identity of the criminal from the reader until the end of the book, when the method and culprit are revealed. "The golden age of detective fiction began with high-class amateur detectives sniffing out murderers lurking in rose gardens, down country lanes, and in picturesque villages. Many conventions of the detective-fiction genre evolved in this era, as numerous writers – from populist entertainers to respected poets – tried their hands at mystery stories."

The four original *Queens of Crime* were Agatha Christie, Dorothy L. Sayers, Ngaio Marsh and Margery Allingham. Apart from Ngaio Marsh (New Zealand) they were all female British writers; perhaps Josephine Tey could be added.

The most popular writer of the Golden Age whodunnit, and one of the most popular writers of all time, was Agatha Christie, who produced a long series of books featuring her detectives Hercule Poirot and Miss Marple, amongst others, and usually including a complex puzzle for the baffled and misdirected reader to try and unravel. Also popular were the stories featuring Dorothy L. Sayers's Lord Peter Wimsey and S. S. Van Dine's Philo Vance.

The "puzzle" approach was carried even further into ingenious and seemingly impossible plots by John Dickson Carr – also writing as Carter Dickson – who is regarded as the master of the "locked room mystery" and Cecil Street, who also wrote as John Rhode, whose detective Dr. Priestley specialised in elaborate technical devices, while in the US the whodunnit was adopted and extended by Rex Stout and Ellery Queen, among others. The emphasis on formal "rules" during the Golden Age produced a variety of reactions. Most writers were content to follow the rules slavishly, some flouted some or all of the conventions, and some exploited the conventions with genius to produce new and startling results.

Private Eye Novel

Private eye Martin Hewitt, created by British author Arthur Morrison, is perhaps the first example of the modern style of fictional private detective. By the late 1920s, Al Capone and the Mob were inspiring not only fear, but piquing genuine mainstream curiosity about the American underworld. Popular pulp fiction magazines like *Black Mask* capitalized on this, as authors such as Carrol John Daly published violent stories that focused on the mayhem and injustice surrounding the criminals, not the circumstances behind the crime. Very often, no actual mystery even existed: the books simply revolved around justice being served to those who deserved harsh treatment, which was described in explicit detail." In the 1930s, the private eye genre was adopted wholeheartedly by American writers. The tough, stylish detective fiction of Dashiell Hammett, Jonathan Latimer, Erle Stanley Gardner and others explored the "mean streets" and corrupt underbelly of the United States. Their style of crime fiction came to be known as "hardboiled," which encompasses stories with similar attitudes concentrating not on detectives but gangsters, crooks, and other committers or victims of crimes. "Told in stark and sometimes elegant language through the unemotional eyes of new hero-detectives, these stories were an American phenomenon."

In the late 1930s, Raymond Chandler updated the form with his private detective Philip Marlowe, who brought a more intimate voice to the detective than Hammett's distant, third-person viewpoint. His cadenced dialogue and cryptic narrations were musical, evoking the dark alleys and tough thugs, rich women and powerful men about whom he wrote. Several feature and television movies have been made about the Philip Marlowe character. James Hadley Chase wrote a few novels with private eyes as the main hero, including "Blonde's Requiem" (1945), "Lay Her Among the Lilies" (1950), and "Figure It Out for Yourself" (1950). Heroes of these novels are typical private eyes which are very similar to Philip Marlowe.

Ross Macdonald, pseudonym of Kenneth Millar, updated the form again with his detective Lew Archer, while still writing in what is considered the PI's Golden Age of Detective Fiction, begun by Hammett. Archer, like Hammett's fictional heroes, was a camera eye, with hardly any known past. "Turn Archer sideways, and he disappears," one reviewer wrote. Two of Macdonald's strengths were his use of psychology and his beautiful prose, which was full of imagery. Like other 'hardboiled' writers, Macdonald aimed to give an impression of realism in his work through violence, sex and confrontation; this is illusory, however, and any real private eye undergoing a typical fictional investigation would soon be dead or incapacitated. The 1966 movie *Harper* starring Paul Newman was based on the first Lew Archer story *The Moving Target* (1949). Newman reprised the role in *The Drowning Pool* in 1976.

Michael Collins, pseudonym of Dennis Lynds, is generally considered the author who led the form into the Modern Age. His PI, Dan Fortune, was consistently involved in the same sort of David-and-Goliath stories that Hammett, Chandler, and Macdonald wrote, but he took a sociological bent, exploring the meaning of his characters' places in society and the impact society had on people. Full of commentary and clipped prose, his books were more intimate than his predecessors, dramatizing that crime can happen in one's own living room.

The PI novel was a male-dominated field in which female authors seldom found publication until Marcia Muller, Sara Paretsky, and Sue Grafton were finally published in the late 1970s and early 1980s. Each author's detective was brainy, physical, and could hold her own. Their acceptance, then success, caused publishers to seek out other female authors. The PI novel today is rich in variety. The strongest characteristic that binds them is that the detective now has a past and a life, while solving cases.

Subgenres

There is also a subgenre of historical detectives. The first amateur railway detective, Thorpe Hazell, was created by Victor Whitechurch and his stories impressed Ellery Queen and Dorothy L. Sayers.

"Cozy mysteries" began in the late 20th century as a reinvention of the Golden Age whodunnit; these novels generally shy away from violence and suspense and frequently feature female amateur detectives. Modern cozy mysteries are frequently, though not necessarily in either case, humorous and thematic (culinary mystery, animal mystery, quilting mystery, etc.)

Another subgenre of detective fiction is the serial killer mystery, which might be thought of as an outcropping of the police procedural. There are early mystery novels in which a police force attempts to contend with the type of criminal known in the 1920s as a homicidal maniac, such as a few of the early novels of Philip Macdonald and Ellery Queen's *Cat of Many Tails*. However, this sort of story became much more popular after the coining of the phrase "serial killer" in the 1970s and the publication of *The Silence of the Lambs* in 1988. These stories frequently show the activities of many members of a police force or government agency in their efforts to apprehend a killer who is selecting victims on some obscure basis. They are also often much more violent and suspenseful than other mysteries.

Suspense Fictions

A beginner to detective fiction would generally be advised against reading anything about a piece of work in the genre (such as a review or even a blurb) before starting the story itself. Even if they do not mean to, advertisers, reviewers, scholars and aficionados usually have a habit of giving away details or parts of the plot, and sometimes — for example in the case of Mickey Spillane's novel *I, the Jury* — even the solution. (After the credits of Billy Wilder's film *Witness for the Prosecution,* the cinemagoers are asked not to talk to anyone about the plot so that future viewers will also be able to fully enjoy the unravelling of the mystery.)

Unresolved Problem of Plausibility and Coincidence

Up to the present, some of the problems inherent in crime fiction have remained unsolved (and possibly also insoluble). After all, this is just part of the game of crime fiction. Still the fact that an old spinster like Miss Marple meets with an estimated two bodies per year does raise a few doubts as to the plausibility of the Miss Marple mysteries.

De Andrea has described the quiet little village of St. Mary Mead as having "put on a pageant of human depravity rivaled only by that of Sodom and Gomorrah". Similarly, TV heroine Jessica Fletcher is confronted with bodies wherever she goes, but over the years people who have met violent deaths have also piled up in the streets of Cabot Cove, Maine, the cozy little village where she lives. Generally, therefore, it is much more convincing if a policeman, private eye, forensic expert or similar professional is made the hero or heroine of a series of crime novels.

This implausibility is satirized frequently on the TV show *Monk,* in which the main character, Adrian Monk, is frequently accused of being a "bad luck charm" and a "murder magnet" as the result of the frequency with which otherwise normal people attempt to pull off elaborate schemes for perfect murders when he is in the vicinity. Likewise Kogoro Mori of Detective Conan got that kind of unflattering reputation. Although Mori is actually a private investigator with his own agency, the police has never been intentionally consulting him and he just keeps stumbling from one crime scene to another.

Also, the role and legitimacy of coincidence has frequently been the topic of heated arguments ever since Ronald A. Knox categorically stated that "no accident must ever help the detective."

Effects of Technology

Technological progress has also rendered many plots implausible and antiquated. For example, the predominance of mobile phones, pagers, and PDAs has significantly altered the previously dangerous situations in which investigators traditionally might have found themselves. Some authors have not succeeded in adapting to the changes brought about by modern technology; others, such as Carl Hiaasen, have.

One tactic that avoids the issue of technology altogether is the historical detective genre. As global interconnectedness makes legitimate suspense more difficult to achieve, several writers—including Elizabeth Peters, P. C. Doherty, Steven Saylor, and Lindsey Davis—have eschewed fabricating convoluted plots in order to manufacture tension, instead opting to set their characters in some former period. Such a strategy forces the protagonist to rely on more inventive means of investigation, lacking as they do the scientific tools available to modern detectives.

The earliest known example of a detective story was "The Three Apples", one of the tales narrated by Scheherazade in the *One Thousand and One Nights* (*Arabian Nights*). In this tale, a fisherman discovers a heavy locked chest along the Tigris river and he sells it to the Abbasid Caliph, Harun al-Rashid, who then has the chest broken open only to find inside it the dead body of a young woman who was cut into pieces. Harun orders his vizier, Ja'far ibn Yahya, to solve the crime and find the murderer within three days, or be executed if he fails his assignment. Suspense is generated through multiple plot twists that occur as the story progresses. This may thus be considered an archetype for detective fiction.

The main difference between Ja'far in "The Three Apples" and later fictional detectives such as Sherlock Holmes and Hercule Poirot, however, is that Ja'far has no actual desire to solve the case. The whodunit mystery is solved by the murderer himself confessing his crime, which in turn leads to another assignment in which Ja'far has to find the culprit who instigated the murder within three days or else be executed. Ja'far again fails to find the culprit before the deadline, but due to his chance discovery of a key item, he eventually manages to solve the case through reasoning, in order to prevent his own execution.

6

American Romance Novels

The romance novel is a literary genre developed in Western culture, mainly in English-speaking countries. Novels in this genre place their primary focus on the relationship and romantic love between two people, and must have an "emotionally satisfying and optimistic ending." Through the late 20th and early 21st centuries, these novels are commercially in two main varieties: category romances, which are shorter books with a one-month shelf-life, and single-title romances, which are generally longer with a longer shelf-life. Separate from their type, a romance novel can exist within one of many subgenres, including contemporary, historical, science fiction and paranormal.

One of the earliest romance novels was Samuel Richardson's popular 1740 novel *Pamela, or Virtue Rewarded,* which was revolutionary on two counts: it focused almost entirely on courtship and did so entirely from the perspective of a female protagonist. In the next century, Jane Austen expanded the genre, and her *Pride and Prejudice* is often considered the epitome of the genre. Austen inspired Georgette Heyer, who introduced historical romances in 1921. A decade later, British company Mills and Boon began releasing the first category romance novels. Their books were resold in North America by Harlequin Enterprises Ltd, which began direct marketing to readers and allowing mass-market merchandisers to carry the books.

The modern romance genre was born in 1972 with Avon's publication of Kathleen Woodiwiss's *The Flame and the Flower*, the first single-title romance novel to be published as an original paperback. The genre boomed in the 1980s, with the addition of many category romance lines and an increased number of single-title romances. Popular authors began pushing the boundaries of the genre and plots and characters began to modernize.

In North America, romance novels are the most popular genre in modern literature, comprising almost 55% of all paperback books sold in 2004. The genre is also popular in Europe and Australia, and romance novels appear in 90 languages. Most of the books, however, are written by authors from English-speaking countries, leading to an Anglo-Saxon perspective in the fiction. Despite the popularity and widespread sales of romance novels, the genre has attracted significant derision, skepticism and criticism.

According to the Romance Writers of America, the main plot of a romance novel must revolve around the two people as they develop romantic love for each other and work to build a relationship together. Both the conflict and the climax of the novel should be directly related to that core theme of developing a romantic relationship, although the novel can also contain subplots that do not specifically relate to the main characters' romantic love. Furthermore, a romance novel must have an "emotionally satisfying and optimistic ending." Others, including Leslie Gelbman, a president of the Berkley Group, use a more shortened definition, that a romance must make the "romantic relationship between the hero and the heroine ... the core of the book." In general, romance novels reward characters who are good people and penalize those who are evil, and a couple who fights for and believes in their relationship will likely be rewarded with unconditional love. Bestselling author Nora Roberts sums up the genre, saying "The books are about the celebration of falling in love and emotion and commitment, and all of those things we really want." Women's fiction (including chick lit) is not directly a subcategory of the romance novel genre, because in women's fiction the heroine's relationship with her family or friends may be equally as important as her relationship with the hero.

Some romance novel authors and readers believe the genre has additional restrictions, from plot considerations such as the protagonists meeting early on in the story, to avoiding themes such as adultery. Other disagreements have centered on the firm requirement for a happy ending, or the place of same-sex relationships within the genre. Some readers admit stories without a happy ending, if the focus of the story is on the romantic love between the two main characters (e.g. Romeo and Juliet). Others believe the definition should be more strictly worded to include only heterosexual pairing. While the majority of romance novels meet the stricter criteria, there are also many books that are widely considered to be romance novels that deviate from these rules. Therefore, the general definition, as embraced by the RWA and publishers, includes only the focus on a developing romantic relationship and an optimistic ending. As long as a romance novel meets those twin criteria, it can be set in any time period and in any location. There are no specific restrictions on what can or cannot be included in a romance novel. Even controversial subjects are addressed in romance novels, including topics such as date rape, domestic violence, addiction, and disability.

The combination of time frame, location, and plot elements does, however, help a novel to fit into one of several romance subgenres. Despite the numerous possibilities this framework allows, many people in the mainstream press claim that "all [romance novels] seem to read alike." Stereotypes of the romance genre abound. For instance, some believe that all romance novels are similar to those of Danielle Steel, featuring rich, glamorous people traveling to exotic locations. Many romance readers disagree that Steel writes romance at all, considering her novels more mainstream fiction.

Romance novels are sometimes referred to as "smut" or female pornography. While some romance novels do contain more erotic acts, in other romance novels the characters do no more than kiss chastely. The romance genre runs the spectrum between these two extremes. Because the vast majority of the romance novel audience are women, most romance novels are told from a woman's viewpoint, in either first or third person.

Formats

Note the number 1 in the upper right corner, indicating that this book was the first release in the Dell Candlelight Ecstasy category.

Romance novels are divided into two sub-sets, category romances, also known as series romances, and single title romances. Many authors write only within one of the formats, but others, including Jayne Ann Krentz and Jennifer Crusie, have achieved success in both formats.

Category Romance

Category romances are short, usually no more than 200 pages, or about 55,000 words. The books are published in clearly delineated lines, with a certain number of books published in each line every month. In many cases, the books are numbered sequentially within the line. These novels have widespread distribution—often worldwide—but a single U.S. print run, remaining on a bookseller's shelves until they are sold out or until the next month's titles are released and take their place. Writers for the largest publisher of category romance, Harlequin/Mills & Boon, can find their novels translated into 26 languages and sold in over 100 international markets.

To write a successful novel of this length, the "author must pare the story down to its essentials. Subplots and minor characters are eliminated or relegated to the backstory." Nonetheless, category romance lines each have a distinct identity which may involve similar settings, characters, time periods, levels of sensuality, or types of conflict. Publishers of category romances usually issue guidelines for each line, specifying the elements necessary for a novel to be included in each line. Depending on the current market and perceived reader preferences, publishers frequently begin new lines or end existing ones. Most recently, erotic and Christian lines have been introduced while traditional Regency romance lines have ended.

Single Title Romances

Romance novels which are not published as part of a publisher's category are known as single-title novels. These novels are longer than category romances and average between 350 and 400 pages. Publishers may release the novels over a shorter space of time for sales velocity and publicity reasons, but on average authors write 1.5 novels per year and have one each year published. Single-title novels remain on the booksellers' shelves at the discretion of the store. Despite their name, single-title novels are not always stand-alone novels. Some authors prefer to write several interconnected books, ranging in number from trilogies to long-running series, so that they can revisit characters or worlds. Such sets of books often have similar titles, and may be labelled as "Number 1 in the XXX Series", but they are not considered series romances because they are not part of a particular line.

Subgenres

Because the definition of a romance novel does not limit the types of plot devices, time frames, or locations that can be included, the genre has grown to encompass a wide variety of material and spawned multiple sub-genres. Sub-genres of romance are often closely related to other literature genres, and some books could be considered a romance subgenre novel and another genre novel at the same time. For example, romantic suspense novels are often similar to mysteries, crime fiction and thrillers, and paranormal romances use elements popular in science fiction and fantasy novels.

Contemporary Romance

Contemporary romance, which is set after World War II, is often what people mean when they refer to a romance novel. The largest of the romance novel subgenres, contemporary romance novels are set in the time in which they are written and usually reflect the mores of that time. Heroines in the contemporary romances written prior to 1970 usually quit working when they married or had children, while those novels written after 1970 usually have, and keep, a career. As contemporary romance novels have grown to contain more complex plotting and more realistic characters, the line between this subgenre and the genre of women's fiction has blurred.

Most contemporary romance novels contain elements which date the books, and the majority of them eventually become irrelevant to more modern readers and go out of print. Those which survive the test of time, such as the works of Jane Austen, are often reclassified as historical romances. Over half of the romantic fiction published in the United States in 2004 (1468 out of 2,285 books) were contemporary romance novels. Contemporary romance novels have twice been chosen by Kelly Ripa to be featured in her Reading with Ripa book club.

Historical Romance

Historical romance is set before World War II. This subgenre includes a wide variety of other subgenres, including Regency romance. Historical romance novels are rarely published in hardcover, with fewer than 15 receiving that status each year, less than one-fifth of the number of contemporary romance novels published in that format. Because historical romances are primarily published in mass-market format, their fortunes are tied to a certain extent to the mass-market trends. Booksellers and large merchandisers are selling fewer mass market paperbacks, preferring trade paperbacks or hardcovers, which prevent historical romances from being sold in some price clubs and other mass merchandise outlets.

In 2001, historical romance reached a 10-year high as 778 were published. By 2004, that number had dropped to 486, which was still 20% of all romance novels published. Kensington Books claims that they are receiving fewer submissions of historical novels, and that their previously published authors are switiching to contemporary.

Romantic Suspense

Romantic suspense involves an intrigue or mystery for the protagonists to solve. Typically, however, the heroine is the victim of a crime or attempted crime, and works with a hero, who tends to be in a field where he would serve as a protector, such as a police officer, FBI agent, bodyguard, or Navy SEAL. By the end of the novel, the mystery is resolved and the interaction between the hero and heroine has evolved into a solid relationship. These novels primarily take place in contemporary times, but authors such as Amanda Quick have broadened the genre to also include historical timeframes.

Like all romances, romantic suspense novels must place the development of a relationship between the protagonists at the heart of the story. The relationship "must impact each decision they make and increase the tension of the suspense as it propel the story. In turn, the events of suspense must also directly affect the relationship and move the story forward." Romantic suspense novels tend to have more "clean" language, without the "emotional, intimate" descriptions often used in more traditional romances. Because the mystery is a crucial aspect of the plot, these novels are more plot-driven instead of character-driven.

This blend of the romance and mystery was perfected by Mary Stewart, who wrote ten romantic suspense novels between 1955 and 1967. Stewart was one of the first to seamlessly combine the two genres, maintaining a full mystery while focusing on the courtship between two people. In her novels, the process of solving the mystery "helps to illuminate" the hero's personality, helping the heroine to fall in love with him.

Paranormal Romance

Paranormal romance blends the real with the fantastic or science fictional. The fantastic elements may be woven into an alternate version of our own world in an urban fantasy involving vampires, demons, and/or werewolves, or they may be more "normal" manifestations of the paranormal—humans with psychic abilities, witches, or ghosts. Time-travel, futuristic, and extraterrestrial romances also fall beneath the paranormal umbrella.

These novels often blend elements of other subgenres—including suspense, mystery, or chick lit—with their fantastic themes. A few paranormals are set solely in the past and are structured much like any historical romance novel. Others are set in the future, sometimes on different worlds. Still others have a time-travel element with either the hero or the heroine traveling into the past or the future. Between 2002 and 2004, the number of paranormal romances published in the United States doubled to 170 per year. A popular title in the genre can sell over 500,000 copies.

Many paranormal romances rely on the blend of contemporary American life with the existence of supernatural or magically empowered beings, human or otherwise; sometimes the larger culture is aware of the magical in its midst, sometimes it isn't. Some paranormal romances focus less on the specifics of their alternative worlds than do traditional science fiction or fantasy novels, keeping the attention strongly on the underlying romance. Others develop the alternate reality meticulously, combining well-planned magical systems and inhuman cultures with contemporary reality.

Science Fiction Romance

The first futuristic romance to be marketed by a mainstream romance publisher, Jayne Ann Krentz's *Sweet Starfire*, was published in 1986 and was a "classic road trip romance" which just happened to be set in a separate galaxy. This genre has become much more popular since 2000. Krentz attributes the popularity of this romance genre to the fact that the novels "are, at heart, classic historical romances that just happen to be set on other worlds."

Fantasy Romance

Fantasy Romance, also known as Romantic Fantasy, is a subgenre of fantasy fiction, describing a fantasy story using many of the elements and conventions of the romance genre. Romantic fantasy has been published by both fantasy and romance lines, with some publishers distinguishing between "fantasy romance" being more like a contemporary fantasy novel with romantic elements, and "romantic fantasy" with more emphasis on the romance elements of the story.

Time-Travel Romances

Time-travel romances are a version of the classic "fish out of water" story. In most, the heroine is from the present day and travels into the past to meet the hero. In a smaller subset of these novels, the hero, who lives in the past, travels forward into his future to meet the heroine. A successful time-travel romance must have the characters react logically to their experience and should investigate some of the differences, both physical and mental, between the world the character normally inhabits and the one in which they have landed. Some writers choose to end their novels with the protagonists trapped in different time periods and unable to be together—to the displeasure of many readers of the genre.

Inspirational Romance

Inspirational romance, as the market exists today, combines explicitly Christian themes with the development of a romantic relationship. In 2004, 167 novels were published in the inspirational romance subgenre. These novels typically do not include gratuitous violence or swearing, and the central courtship is chaste. Sex, if it is present at all, occurs after marriage and is not explicitly detailed. Many novels in this genre also focus on the hero or heroine's faith, turning the love story into "a triangle: the man and the woman and also their relationship with God." Themes such as forgiveness, honesty, and fidelity are common.

The first line of series inspirational romances debuted shortly after the 1980 U.S. presidential election, when Silhouette launched their Silhouette Inspirations line. The books were aimed at born-again Christians and were marketed in religious bookstores. The Silhouette Inspirations line was closed after Harlequin acquired Silhouette in 1984 because it was not profitable. However, Christian publishers continue to produce romance novels, including historical and contemporary.

Multicultural Romance

Multicultural romance typically features a hero and/or heroine who is African-American, although some multicultural lines also include Asian or Hispanic heroes or heroines or interracial relationships. The first line of multicultural romance novels, Arabesque, was launched by Kensington books in 1994. BET Books purchased the line in 1998, and the number of new authors that they publish has continued to expand each year. BET has also developed some of the Arabesque novels into made-for-television movies.

In 1999, Kensington Publishing launched the first line of Latino romance novels - ENCANTO. The ENCANTO novels were originally released in two ways - a bilingual Spanish/English version and a Spanish only version. Two novels were published every month until late 2001 when the line went into hiatus. Despite the demise of the line, several of the ENCANTO authors have continued writing novels with Latino protagonists namely, Sylvia Mendoza, Tracy Montoya, Caridad Pineiro, Berta Platas, Lara Rios and Lynda Sandoval.

Although romance novels featuring African-Americans and Hispanic protagonists are becoming more popular, those featuring Asian or Asian-American characters are rare. Author Tess Gerritsen believes this is due to the fact that there are fewer Asian-American women who read romances: "We read romances because we want to feel good about love...in order to do that, the reader must identify with the heroine."

Erotic Romance

Erotic romance, sometimes called romantica, is a blend of romance and erotica. Erotic romance novels are characterized by strong sexual content, but can contain elements of any of the other romance subgenres. Erotic romance novels tend to use more frank language, avoiding many of the euphemisms used in books with milder content. These novels also usually include more sex scenes, often focusing more on the sex act rather than being a more traditional love scene, and may include more unusual positions or acts. Despite a greater emphasis on the sex scenes, however, erotic romance is not to be confused with pornography. While pornography would concentrate solely on the sex acts, erotica novels include well-developed characters and a plot which could exist without the sex acts.

Erotic romances lengths run from short stories to single-title novels. Some of these are published as part of a category, such as Harlequin Blaze, while others are published as part of an anthology and are only novella length. Even single-title erotic romances may be as short as a novella, however.

Many of the publishers of erotic romance are either small press publishers or electronic book publishers. Writers often have more leeway in what types of erotic acts can be included when working with an electronic publisher than they would have working with a print publisher. The market for erotic romances has been growing rapidly, leading some publishers to create new lines for these types of books. Some subjects are still considered taboo, even with erotic romance. Themes such as pedophilia, incest, and bestiality are discouraged by all publishers.

The market for erotic romances has been growing rapidly. Ellora's Cave, an electronic publisher which focuses on erotic romance, became the first electronic publisher to be recognized by the Romance Writers of America as a legitimate publisher.

Development of Romance Novels

One of the earliest romance novels was *Pamela, or Virtue Rewarded,* by Samuel Richardson. Published in 1740, *Pamela* was the first popular novel to be based on a courtship as told from the perspective of the heroine. Unlike many of the novels of the time, *Pamela* had a happy ending. The book was one of the first bestsellers, with five editions printed in the first eleven months of release. The genre did not fully take form, however, until the nineteenth century.

Jane Austen is widely considered to be one of the masters of the romance novel genre, with *Pride and Prejudice,* published in 1813, considered "the best romance novel ever written." Critics, however, lamented that Austen's works reinforced the sexist stereotype that women must marry. The Bronte sisters built upon Austen's work with their novels. Charlotte

Brontë's *Jane Eyre,* published in 1847, introduced the orphaned heroine. Incorporating elements of both gothic novels and Elizabethan drama, *Jane Eyre* "demonstrate[d] the flexibility of the romance novel form."

The genre continued to be popular into the twentieth century. In 1919, E.M. Hull's novel *The Sheik* was published in the United Kingdom. The novel, which became hugely popular, was adapted into a movie, which established star Rudolph Valentino as the top male actor of the time. The hero of this book was an iconic alpha male who kidnapped the heroine and won her admiration through his forceful actions. The novel was one of the first to introduce the rape fantasy. Although women were gaining more independence in life, publishers believed that readers would only accept premarital sex in the context of rape. In this novel and those that followed, the rape was depicted as more of a fantasy; the heroine is rarely if ever shown experiencing terror, stress, or trauma as a result.

The first historical romances appeared in 1921, when Georgette Heyer began writing romances set during the English Regency period (1811–1820), when the Prince Regent ruled England in place of his ill father, George III. Heyer was inspired by Austen's novels. Although Austen had also written romances set in the Regency period, hers were contemporary novels, describing the times in which she lived. Because Heyer's writing was set in the midst of events that had occurred over 100 years previously, she had to include more detail on the time period in order for her readers to understand. Unlike the other romance novels of the time period, Heyer's novels used the setting as a plot device. Her characters often contained more modern-day sensibilities, and more conventional characters in the novels would point out the heroine's eccentricities, such as wanting to marry for love. Heyer was a prolific author, and write one to two historical romance novels per year until her death in 1974.

Rise of Category Romance

In the 1930s, Mills and Boon began releasing hardback romance novels. The books were sold through weekly two-penny libraries and were known as "the books in brown" for their brown binding. In the 1950s, the company began offering the books for sale through newsagents across the United Kingdom.

A Canadian company, Harlequin Enterprises, Ltd., began distributing in North America in 1957 the category romances published by Mills and Boon. Mary Bonneycastle, wife of Harlequin founder Richard Bonneycastle, and her daughter, Judy Burgess, exercised editorial control over which Mills and Boon novels were reprinted by Harlequin. They had a "decency code" and rejected more sexually explicit material that Mills and Boon submitted for reprinting. Upon realizing that the genre was popular, Richard Bonneycastle finally decided to read a romance novel. He chose one of the more explicit novels and enjoyed it. On his orders, the company conducted a market test with the novel he had read and discovered that it outsold a similar, tamer novel. Overall, the novels were short and formulaic, featuring heroines who were sweet, compassionate, pure and innocent. The few heroines who worked did so in traditional female jobs, including as nurses, governesses and secretaries. Intimacy in the novels never extended beyond a chaste kiss between the protagonists. On October 1, 1971, Harlequin purchased Mills and Boon. By this point, the romance novel genre "had been popularized and distributed widely to an enthusiastic audience" in Great Britain. In an attempt to duplicate Mills and Boon's success in North America, Harlequin had improved their distribution and marketing system. By choosing to sell their books "where the women are", they allowed many mass-market merchandisers and even supermarkets to sell the books, all of which were exactly 192 pages. Harlequin then began a reader service, selling directly to readers who agreed to purchase a certain number of books each month.

Birth of Modern Romance

The modern romance genre was born in 1972 with Avon's publication of Kathleen Woodiwiss's *The Flame and the Flower*, the first romance novel "to [follow] the principals into the bedroom." Aside from its content, the book was revolutionary in that it was one of the first single-title romance novels to be published as an original paperback, rather than being first published in hardcover, and, like the category romances, was distributed in drug stores and other mass-market merchandising outlets. The novel went on to sell 2.35 million copies. Avon followed its release with the 1974 publication of Woodiwiss's second novel, *The Wolf and the Dove* and two sexy novels by newcomer Rosemary Rogers, *Sweet Savage Love* and *Dark Fires*. The latter sold two million copies in its first three months of release. By 1975, *Publishers Weekly* had reported that the "Avon originals" had sold a combined 8 million copies. The following year over 150 historical romance novels, many of them paperback originals, were published, selling over 40 million copies.

The success of these novels prompted a new style of writing romance, concentrating primarily on historical fiction tracking the monogamous relationship between a helpless heroine and the hero who rescued her, even if he had been the one to place her in danger. The covers of these novels tended to feature scantily clad women being grabbed by the hero, and caused the novels to be referred to as "bodice-rippers." A *Wall St. Journal* article in 1980 referred to these bodice rippers as "publishing's answer to the Big Mac: They are juicy, cheap, predictable, and devoured in stupefying quantities by legions of loyal fans." The term bodice-ripper is now considered offensive to many in the romance industry.

In this new style of historical romance, heroines were independent and strong-willed and were often paired with heroes who evolved into caring and compassionate men who truly admired the women they loved. This was in contrast to the contemporary romances published during this time, which were often characterized by weak females who fell in love with overbearing alpha males. Although these heroines had active roles in the plot, they were "passive in relationships with the heroes." Across the genre, heroines during this time were usually aged 16–21, with the heroes slightly older, usually around 30. The women were virgins, while the men were not, and both members of the couple were described as beautiful.

Category romance lines were slower to react to some of the changes that had swept the historical romance subgenre. Despite the fact that the former Mills & Boon lines were now owned by a North American company, the lines did not have any

American writers until 1975, when Harlequin purchased a novel by Janet Dailey. Dailey's novels provided the romance genre's "first look at heroines, heroes and courtships that take place in America, with American sensibilities, assumptions, history, and most of all, settings." Harlequin was unsure how the market would react to this new type of romance, and was unwilling to fully embrace it. In the late 1970s, a Harlequin editor rejected a manuscript by Nora Roberts, who has since become the top-selling romance author, because "they already had their American writer."

In 1980, Simon and Schuster formed Silhouette Books to take advantage of the untapped talent of the American writers. They published several lines of category romance, and encouraged their writers to create stronger heroines and less dominant heroes. Authors were also expected to address contemporary issues where appropriate. Silhouette soon saw their market share expand, and in 1984, Harlequin acquired them. Despite the acquisition, Silhouette continued to retain editorial control and to publish various lines under their own imprint.

Harlequin had also failed to adapt quickly to the signs that readers appreciated novels with more explicit sex scenes, and in 1980, several publishers entered the category romance market to fill that gap. That year, Dell launched their Candlelight Ecstasy line with Amii Lorin's *The Tawny Gold Man,* becoming the first line to waive the requirement that heroines be virgins. By the end of 1983 sales for the Candlelight Ecstasy line totaled $30 million. Silhoeutte also launched similar lines, Desire (sexually explicit) and Special Edition (sexually explicit and longer stories, up to 250 pages), each of which had a 90–100% sellout rate each month.

A 1982 survey of romance readers confirmed that the new styles of writing were attracting new readers to the genre. 35% of the readers surveyed had begun reading romances after 1977. An additional 31% of those surveyed had been readers for between 6 and 10 years, meaning they had become interested in the genre after 1972, when Woodiwiss's revolutionary novel was published. This means that two-thirds of those surveyed joined the genre after it had begun to change.

The number of category romance lines increased at a rapid pace, and by 1985 there were 16 separate lines producing a total of 80 novels per month. The sudden increase in category romance lines meant an equally sudden increase in demand for writers of the new style of romance novel. This tight market caused a proportionate decrease in the quality of the novels that were being released. By 1984, the market was saturated with category lines and readers had begun to complain of redundancy in plots. The following year, the "dampening effect of the high level of redundancy associated with series romances was evident in the decreased number of titles being read per month." Harlequin's return rate, which had been less than 25% in 1978, when it was the primary provider of category romance, swelled to 60%.

The genre continued to expand in the mid-to-late 1980s, as publishers realized that the more popular authors were often those who stretched the boundaries of the genre. A 1984 novel by LaVyrle Spencer featured an overweight, middle-aged hero who had to make drastic changes to his lifestyle to win the heroine, while a 1987 Dailey novel involved an ugly hero and a heroine who was searching for her birth mother. Jayne Ann Krentz's 1986 novel *Sweet Starfire* became the first futuristic romance, combining elements of traditional romance novels and science fiction. The relationships had also modernized: by the 1990s, it was rare to see a book which featured a man raping his future wife.

In the mid-to-late 1980s, contemporary romances began to feature women in more male-dominated jobs, such as offshore oil rigs and the space program. By the early 1990s, the pendulum had swung back to feature heroines who were self-employed. The age range of heroines also began to expand, so that books began to feature women who had already reached 30 and even 40. Heroes also changed, with some authors veering towards a more sensitive man. Despite the broadening of some aspects of the plot, other taboos remained, and publishers discouraged authors from writing about controversial subjects such as terrorism, warfare, and masculine sports. Romance novels began to contain more humor beginning in the 1990s, as Julie Garwood began introducing a great deal of humor into her historical romances.

The romance novel began to expand in other ways as well. In 1989, author Jude Deveraux became the first romance author to transition from writing original mass market paperbacks to being published in hardcover. Her novel, *A Knight in Shining Armor,* "became a natural bestseller." Several authors found success writing single-title romances set in contemporary times, and publishing houses began to encourage the growth in the genre. Because the novels were set in modern times, they could include more of the elements that modern women could relate to, and soon began to touch on themes such as single parenthood, adoption, and abuse. By 2000, the covers had begun to evolve from featuring a scantily clad couple to instead showing a view of the landscape featured in the novel.

As women's career options have expanded in real life, so have those of their fictional counterparts. In the earliest Harlequin romance novels, heroines were typically nurses and secretaries. As time has passed and women have entered the workforce in larger numbers, romance heroines have spanned the career spectrum. Modern romance novels now feature more balanced relationships between men and women.

American Romance Fiction Market

The romance fiction market "has been impervious to the overall economic recession, with faithful readers spending up to $40 a month" on romance novels in 1982. That year, paperback romances totaled $300 million in sales, and the total audience was estimated at 20 million readers. A survey of 600 regular romance readers the same year "found that they mirror the general population in age, education, and marital and socioeconomic status." Over half of the women had at least some college education, and 40% were employed full-time. 60% of the women surveyed read at least one romance every two days. The women admitted to reading romances as an antidote to stress, for mental escape, and to learn about history and new careers.

The romance novel market continued to expand, so that by 1991, they comprised 46% of all mass market paperbacks sold in the US. This expansion was due in part to voracious readers, with over half of Harlequin's customers purchasing 30 novels per month. By this time, the romance novel audience had become more educated, with 45% having a college degree, and more than half of the audience worked outside the home.

By the 2000s, romance had become the most popular genre in modern literature. In 2004, romantic fiction generated $1.2 billion in sales, with 2,285 romance novels published. Almost 55% of all paperback books sold in 2004 were romance novels, and this genre made up 39% of all fiction sold that year. Over 64 million people claimed to have read at least one romance novel in 2004, according to a Romance Writers of America study, a 26% increase over their 2001 study. Twenty-two percent of romance readers identified themselves as male, and the romance readers were split evenly between people who were married and those who were single. People of all ages read romance novels, with one percent of readers younger than 13, and forty-two percent of them have at least a bachelor's degree.

International Markets

Harlequin sells more than 4 books per second, half of them internationally. Author Heather Graham attributes this to the fact that "emotions translate easily." In the United Kingdom, over 20% of all fiction books sold each year are romance novels. Although romance novels are translated into over 90 languages, the majority of authors of these works are from Great Britain, the United States, Canada, or, to a lesser extent, Australia. Even in France, where over 12 million romance novels are sold each year, all of the books are translations. This leads to a more Anglo-Saxon perspective in the fiction, which at times can be much less successful in a European market. Although Italy is the strongest foreign market for the chick lit sold by single-title imprint Red Dress Ink, in that country romance readers do not care to read books about cowboys, as this type of occupation was not common in their culture. The paranormal romance genre is not popular in countries such as Poland and Russia, although historical romance tends to be very successful. Inspirational romance does not sell well in Europe, where romances that feature babies are very popular.

Some publishing companies in Germany refuse to allow their romance authors to use their own names, fearing that the German audience will not buy a romance novel that does not have an Anglo-American pseudonym. German readers enjoy reading more erotic romance novels, and some German translations of English romance novels expand or insert love scenes into otherwise tame stories. The alternate scenario also occurs, as other German translators censor the love scenes.

In 2004, sales of romance novels in Australia increased 28% over the year before. Between 1999 and 2004 there was an increase of 40–50% in the number of new titles released. Harlequin received 20,000 unsolicited manuscripts each year.

The romance genre has been popularly derided and critically ignored, in company with other popular genres (men's adventure, science fiction, westerns). Despite recent rehabilitation and merging of the genre with other genres, the stigma attached to the romance genre continues to be strong, with some dedicated readers embarrassed to admit to buying or even reading the books. The romance genre has over the years generated significant derision, skepticism and criticism. Some critics point to a lack of suspense, as it is obvious that the hero and heroine will eventually resolve their issues, and wonder whether it is beneficial "for women to be whiling away so many hours reading impossibly glamorized love stories." According to fiction author Melissa Pritchard, a romance novel "perpetuates something slightly dangerous, that there's this notion, that there's this perfect love out there, and it can distract you from the work of loving yourself."

However, with the growth of popular culture studies, academic attention has turned to the romance genre and other forms of popular entertainment. Scholars such as Janice Radway, Nancy Chodorow, and Ann Douglas have looked at the genre in a broader social context, as other scholars have done with soap operas, western novels, science fiction, and other popular entertainment.

Romance novelists attribute the stigma to the fact that romance is the only genre "written almost exclusively by women for women." Romance novelist Jennifer Crusie counters that in the modern romance novel "a woman is rewarded with unconditional love [only] if she remains true to herself", while novelist Susan Elizabeth Phillips believes that romance novels are popular because the heroine always wins, sometimes overcoming great odds so that she is no longer a victim.

7

American Science Fictions

Science fiction is a genre of fiction. It differs from fantasy in that, within the context of the story, its imaginary elements are largely possible within scientifically established or scientifically postulated laws of nature (though *some* elements in a story might still be pure imaginative speculation). Exploring the consequences of such differences is the traditional purpose of science fiction, making it a "literature of ideas". Science fiction is largely based on writing rationally about alternative possibilities. The settings for science fiction are often contrary to known reality.

These may include:

1) A setting in the future, in alternative timelines, or in a historical past that contradicts known facts of history or the archaeological record
2) A setting in outer space, on other worlds, or involving aliens.
3) Stories that involve technology or scientific principles that contradict known laws of nature
4) Stories that involve discovery or application of new scientific principles, such as time travel or psionics, or new technology, such as nanotechnology, faster-than-light travel or robots, or of new

and different political or social systems (e.g., a dystopia, or a situation where organized society has collapsed)

Science fiction is difficult to define, as it includes a wide range of subgenres and themes. Author and editor Damon Knight summed up the difficulty by stating that "science fiction is what we point to when we say it", a definition echoed by author Mark C. Glassy, who argues that the definition of science fiction is like the definition of pornography: you don't know what it is, but you know it when you see it. Vladimir Nabokov argued that if we were rigorous with our definitions, Shakespeare's play *The Tempest* would have to be termed science fiction.

According to science fiction writer Robert A. Heinlein, "a handy short definition of almost all science fiction might read: realistic speculation about possible future events, based solidly on adequate knowledge of the real world, past and present, and on a thorough understanding of the nature and significance of the scientific method." Rod Serling's definition is "fantasy is the impossible made probable. Science Fiction is the improbable made possible." Lester del Rey wrote, "Even the devoted aficionado– or fan- has a hard time trying to explain what science fiction is", and that the reason for there not being a "full satisfactory definition" is that "there are no easily delineated limits to science fiction."

Forrest J Ackerman used the term "sci-fi" at UCLA in 1954. As science fiction entered popular culture, writers and fans active in the field came to associate the term with low-budget, low-tech "B-movies" and with low-quality pulp science fiction. By the 1970s, critics within the field such as Terry Carr and Damon Knight were using "sci-fi" to distinguish hack-work from serious science fiction, and around 1978, Susan Wood and others introduced the pronunciation "skiffy". Peter Nicholls writes that "SF" (or "sf") is "the preferred abbreviation within the community of sf writers and readers". David Langford's monthly fanzine *Ansible* includes a regular section "As Others See Us" which offers numerous examples of "sci-fi" being used in a pejorative sense by people outside the genre.

History of Science Fictions

As a means of understanding the world through speculation and storytelling, science fiction has antecedents back to mythology, though precursors to science fiction as literature can be seen in Lucian's *True History* in the 2nd century, some of the *Arabian Nights* tales, *The Tale of the Bamboo Cutter* in the 10th century, Ibn al-Nafis' *Theologus Autodidactus* in the 13th century, and Cyrano de Bergerac' *Voyage de la Terre à la Lune* and *Des états de la Lune et du Soleil* in the 17th century. Following the Age of Reason and the development of modern science itself, Jonathan Swift's *Gulliver's Travels* was one of the first true science fiction works, together with Voltaire's *Micromégas* and Kepler's Somnium. This latter work is considered by Carl Sagan and Isaac Asimov to be the first science fiction story. It depicts a journey to the Moon and how the Earth's motion is seen from there. Another example is Ludvig Holberg's novel *Nicolai Klimii iter subterraneum*, 1741.

Following the 18th century development of the novel as a literary form, in the early 19th century, Mary Shelley's books *Frankenstein* and *The Last Man* helped define the form of the science fiction novel; later Edgar Allan Poe wrote a story about a flight to the moon. More examples appeared throughout the 19th century.

Then with the dawn of new technologies such as electricity, the telegraph, and new forms of powered transportation, writers like Jules Verne and H. G. Wells created a body of work that became popular across broad cross-sections of society Wells' *The War of the Worlds* describing an invasion of late Victorian England by Martians using tripod fighting machines, equipped with advanced weaponry. It is a seminal depiction of an alien invasion of Earth.

In the late 19th century, the term "scientific romance" was used in Britain to describe much of this fiction. This produced additional offshoots, such as the 1884 novella *Flatland: A Romance of Many Dimensions* by Edwin Abbott Abbott. The term would continue to be used into the early 20th century for writers such as Olaf Stapledon.

In the early 20th century, pulp magazines helped develop a new generation of mainly American SF writers, influenced by Hugo Gernsback, the founder of *Amazing Stories* magazine. In the late 1930s, John W. Campbell became editor of *Astounding Science Fiction*, and a critical mass of new writers emerged in New York City in a group called the Futurians, including Isaac Asimov, Damon Knight, Donald A. Wollheim, Frederik Pohl, James Blish, Judith Merril, and others. Other important writers during this period included E.E. (Doc) Smith, Robert A. Heinlein, Arthur C. Clarke, A. E. van Vogt and Stanis³aw Lem. Campbell's tenure at *Astounding* is considered to be the beginning of the Golden Age of science fiction, characterized by hard SF stories celebrating scientific achievement and progress. This lasted until postwar technological advances, new magazines like *Galaxy* under Pohl as editor, and a new generation of writers began writing stories outside the Campbell mode.

In the 1950s, the Beat generation included speculative writers like William S. Burroughs. In the 1960s and early 1970s, writers like Frank Herbert, Samuel R. Delany, Roger Zelazny, and Harlan Ellison explored new trends, ideas, and writing styles, while a group of writers, mainly in Britain, became known as the New Wave. In the 1970s, writers like Larry Niven and Poul Anderson began to redefine hard SF. Ursula K. Le Guin and others pioneered soft science fiction.

In the 1980s, cyberpunk authors like William Gibson turned away from the traditional optimism and support for progress of traditional science fiction. *Star Wars* helped spark a new interest in space opera, focusing more on story and character than on scientific accuracy. C.J. Cherryh's detailed explorations of alien life and complex scientific challenges influenced a generation of writers. Emerging themes in the 1990s included environmental issues, the implications of the global Internet and the expanding information universe, questions about biotechnology and nanotechnology, as well as a post-Cold War interest in post-scarcity societies; Neal Stephenson's *The Diamond Age* comprehensively explores these themes. Lois McMaster Bujold's *Vorkosigan* novels brought the character-driven story back into prominence. The television series *Star Trek: The Next Generation* (1987) began a torrent of new SF shows, including three further *Star Trek* spin-off shows and *Babylon 5*. Concern about the rapid pace of technological change crystallized around the concept of the technological singularity, popularized by Vernor Vinge's novel

Marooned in Realtime and then taken up by other authors.

Innovation

While SF has provided criticism of developing and future technologies, it also produces innovation and new technology. The discussion of this topic has occurred more in literary and sociological than in scientific forums. Cinema and media theorist Vivian Sobchack examines the dialogue between science fiction film and the technological imagination. Technology does impact how artists portray their fictionalized subjects, but the fictional world gives back to science by broadening imagination. While more prevalent in the beginning years of science fiction with writers like Arthur C. Clarke, new authors still find ways to make the currently impossible technologies seem so close to being realized.

Subgenres

Authors and filmmakers draw on a wide spectrum of ideas, but marketing departments and literary critics tend to separate such literary and cinematic works into different categories, or "genres", and subgenres. These are not simple pigeonholes; works can be overlapped into two or more commonly-defined genres, while others are beyond the generic boundaries, either outside or between categories, and the categories and genres used by mass markets and literary criticism differ considerably.

Hard science fiction, or "hard SF", is characterized by rigorous attention to accurate detail in quantitative sciences, especially physics, astrophysics, and chemistry, or on accurately depicting worlds that more advanced technology may make possible. Many accurate predictions of the future come from the hard science fiction subgenre, but numerous inaccurate predictions have emerged as well. Some hard SF authors have distinguished themselves as working scientists, including Gregory Benford and Geoffrey A. Landis, while mathematician authors include Rudy Rucker and Vernor Vinge. Other noteworthy hard SF authors include Hal Clement, Greg Bear, Larry Niven, Robert J. Sawyer, Stephen Baxter, and Greg Egan.

Soft and Social SF

The description "soft" science fiction may describe works based on social sciences such as psychology, economics, political science, sociology, and anthropology. Noteworthy writers in this category include Ursula K. Le Guin and Philip K. Dick. The term can describe stories focused primarily on character and emotion; SFWA Grand Master Ray Bradbury is an acknowledged master of this art. The Soviet Union produced a quantity of social science fiction, including works by the Strugatsky brothers, Kir Bulychov and Ivan Yefremov. Some writers blur the boundary between hard and soft science fiction.

Related to Social SF and Soft SF are the speculative fiction branches of utopian or dystopian stories; *The Handmaid's Tale, Nineteen Eighty-Four,* and *Brave New World* are examples. Satirical novels with fantastic settings such as *Gulliver's Travels* may be considered speculative fiction.

Cyberpunk

The *Cyberpunk* genre emerged in the early 1980s; its the name combining "cybernetics" and "punk", and was first coined by author Bruce Bethke in his 1980 short story "Cyberpunk". The time frame is usually near-future and the settings are often dystopian (characterized by misery). Common themes in cyberpunk include advances in information technology and especially the Internet (visually abstracted as cyberspace), artificial intelligence and prosthetics and post-democratic societal control where corporations have more influence than governments. Nihilism, post-modernism, and film noir techniques are common elements, and the protagonists may be disaffected or reluctant anti-heroes. Noteworthy authors in this genre are William Gibson, Bruce Sterling, Neal Stephenson, and Pat Cadigan. James O'Ehley has called the 1982 film *Blade Runner* a definitive example of the *cyberpunk* visual style.

Time Travel

Time travel stories have antecedents in the 18th and 19th centuries. The first major time travel novel was Mark Twain's *A Connecticut Yankee in King Arthur's Court*. The most famous is H. G. Wells's *The Time Machine,* which uses a vehicle that allows an operator to travel purposefully and selectively, while Twain's time traveler is struck by lightening. The term "*time machine*", coined by Wells, is now universally used to refer to such a vehicle. Stories of this type are complicated by logical problems such as the grandfather paradox. Time travel is a popular subject in modern science fiction, in print, movies, and television.

Alternative History

Alternative (or alternate) history stories are based on the premise that historical events might have turned out differently. These stories may use time travel to change the past, or may simply set a story in a universe with a different history from our own. Classics in the genre include *Bring the Jubilee* by Ward Moore, in which the South wins the American Civil War, and *The Man in the High Castle* by Philip K. Dick, in which Germany and Japan win World War II. The Sidewise Award acknowledges the best works in this subgenre; the name is taken from Murray Leinster's early story *Sidewise in Time*. Harry Turtledove is one of the most prominent authors in the subgenre and is often called the "master of alternate history".

Military SF

Military science fiction is set in the context of conflict between national, interplanetary, or interstellar armed forces; the primary viewpoint characters are usually soldiers. Stories include detail about military technology, procedure, ritual, and history; military stories may use parallels with historical conflicts. Heinlein's *Starship Troopers* is an early example, along with the Dorsai novels of Gordon Dickson. Joe Haldeman's *The Forever War* is a critique of the genre, a Vietnam-era response to the World War II-style stories of earlier authors. Prominent military SF authors include David Drake, David Weber, and S. M. Stirling. Baen Books is known for cultivating military science fiction authors.

Superhuman

Superhuman stories deal with the emergence of humans who have abilities beyond the norm. This can stem either from natural causes such as in Olaf Stapledon's novel *Odd John*, and Theodore Sturgeon's *More Than Human*, or be the result of intentional augmentation such as in A.E. Van Vogt's novel *Slan*.

These stories usually focus on the alienation that these beings feel as well as society's reaction to them. These stories have played a role in the real life discussion of human enhancement.

Apocalyptic

Apocalyptic fiction is concerned with the end of civilization through war (*On The Beach*), pandemic (*The Last Man*), astronomic impact (*When Worlds Collide*), ecological disaster (*The Wind From Nowhere*), or mankind's self-destruction (*Oryx and Crake*), or some other general disaster or with a world or civilization after such a disaster. Typical of the genre are George R. Stewart's novel *Earth Abides* and Pat Frank's novel *Alas, Babylon*. Apocalyptic fiction generally concerns the disaster itself and the direct aftermath, while post-apocalyptic can deal with anything from the near aftermath (as in Cormac McCarthy's *The Road*) to 375 years in the future (as in *By The Waters of Babylon*) to hundreds or thousands of years in the future, as in Russell Hoban's novel *Riddley Walker*.

Space Opera

Space opera is adventure science fiction set in outer space or on distant planets, where the emphasis is on action rather than either science or characterization. The conflict is heroic, and typically on a large scale. Space opera is sometimes used pejoratively, to describe improbable plots, absurd science, and cardboard characters. But it is also used nostalgically, and modern space opera may be an attempt to recapture the sense of wonder of the golden age of science fiction. The pioneer of this subgenre is generally recognized to be Edward E. (Doc) Smith, with his *Skylark* and *Lensman* series. Alastair Reynolds'

Revelation Space series and the immensely popular *Star Wars* trilogies are newer examples of this genre.

Space Western

Space Western could be considered a sub-genre of Space Opera that transposes themes of the American Western books and film to a backdrop of futuristic space frontiers. These stories typically involve "frontier" colony worlds (colonies that have only recently been terraformed and/or settled) serving as stand-ins for the backdrop of lawlessness and economic expansion that were predominant in the American west. Examples include *Firefly* and the accompanying movie *Serenity* by Joss Whedon, as well as the animes *Cowboy Bebop* and *Outlaw Star*. The *Star Wars* character Han Solo is often considered elemental to this genre.

Other Sub-genres

Feminist Science Fictions

Feminist science fiction poses questions about social issues such as how society constructs gender roles, the role reproduction plays in defining gender and the unequal political and personal power of men and women. Some of the most notable feminist science fiction works have illustrated these themes using utopias to explore a society in which gender differences or gender power imbalances do not exist, or dystopias to explore worlds in which gender inequalities are intensified, thus asserting a need for feminist work to continue.

New Wave

New Wave is a term applied to science fiction writing

characterized by a high degree of experimentation, both in form and in content, and a highbrow and self-consciously "literary" or artistic sensibility.

Steampunk

Steampunk is set in an era or world where steam power is still widely used—usually the 19th century, and often set in Victorian era England—but with prominent elements of either science fiction or fantasy, such as fictional technological inventions like those found in the works of H.G. Wells and Jules Verne, or real technological developments like the computer occurring at an earlier date. A popular example is the Girl Genius series by Phil and Katya Foglio.

Religious or Spiritual science fiction

Religious or Spiritual science fiction is an established sub-genre. There are magazines like *Solaris Science Fiction* that cater specifically to this sub-genre. Of the sub-sub-genres in this category, Christian SF has been quite prominent. On the other hand, Islamic SF has been coming to prominence only of late, particularly through websites, and publications such as the anthology, *A Mosque Among the Stars.*

Speculative Fiction, Fantasy and Horror

The broader category of speculative fiction includes science fiction, fantasy, alternate histories (which may have no particular scientific or futuristic component), and even literary stories that contain fantastic elements, such as the work of Jorge Luis Borges or John Barth. For some editors, magic realism is considered to be within the broad definition of speculative fiction.

Fantasy

Fantasy is closely associated with science fiction, and many writers have worked in both genres, while writers such as Anne McCaffrey and Marion Zimmer Bradley have written works that appear to blur the boundary between the two related genres. The authors' professional organization is called the Science Fiction and Fantasy Writers of America (SFWA). SF conventions routinely have programming on fantasy topics, and fantasy authors such as J. K. Rowling have won the highest honor within the science fiction field, the Hugo Award. Some works show how difficult it is to draw clear boundaries between subgenres; however authors and readers often make a distinction between fantasy and SF. In general, science fiction is the literature of things that might someday be possible, and fantasy is the literature of things that are inherently impossible. Magic and mythology are popular themes in fantasy. Some narratives are described as being essentially science fiction but "with fantasy elements". The term "science fantasy" is sometimes used to describe such material.

Horror Fiction

Horror fiction is the literature of the unnatural and supernatural, with the aim of unsettling or frightening the reader, sometimes with graphic violence. Historically it has also been known as weird fiction. Although horror is not per se a branch of science fiction, many works of horror literature incorporates science fictional elements. One of the defining classical works of horror, Mary Shelley's novel Frankenstein, is the first fully-realized work of science fiction, where the manufacture of the monster is given a rigorous science-fictional grounding. The works of Edgar Allan

Poe also helped define both the science fiction and the horror genres. Today horror is one of the most popular categories of films. Horror is often mistakenly categorized as science fiction at the point of distribution by libraries, video rental outlets, etc. For example, the Sci fi Channel (distributed via cable and satellite television in the United States) currently devotes a majority of its air time to horror films with very few

Mystery Fiction

Works in which science and technology are a dominant theme, but based on current reality, may be considered mainstream fiction. Much of the thriller genre would be included, such as the novels of Tom Clancy or Michael Crichton, or the James Bond films. Modernist works from writers like Kurt Vonnegut, Philip K. Dick, and Stanis³aw Lem have focused on speculative or existential perspectives on contemporary reality and are on the borderline between SF and the mainstream. According to Robert J. Sawyer, "Science fiction and mystery have a great deal in common. Both prize the intellectual process of puzzle solving, and both require stories to be plausible and hinge on the way things really do work." Isaac Asimov, Walter Mosley, and other writers incorporate mystery elements in their science fiction, and vice versa.

Superhero Fiction

Superhero fiction is a genre characterized by beings with much higher than usual capability and prowess, generally with a desire or need to help the citizens of their chosen country or world by using his or her powers to defeat natural or superpowered threats. Many superhero fiction characters involve themselves (either intentionally or accidentally) with science fiction and fact, including advanced technologies, alien worlds, time travel, and interdimensional travel; but the standards of scientific plausibility are lower than with actual science fiction. Authors of this genre include Stan Lee (co-creator of Spider-Man, the Fantastic Four, the X-Men, and the Hulk); Marv Wolfman, the creator of *Blade* for Marvel Comics, and *The New Teen Titans* for DC Comics; Dean Wesley Smith (*Star Trek, Smallville, Spider-Man,* and *X-Men* novels) and *Superman* writers Roger Stern and Elliot S! Maggin.

8

Fantasy Writings

Fantasy is a genre that uses magic and other supernatural forms as a primary element of plot, theme, and/or setting. Many works within the genre take place on fictional planes or planets where magic is common. Fantasy is generally distinguished from science fiction and horror by the expectation that it steers clear of scientific and macabre themes, respectively, though there is a great deal of overlap between the three.

In popular culture, the genre of fantasy is dominated by its medievalist form, especially since the worldwide success of the *The Lord of the Rings* by J.R.R. Tolkien. In its broadest sense however, fantasy comprises works by many writers, artists, filmmakers, and musicians, from ancient myths and legends to many recent works embraced by a wide audience today.

Fantasy is a vibrant area of academic study in a number of disciplines. Work in this area ranges widely, from the structuralist theory of Tzvetan Todorov, which emphasizes the fantastic as a liminal space, to work on the connections (political, historical, literary) between medievalism and popular culture.

Traits of Fantasy

The identifying traits of fantasy are the inclusion of fantastic elements in a self-coherent (internally consistent) setting, where inspiration from mythology and folklore remains a consistent theme. Within such a structure, any location of the fantastical element is possible: it may be hidden in, or leak into the apparently real world setting, it may draw the characters into a world with such elements, or it may occur entirely in a fantasy world setting, where such elements are part of the world. American fantasy, starting with the stories chosen by John W. Campbell, Jr. for the magazine *Unknown,* is often characterized by internal logic. That is, the events in the story are impossible, but follow "laws" of magic, and have a setting that is internally consistent.

History

Beginning perhaps with the *Epic of Gilgamesh* and the earliest written documents known to humankind, mythic and other elements that would eventually come to define fantasy and its various subgenres have been a part of some of the grandest and most celebrated works of literature.

From *The Odyssey* to *Beowulf,* from the *Mahabharata* to *The Book of One Thousand and One Nights,* from the *Ramayana* to the *Journey to the West,* and from the Arthurian legend and medieval romance to the epic poetry of the *Divine Comedy,* fantastical adventures featuring brave heroes and heroines, deadly monsters, and secret arcane realms have inspired many audiences. In this sense, the history of fantasy and the history of literature are inextricably intertwined.

There are many works where the boundary between fantasy and other works is not clear; the question of whether the writers believed in the possibilities of the marvels in *A Midsummer Night's Dream* or *Sir Gawain and the Green Knight* makes it difficult to distinguish when fantasy, in its modern sense, first began.

Although pre-dated by John Ruskin's *The King of the Golden River* (1841), the history of modern fantasy literature is usually said to begin with George MacDonald, the Scottish author of such novels as *The Princess and the Goblin* and *Phantastes* (1858), the latter of which is widely considered to be the first fantasy novel ever written for adults. MacDonald was a major influence on both J.R.R. Tolkien and C. S. Lewis. The other major fantasy author of this era was William Morris, a popular English poet who wrote several novels in the latter part of the century, including *The Well at the World's End*.

Despite MacDonald's future influence with *At the Back of the North Wind* (1871), and Morris's popularity with his contemporaries, it wasn't until the turn of the century that fantasy fiction began to reach a large audience. Lord Dunsany established the genre's popularity in both the novel and the short story form. Many popular mainstream authors also began to write fantasy at this time, including H. Rider Haggard, Rudyard Kipling and Edgar Rice Burroughs. These authors, along with Abraham Merritt, established what was known as the "lost world" sub-genre, which was the most popular form of fantasy in the early decades of the 20th century, although several classic children's fantasies, such as *Peter Pan* and *The Wonderful Wizard of Oz*, were also published around this time.

Indeed, juvenile fantasy was considered more acceptable than fantasy intended for adults, with the effect that writers who wished to write fantasy had to fit their work in a work for children. Nathaniel Hawthorne wrote many early works verging on fantasy, but in *A Wonder-Book for Girls and Boys,* intended for children, wrote fantasy. For many years, this and successes such as *Alice's Adventures in Wonderland* (1865), created the circular effect that all fantasy works, even the later *The Lord of the Rings,* were therefore classified as children's literature.

In 1923 the first all-fantasy fiction magazine, *Weird Tales,* was created. Many other similar magazines eventually followed, most noticeably *The Magazine of Fantasy and Science Fiction.* The pulp magazine format was at the height of its popularity at this time and was instrumental in bringing fantasy fiction to a wide audience in both the U.S. and Britain. Such magazines were also instrumental in the rise of science fiction, and it was at this time the two genres began to be associated with each other.

By 1950 "sword and sorcery" fiction had begun to find a wide audience, with the success of Robert E. Howard's Conan the Barbarian and Fritz Leiber's Fafhrd and the Gray Mouser stories. However, it was the advent of high fantasy, and most of all the popularity of J. R. R. Tolkien's *The Hobbit* and *The Lord of the Rings* in the late 1960s, that allowed fantasy to truly enter the mainstream. Several other series, such as C. S. Lewis's *Chronicles of Narnia* and Ursula K. Le Guin's Earthsea books, helped cement the genre's popularity.

The popularity of the fantasy genre has continued to increase in the 21st century, as evidenced by the best-selling status of J.K. Rowling's Harry Potter books. Several fantasy film adaptations have achieved blockbuster status, most notably *The Lord of the Rings* film trilogy directed by Peter Jackson.

Criticism of fantasy includes its being called "second rate" literature; but author Terry Brooks rebutted this when he answered a question on his official website.

People who view fantasy as second rate or childish are usually people who don't read or understand it. I like to tell them that good fantasy is social commentary combined with good storytelling - Tolkien, C.S. Lewis, the Oz stories and so many others. Sure, the stories take place in an imaginary world. But those worlds mirror our own and tell us things about ourselves that need to be said and understood. I also like to tell them how often other forms of literature use fantasy as the bedrock of their own stories. Fantasy transcends its own form in wider scope than any other type of writing.

Media

Fantasy is a popular genre, having found a home for itself in almost every medium. While fantasy art and recently fantasy films have been increasingly popular, it is fantasy literature which has always been the genre's primary medium.

Fantasy role-playing games cross several different media. The "pen & paper" role-playing game Dungeons & Dragons was the first and is the most successful and influential, and the science fantasy role-playing game series *Final Fantasy* has been an icon of the console RPG genre.

Subgenres

Modern fantasy, including early modern fantasy, has also spawned many new subgenres with no clear counterpart in mythology or folklore, although inspiration from mythology and folklore remains a consistent theme. Fantasy subgenres are numerous and diverse, frequently overlapping with other forms of speculative fiction in almost every medium in which they are produced. A couple of examples are the science fantasy and dark fantasy subgenres, which the fantasy genre shares with science fiction and horror, respectively.

Professionals such as publishers, editors, authors, artists, and scholars within the fantasy genre get together yearly at the World Fantasy Convention. The World Fantasy Awards are presented at the convention. The first WFC was held in 1975, and it has occurred every year since. The convention is held at a different city each year. Additionally, many science fiction conventions, such as Florida's FX Show and MegaCon, cater to fantasy and horror fans. Anime conventions, such as Ohayocon or Anime Expo frequently feature showings of fantasy, science fantasy, and dark fantasy series and films, such as *Majutsushi Orphen* (fantasy), *Sailor Moon* (science fantasy), *Berserk* (dark fantasy), and *Spirited Away* (fantasy).

Many science fiction/fantasy and anime conventions also strongly feature or cater to one or more of the several subcultures within the main subcultures, including the cosplay subculture, the fan fiction subculture, and the fan vid or AMV subculture, as well as the large internet subculture devoted to reading and writing prose fiction and/or doujinshi in or related to those genres.

9

Western American Fiction

Western fiction is a genre of literature set in the American Old West frontier and typically set during the late nineteenth century. Well-known writers of Western fiction include Zane Grey from the early 1900s and Louis L'Amour from the mid 20th century. The genre peaked around the early 1960s, largely due to the popularity of televised Westerns such as *Bonanza*. Readership began to drop off in the mid- to late 1970s and has reached a new low in the 2000s. Most book stores. outside of a few western states, only carry a small number of Western fiction books.

Historical Development

The western in American literature emerged early in the nineteenth century with the novels of James Fenimore Cooper, particularly the five novels that comprise his *Leatherstocking Tales*. Cooper's novels were largely set in what was at the time the American frontier, the Appalachian Mountains and areas west of there. Most later westerns would typically take place west of the Mississippi River.

The Western as a specialized genre got its start in the "penny dreadfuls" and later the "dime novels" that first began to be published in the mid-nineteenth century. These cheaply made books were published to capitalize on the many fanciful yet supposedly true stories that were being told about the mountain men, outlaws, settlers and lawmen who were taming the western frontier.

By 1900, the new medium of pulp magazines also helped to relate these adventures to easterners. Meanwhile, non-American authors like the German Karl May picked up the genre, went to full novel length, and made it hugely popular and successful in continental Europe from about 1880 on, though they were generally dismissed as trivial by the literary critics of the day.

Popularity grew with the publication of Owen Wister's The Virginian in 1902 and especially Zane Grey's *Riders of the Purple Sage* in 1912. When pulp magazines exploded in popularity in the 1920s, western fiction greatly benefited (as did the author Max Brand, who excelled at the western short story). The simultaneous popularity of Western movies in the 1920s also helped the genre.

In the 1940s several seminal westerns were published including *The Ox-Bow Incident* (1940) by Walter van Tilburg Clark, *The Big Sky* (1947) and *The Way West* (1949) by A.B. Guthrie, Jr., and *Shane* (1949) by Jack Schaefer. Many other western authors gained readership in the 1950s, such as Luke Short, Ray Hogan, and Louis L'Amour.

The genre peaked around the early 1960s, largely due to the tremendous number of westerns on television. The burnout of the American public on television westerns in the late 1960s seemed to have an effect on the literature as well, and interest in western literature began to wane.

In the 1970s, the work of Louis L'Amour began to catch hold of most western readers and he has tended to dominate the western reader lists ever since. George G. Gilman also maintained a cult following for several years in the 1970s and 1980s. Larry McMurtry's and Cormac McCarthy's works remain notable. Specifically, McMurtry's *Lonesome Dove* and McCarthy's *Blood Meridian* (both published in 1985) are recognized as major masterpieces both within and beyond the genre. Elmer Kelton, mostly noted for his novels *The Good Old Boys* and *The Time it Never Rained,* was voted by the Western Writers of America as the "Best Western Writer of All Time". Western readership as a whole began to drop off in the mid- to late 1970s.

Readership of western fiction reached a new low in the 2000s, and most bookstores, outside of a few western states, only carry a small number of Western fiction books. Nevertheless, several Western fiction series are published monthly, such as *The Trailsman, Slocum,* and *Longarm.* The genre has seen the rumblings of a revival, and 2008 saw the publication of an all-Western short story magazine Great Western Fiction which was published by Dry River Publishing in Colorado. Unfortunately the magazine was short lived and folded after only two issues.

10

Lovecrafting Horror

Lovecraftian horror is a sub-genre of horror fiction which emphasizes the psychological horror of the unknown (in some cases, unknowable) over gore or other elements of shock, though these may still be present. It is named after American author H. P. Lovecraft (1890 – 1937).

Origin

Lovecraft refined this style of story-telling into his own mythos that involved a set of supernatural, pre-human and extraterrestrial elements. His work was informed by and similar to that of previous authors such as Edgar Allan Poe and Algernon Blackwood. The hallmark of Lovecraft's work was the sense that ordinary life was a thin shell over a reality which was so alien and abstract in comparison that merely contemplating it would damage the sanity of the ordinary person.

Lovecraft's work was also steeped in the insular feel of rural New England, and much of the genre continues to maintain this sense that "that which man was not meant to know" might be closer to the surface of ordinary life outside of the crowded cities of modern civilization. However, Lovecraftian horror is by no means restricted to the countryside; 'The Horror at Red Hook', for instance, is set in a crowded ethnic ghetto.

Themes

Several themes found in Lovecraft's writings are considered to be a component of a "Lovecraftian" work:

1) *Anti-anthropocentrism,* misanthropy in general. Lovecraft's works tend not to focus on characterization of humans, in line with his view of humanity's insignificant place in the universe, and the general Modernist trend of literature at the time of his writings.
2) *Preoccupation with viscerate texture.* The horror features of Lovecraft's stories tend to involve semi-gelátinous substances, such as slime, as opposed to standard horror tropes such as blood, bones, or corpses.
3) *Antiquarian writing style.* Even when dealing with up-to-date technology, Lovecraft tended to use anachronisms as well as old-fashioned words when dealing with such things. For example, he used the term "men of science" rather than the modern word, "scientist" and often spelled "show" as "shew".
4) *Detachment.* Lovecraftian heroes (both in original writings and in more modern adaptations) tend to be isolated individuals, usually with an academic or scholarly bent.
5) *Helplessness and hopelessness.* Although Lovecraftian heroes may occasionally deal a "setback" to malignant forces, their victories are temporary,

and they usually pay a price for it. Otherwise, subjects often find themselves completely unable to simply run away, instead driven by some other force to their desperate end.

6) *Unanswered questions.* Characters in Lovecraft's stories rarely if ever fully understand what is happening to them, and often go insane if they try.

7) *Sanity's fragility and vulnerability.* Characters in many of Lovecraft's stories are unable to mentally cope with the extraordinary and almost unreasonable truths they witness or hear. The strain of trying to cope, as Lovecraft often illustrates, is too impossible to bear and insanity takes hold.

Collaborators and Followers

Much of Lovecraft's influence is secondary, as he was a friend, inspiration, and correspondent to many authors who would gain fame through their creations. Many of these also worked with Lovecraft on jointly-written stories. His more famous friends and collaborators include Robert Bloch, author of *Psycho*; Robert E. Howard, creator of Conan the Barbarian; and August Derleth, who codified and added to the Cthulhu Mythos.

Subsequent horror writers also heavily drew on Lovecraft's work. While many made direct references to elements of Lovecraft's mythos, either to draw on its associations or to acknowledge his influence, many others drew on the feel and tone of his work without specifically referring to mythos elements. Some have said that Lovecraft, along with Edgar Allan Poe, is the most influential author on modern horror. Author Stephen King has said: "Now that time has given us some perspective on his work, I think it is beyond doubt that H. P. Lovecraft has yet to be surpassed as the Twentieth Century's greatest practitioner of the classic horror tale."

By the late 20th century, Lovecraft had become something of a pop-culture icon, resulting in countless reinterpretations of and references to his work. Many of these fall outside the sphere of 'Lovecraftian horror' proper and are not discussed here; see instead Cthulhu Mythos in popular culture.

Literature and Art

Lovecraft's work, mostly published in pulp magazines, has never had the same sort of influence on literature as his high-modernist literary contemporaries such as Ernest Hemingway and F. Scott Fitzgerald – some of the most influential authors in American history. However, his impact is still broadly and deeply felt in some of the most celebrated authors of contemporary fiction. The fantasias of the Argentinian short story writer and essayist Jorge Luis Borges display a marked resemblance to some of Lovecraft's more dream influenced work, and Borges dedicated his story, "There Are More Things" to Lovecraft. The controversial French novelist Michel Houellebecq has also cited Lovecraft as an influence and has written a lengthy essay on Lovecraft entitled *H. P. Lovecraft: Against the World, Against Life* in which he refers to the Cthulhu cycle as "the great texts".

Lovecraft's penchant for dreamscapes and for the biologically macabre has also profoundly influenced visual artists such as Jean "Moebius" Giraud and H.R.

Giger. Giger's book of paintings which led directly to many of the designs for the film *Alien* was named *Necronomicon,* the name of a fictional book in several of Lovecraft's mythos stories. Dan O'Bannon, the original writer of the *Alien* screenplay, has also mentioned Lovecraft as a major influence on the film. With Ronald Shusset, he would later write *Dead & Buried* and *Hemoglobin,* both of which were admitted pastiches of Lovecraft.

Comics

Lovecraft has cast a long shadow across the comic world. This has included not only adaptations of his stories, like *H. P. Lovecraft's Cthulhu: The Whisperer in Darkness, Graphic Classics: H.P. Lovecraft* and MAX's *Haunt of Horror,* but also the incorporation of the Mythos into new stories.

Alan Moore has touched on Lovecraftian themes, most obviously in his *The Courtyard* and *Yuggoth Cultures and Other Growths,* but also in his *Black Dossier.* Gordon Rennie not only used various Lovecraft creations, like Tcho-Tcho, in his *Necronauts,* but he also included Lovecraft himself as a character, teaming up with an influence of his Charles Fort, a combination that would occur again in *Fort: Prophet of the Unexplained. Necronauts* wasn't the first appearance of Lovecraftian horror in *2000 AD* as Grant Morrison's *Zenith* involved the eponymous hero trying to stop the Lloigor.

Boom! Studios have also run a number of series based on Cthulhu and other characters from the mythos, including *Cthulhu Tales* and *Fall of Cthulhu.*

The creator of *Hellboy,* Mike Mignola, has described the books as being influenced primarily by the works of Lovecraft, in addition to those of Robert E. Howard and the legend of Dracula. This was adapted into the 2004 film *Hellboy*.

A new webcomic, Lovecraft is Missing, debuted Oct. 1, 2008. It takes place in 1926, before the publication of The Call of Cthulhu, and weaves in elements of Lovecraft's earlier stories.

The manga artist Junji Ito was heavily influenced by Lovecraft. Arkham Asylum, from Batman comics, was named for the fictitious town of Arkham, Massachusetts. Arkham is a major setting in the Mythos and appears in many of Lovecraft's works.

Movies and Television

With the advent of film, Lovecraftian horror truly became a sub-genre, fueling not only direct adaptations of Poe and Lovecraft, but providing the foundation upon which many of the horror films of the 1950s and 1960s were constructed. One notable movie-maker to dip into the Lovecraftian well was 1960s B-movie maker, Roger Corman, though in 1965 *Die, Monster, Die!* (an adaptation of The Colour Out of Space so loose that it was nearly unrelated), caused movie makers to re-consider the value of Lovecraftian horror.

Rod Serling's 1969-73 series, *Night Gallery*, adapted at least two Lovecraft stories, "Pickman's Model" and "Cool Air". The episode "Professor Peabody's Last Lecture", concerning the fate of a man who read the *Necronomicon*, included a student named "Mr. Lovecraft". Another five minute short was called "Ms. Lovecraft Sent Me", about a babysitter and her strange client. Peabody is also a name used by Lovecraft in "At the Mountains of Madness".

In the late 1970s a revival of the horror movie genre was based on the success of Stephen King and Brian de Palma's *Carrie*; John Carpenter's *Halloween*; and Dan O'Bannon and Ridley Scott's *Alien*. All three movies bore Lovecraftian influences to one degree or another, and their authors were deeply influenced by Lovecraft's works. As the 1980s and 1990s played out, Lovecraftian horror became a recognizable film staple in such varied films as the self-referential *In the Mouth of Madness*, *Necronomicon*, the comedic *Re-Animator*, and Carpenter's Antarctic horror *The Thing*. Even in the works of Chiaki J. Konaka's anime including Digimon Tamers with the main antagonist the D-Reaper, sleeping until they wake and destroy the world.

Roleplaying

In the early 1970s, Dungeons and Dragons drew from many of the most popular fantasy settings including those of some of Lovecraft's contemporaries. However, Lovecraftian elements in the game would wait until *Dragon* magazine issue #12 in 1978 with Robert J. Kuntz's, "The Lovecraftian Mythos in Dungeons & Dragons". In 1980 a hardcover collection of the various fantasy and historical pantheons available for the game was published under the title, *Deities & Demigods*. The first and second printings contained a version of the Cthulhu mythos, but that section was removed in the third and subsequent printings for copyright reasons.

As the game has evolved, many of the creatures (e.g. the illithid) and even gods (e.g. Tharizdun) that were introduced were inspired by Lovecraft's works; and in October 2004, *Dragon* magazine published a lengthy article titled "The Shadow Over D&D: H. P. Lovecraft's Influence on Dungeons & Dragons" discussing these influences. Dungeons & Dragons was not the only roleplaying game to incorporate Lovecraftian horror, however. The most overt example was published in 1980 by Chaosium. Call of Cthulhu is directly based on the Cthulhu mythos. In keeping with its source material, and unlike most other role-playing games, characters who attempt to confront its monsters directly are likely to die or be driven insane rather than succeed. This is reinforced by the game's best-known feature, a mechanic by which knowledge about mythos entities can only be gained at a permanent cost to one's sanity. Following this roleplaying game into a modern era with an emphasis on military hardware and espionage wetware is Delta Green, in which characters fight the conspiracies behind which the Mythos hides rather than facing the Mythos more directly.

Steve Jackson Games' GURPS, a genre-neutral game system, was first published in 1986 and brought diverse elements of fiction and non-fiction together across their lengthy list of published supplements which included *Cthulhupunk*, a licensed adaptation of Call of Cthulhu into a cyberpunk setting.

Video Games

Video games, like films have a rich history of Lovecraftian elements and adaptations. In 1987, *The Lurking Horror* was the first to bring the Lovecraftian horror sub-genre to the multiple computer platforms. This was a text based adventure game, released by Infocom, who are best known for the Zork series. As 3-D computer graphics games developed, so too did the Lovecraftian influences. In 1992, *Alone in the Dark* was published by Infogrames for the PC, claiming to be inspired by the works of Lovecraft on its retail box.The plot of Quest for Glory IV: Shadows of Darkness involves an attempt to summon a creature named Avoozl to bring permanent darkness over the world. Both the Necromonicon and the chant "Ia!" are borrowed directly from Lovecraft.

In 1995 the second installment of the X-Com Series, Terror from the deep which featured references to Cthulhu and R'lyeh and conveyed a general sense of lovecraftian horror atmosphere, integrating the Cthulhu myth into the X-Com alien invasion scheme.

In the seminal 3D first person shooter, *Quake* in 1996 environments, creatures (including names such as Shub-Niggurath), and the atmosphere of the game emphasized many traditionally Lovecraftian features, with the architecture of the otherworldly dimension resembling many of Lovecraft's descriptions of ancient ruins and alien worlds. The three sequels, as of 2005, contain no Lovecraftian elements, however, and have opted for a more typical science fiction and mainstream horror approach, whose monsters now include only differing types of androids (mechanised alien species).

In 2005 *Call of Cthulhu: Dark Corners of the Earth* was released for PC. The game is a first person shooter horror game chiefly inspired by Lovecraft's stories *The Shadow Over Innsmouth* and *The Shadow Out of Time.*

Overall, the reception of Lovecraftian horror in video games, as with print fiction, has never achieved the same level of recognition as the high fantasy, swords-and-sorcery model games.

11

Writings of John Smith

Captain John Smith (c. January 1580 – June 21, 1631) Admiral of New England was an English soldier, explorer, and author. He is remembered for his role in establishing the first permanent English settlement in North America at Jamestown, Virginia, and his brief association with the Virginia Indian girl Pocahontas during an altercation with the Powhatan Confederacy and her father, Chief Powhatan. He was a leader of the Virginia Colony (based at Jamestown) between September 1608 and August 1609, and led an exploration along the rivers of Virginia and the Chesapeake Bay.

His books and maps may have been as important as his deeds, as they encouraged more Englishmen and women to follow the trail he had blazed and colonize the New World. He gave the name New England to that region, and encouraged people with the comment, "Here every man may be master and owner of his owne labour and land... If he have nothing but his hands, he may... by industrie quickly grow rich." His message attracted millions of people in the next four centuries.

Biography

John Smith was baptized on 6 January 1580 at Willoughby near Alford, Lincolnshire where his parents rented a farm from Lord Willoughby. He was a descendant of the ancient Smith family of Cuerdley and was educated at King Edward VI Grammar School, Louth. After his father died, Smith left home at age 16 and set off to sea. He served as a mercenary in the army of King Henry IV of France against the Spaniards, fought for Dutch independence from the Spanish King Phillip II, then set off for the Mediterranean Sea. There he engaged in both trade and piracy, and later fought against the Ottoman Turks in the Long War. Smith was promoted to captain while fighting for the Austrian Habsburgs in Hungary, in the campaign of Michael the Brave in 1600-1601. After the death of Michael the Brave, he fought for Radu Serban in Wallachia against Ottoman vassal Ieremia Movila.

He is reputed to have defeated, killed and beheaded Turkish commanders in three duels, for which he was knighted by the Transylvanian Prince Sigismund Báthory and given a horse and coat of Arms showing three Turks' heads. However, in 1602 he was wounded in a skirmish with the Tatars, captured and sold as a slave. As Smith describes it: "we all sold for slaves, like beasts in a market-place." Smith claimed his master, a Turkish nobleman, sent him as a gift to his Greek mistress in Constantinople, who fell in love with Smith. He then was taken to Crimea, from where he escaped from the Ottoman lands into Muscovy then on to the Polish-Lithuanian Commonwealth. Smith then traveled through Europe and Northern Africa, returning to England during 1604.

Life at Virginia Colony

In 1606, Smith became involved with plans to colonize Virginia for profit by the Virginia Company of London, which had been granted a charter from King James I of England. The expedition set sail in three small ships, the *Discovery*, the *Susan Constant* and the *Godspeed*, on December 20, 1606. His page was a 12-year-old boy named Samuel Collier.

John Smith was apparently a troublemaker on the voyage, and Captain Christopher Newporthad planned to execute him upon arrival in Virginia. However, upon first landing at what is now Cape Henry on April 26, 1607, sealed orders from the Virginia Company were opened. They designated Smith to be one of the leaders of the new colony, forcing Newport to spare him. The search for a suitable site ended on May 14, 1607, when Captain Edward Maria Wingfield, president of the council, chose the Jamestown site as the location for the colony.

Harsh weather, lack of water and attacks from Algonquian speaking tribes almost destroyed the colony. In December 1607, while seeking food along the Chickahominy River, Smith was captured and taken to meet the Chief of the Powhatans at Werowocomoco, the chief village of the Powhatan Confederacy on the north shore of the York River about 15 miles due north of Jamestown, and 25 miles downstream from where the river forms from the Pamunkey River and the Mattaponi River at West Point, Virginia. Although he feared for his life, Smith was eventually released without harm and later attributed this in part to the chief's daughter, Pocahontas, who, according to Smith, threw herself across his body: "at the minute of my execution, she hazarded [*i.e.* risked] the beating out of her own brains to save mine; and not only that, but so prevailed with her father, that I was safely conducted to Jamestown".

Smith's version of events is the only source, and since the 1860s, scepticism has increasingly been expressed about its veracity. One reason for such doubt is that despite having published two earlier books about Virginia, Smith's earliest surviving account of his rescue by Pocahontas dates from 1616, nearly 10 years later, in a letter entreating Queen Anne to treat Pocahontas with dignity. The time gap in publishing his story raises the possibility that Smith may have exaggerated or invented the event to enhance Pocahontas's image. However, in a recent book, Lemay points out that Smith's earlier writing was primarily geographical and ethnographic in nature and did not dwell on his personal experiences; hence there was no reason for him to write down the story until this point.

Henry Brooks Adams, the pre-eminent Harvard historian of the second half of the 19th century, attempted to debunk Smith's claims of heroism. He said that Smith's recounting of the story of Pocahontas had been progressively embellished, made up of "falsehoods of an effrontery seldom equalled in modern times." Although there is general consensus among historians that Smith tended to exaggerate, his account does seem to be consistent with the basic facts of his life. Adams' attack on Smith, an attempt to deface one of the icons of Southern history, was motivated by political considerations in the wake of the Civil War. Adams had been influenced to write his fusillade against Smith by John G. Palfrey who was promoting New England colonization, as opposed to southern settlement, as the founding of America. The accuracy of Smith's accounts has continued to be a subject of debate over the centuries.

Some experts have suggested that, although Smith believed he had been rescued, he had in fact been involved in a ritual intended to symbolize his death and rebirth as a member of the tribe. However, in *Love and Hate in Jamestown*, David A. Price notes that this is only guesswork, since little is known of Powhatan rituals, and there is no evidence for any similar rituals among other Native American tribes in North America.

Whatever really happened, the encounter initiated a friendly relationship between the natives and Smith and the colonists at Jamestown. As the colonists expanded further, however, some of the tribes felt that their lands were threatened, and conflicts arose again.

In 1608, Pocahontas is said to have saved Smith a second time. Smith and some other colonists were invited to Werowocomoco by Chief Powhatan on friendly terms, but Pocahontas came to the hut where the English were staying and warned them that Powhatan was planning to kill them. Due to this warning, the English stayed on their guard, and the attack never came.

Later, Smith left Jamestown to explore the Chesapeake Bay region and search for badly-needed food, covering an estimated 3,000 miles. In his absence, Smith left his friend Matthew Scrivener, a young gentleman adventurer from Sibton, Suffolk, who was related by marriage to the Wingfield family, as Governor in his place. When he returned, he discovered that Scrivener wasn't cut out to be a leader of the people, and so Smith was eventually elected president of the local council in September 1608 and instituted a policy of discipline, encouraging farming with a famous admonition taken from the New Testament : "He who does not work, will not eat."

Return to New England

In 1614, Smith returned to the Americas in a voyage to the coasts of Maine and Massachusetts Bay, and named the region "New England".He made two attempts in 1614 and 1615 to return to the same coast. The first ended when a storm dismasted his ship, the second when he was captured by French pirates off the Azores. Smith escaped after weeks of captivity and made his way back to England, where he published an account of his two voyages as *A Description of New England*. He never left England again, and spent the rest of his life writing books. He died in the year 1631 in London at the age of 51.

Authorship

Many critics judge Captain John Smith's character and credibility as an author based on a single event, the infamous scene where Pocahontas saved his life from the hand of Powhatan. Additional and likely more accurate judgments should rest upon his relationship with both the Indians and colonists of Jamestown. Smith earned his status as an American hero through his strong work ethic and compromise with the Indians, themes that reappear in his writings such as *The Generall Historie of Virginia* and *The True Travels...of Captain John Smith*. Most of the critical skepticism of Smith's credibility is a result of the differences between his narratives. His earliest text is A True Relation of Virginia, which was submitted for publication in 1608, only a year after Smith's experiences in Jamestown. The second, *The Generall Historie,* was published in

1624, a whole sixteen years later. Compared to the *The Generall Historie,* many events, including the Pocahontas scene, are either left out or changed; this is likely to due to the fact that *The Generall Historie* was composed so much later, and Smith's memories of the colony, the Indians, and their relations were faded. Accordingly, the publishing of letters, journals, and pamphlets from the colonists were regulated by the companies that sponsored the voyage in that they must go "directly to the company," because no one was to "write any letter of anything that may discourage others." Smith is now known to have violated this regulation by first publishing *A True Relation* as an unknown author. Furthermore, the editor of *The Generall Historie* likely "cut out...references to the Indians' hostility, to bickering among the leaders of Virginia Company, and to the early supposed mutiny of...Smith on the voyage to Virginia."

The Pocahontas episode is subject to the most scrutiny by literary critics, for it does not even appear in *A True Relation,* but does so in *The Generall Historie.* According to Lemay, it is probable that "Smith was being ritualistically killed. Reborn, he was adopted into the tribe, with Pocahontas as his sponsor. But Smith, of course, did not realize the nature of the initiation ceremony." Also important evidence to Smith's credibility regarding the story is the fact that "no one in Smith's day ever expressed doubt in [it], and many persons who must have known the truth...including John Rolfe [and] Pocahontas...were in London in 1616 when Smith publicized the story in a letter to the queen."

Smith focuses heavily on American Indians in all of his works concerning the New World. Smith's relationship with the Powhatan Indians is the sole factor that saved the Jamestown colony from sharing the fate of the Roanoke colony. His relations with the Indians were very wise in that:

He was friendly toward them, but never let them forget the might of English weapons...Realizing that the very existence of the colony depended on peace, he never thought of trying to exterminate the natives. Only after his departure were there bitter wars and massacres, the natural results of a more hostile policy. In his writings, Smith reveals the attitudes behind his actions.

However, in *The Generall Historie*, Smith implies that the Virginia colonists resented the Indians and the two peoples had mostly hostile feelings towards each other. He compares Chief Powhatan to the devil, and refers to the Indians as "barbarians." Numerous times, he mentions sending spies to discover the Chief's intent and declining Powhatan's request to relinquish their arms. He also stresses the many experiences where the Indians threatened and attempted to kill him. However, Lemay contests Smith's depiction of the relations between colonists and Indians: "[He] was not only fair, he was surprisingly kind and humanitarian. He treated the Indians as he treated whites...tortured [none], executed none, and saved Indians when others wanted to slay them." Smith's own past as a commoner allowed him to sympathize with the Indians, and he believed that the Indians were not inferior to the whites but just "at a different stage of civilization." The amount of respect that existed between Smith and the Powhatan even earned him the title of a werowance, "a chieftain among the whites." The relationship between Smith and Chief Powhatan is further evidence of the understanding between these two cultures.

In *The Generall Historie,* Smith addresses a number of letters exchanged between him and Powhatan that reflect the respect that existed between them: "Half a dozen years after Smith had left Virginia—and after the whites had repeatedly assured Powhatan that Smith was dead—[the] leader instructed his advisor... [and] Pocahontas to look for Smith in England;" judging from his directions, the Chief seems to have been deeply affected by the Smith's rumored death. This is another indication of the positive relationship held between colonists and Indians: if their associations were as Smith depicted them in *The Generall Historie,* Powhatan would not have been much concerned about his absence or death. Concerning his relationship with the colonists, Smith is considered by historical and literary critics to be an arrogant braggart.

On numerous accounts, he outwardly expressed the colonists were worthless; most of them were gentlemen who felt no need to do physical labor. As a method of survival, Smith blatantly rejected the social order that existed in England, which obviously angered the gentlemen of the colony. Smith became regularly frustrated with the amount of delegation that the colonists went through before a decision could be made. Smith's disgust with the "gentlemen" of Jamestown was clear: he makes several references to them as "useless parasites," for their ignorance in the laborious tasks that are required for beginning a colony. His frustration with them did not end at their inability to work, but also extended to the social order that they believe they were entitled to. The colonists, accustomed to the social order of England, rejected the social construct that Smith created in Jamestown. They perceived Smith's establishment of this new structure as a challenge to their "deserved" respect. Smith mentions several times in his works that having actual workers would have been better than what the Virginia Company sent over: "twentie good workmen had been better than all them all."

In Smith's hopes to better colonize the Americas, he urges to the Massachusetts Bay Company not to make the same mistake that the Virginia Company made: "...nor such multitude of Officers, neither masters, gentlemen, gentlewomen and children as you have men to work, which idle chares you will fine very troublesome, and the effects dangerous, and one hundred good labourers better than a thousand such Gallants as we were sent me that could do nothing." In reality, Smith was discontent with only a few colonists who acted this way: he "claimed the early colonists were heroes. His primary purpose in writing The *Generall Historie*...was to eternalize 'the memory of those that effected' the settlement of Virginia."

In Smith's publication, *A Description of New England* (1616), he goes so far as to compare the colonists to Adam and Eve; just as Adam and Eve spread productivity throughout the world, the colonists created life in the Virginia colony. Smith essentially sympathized with gentlemen; he knew it was not their fault they were useless and that this trait was merely a product of the imposed standards of English society. He recognized that "they were imprisoned by their own self-imposed limitations. What they could and could not do was decided by their awareness of traditional roles and by the shame that they would feel if others saw them engaged in physical work." Lemay speculates that as a result of Smith's strict rules and the emigration to America, these men could shed these roles and create new lives for themselves in which they could celebrate the products of their labors and not feel humiliated.

Promoter of American Colonization

One of John Smith's main incentives in writing about his New World experiences and observances was to promote the colonization of America by England. Many promotional writers sugarcoated their depictions of America in order to heighten its appeal, but Smith was not one to exaggerate the facts. He was very straightforward with his readers about both the dangers and the possibilities of colonization: instead of proclaiming that there was an abundance of gold in the New World—as many writers did—Smith illustrated that what was truly abundant within America was monetary opportunity in the form of industry. Smith was realistic about his proposition for colonization and the benefits that it could yield. He recognized that no "other motive [besides] wealth...would draw [potential colonists] from their ease and humours at home." Therefore, he presented in his writings actual industries that could yield significant capital within the New World: fishing, farming, shipbuilding, and fur trading."

In *A Description of New England,* Smith illustrates America as an ideal environment for such trades and enumerates the monetary benefits that they would bring. Rather than making false promises of abounding gold to his readers, Smith attempted to attract interest for colonization by depicting the opportunities that fertile soil and abundant resources would bring. He insists, however, that only hard workers will be able to reap such benefits. Just as Smith did not exaggerate the possibilities for wealth within America, he did not deemphasize the dangers and toil associated with colonization. He declared that only those with a strong work ethic would be able to "live and succeed in America" in the face of such dangers. Colonists would have to risk their lives in order to benefit from the "phenomenal possibilities" that the New World offered. As a promoter of American colonization, Smith did not placate his readers: he wished for potential colonists to be aware of the dangers that they faced, the work that colonization would require, and the benefits that they stood to gain.

Additional Works

A Map of Virginia is focused centrally on the observations that Smith made about the Indians, particularly regarding their religion and government. This specific focus would have been Smith's way of adapting to the new world by assimilating to the best part of their culture and to incorporating it into the colony.

A Map of Virginia was not just a pamphlet discussing the observations that Smith made, but also a map by which Smith had draws himself to help make the Americas seem more domestic. As Lemay remarks, "maps tamed the unknown, reduced it to civilization and harnessed it for Western consciousness," promoting Smith's central theme of encouraging the settlement of America. Many "naysayers of the late nineteenth and early twentieth century" have made the argument that Smith's maps weren't reliable because he "lacked a formal education in cartography." That allegation, however, was proved false by the fact that Smith was a "master in his chosen fields of experience." *The Proceedings of English Colonie In Virginia* was a compilation of other writings; it narrates the colony's history from Dec. 1609 to summer 1610, and Smith left the colony in Oct. 1609 due to a gun-powder accident. The writing style of *The Proceedings* is better constructed than *A Map of Virginia.* It is well organized and more focused, and this could've been a result of Smith's ever conscious self promotion by allocating it to a wider reader base: "Books stood a better change...if they had been Testimonial."

12

Works of Walt Whitman

Walter Whitman (May 31, 1819 – March 26, 1892) was an American poet, essayist, journalist, and humanist. He was a part of the transition between Transcendentalism and realism, incorporating both views in his works. Whitman is among the most influential poets in the American canon, often called the father of free verse. His work was very controversial in its time, particularly his poetry collection *Leaves of Grass*, which was described as obscene for its overt sexuality.

Born on Long Island, Whitman worked as a journalist, a teacher, a government clerk, and a volunteer nurse during the American Civil War in addition to publishing his poetry. Early in his career, he also produced a temperance novel, *Franklin Evans* (1842). Whitman's major work, *Leaves of Grass*, was first published in 1855 with his own money. The work was an attempt at reaching out to the common person with an American epic. He continued expanding and revising it until his death in 1892. After a stroke towards the end of his life, he moved to Camden, New Jersey where his health further declined. He died at age 72 and his funeral became a public spectacle.

Whitman's sexuality is often discussed alongside his poetry. Though biographers continue to debate his sexuality, he is usually described as either homosexual or bisexual in his feelings and attractions. However, there is disagreement among biographers as to whether Whitman had actual sexual experiences with men. Whitman was concerned with politics throughout his life. He supported the Wilmot Proviso and opposed the extension of slavery generally. His poetry presented an egalitarian view of the races, and at one point he called for the abolition of slavery, but later he saw the abolitionist movement as a threat to democracy

Biography

Walter Whitman was born on May 31, 1819, in West Hills, Town of Huntington, Long Island, to parents with interest in Quaker thought, Walter and Louisa Van Velsor Whitman. He was the second of nine children and was immediately nicknamed "Walt" to distinguish him from his father. Walter Whitman Sr. named three of his seven sons after American leaders: Andrew Jackson, George Washington, and Thomas Jefferson. The oldest was named Jesse and another boy died unnamed at the age of six months. The couple's sixth son, the youngest, was named Edward. At age four, Whitman moved with his family from West Hills to Brooklyn, living in a series of homes in part due to bad investments. Whitman looked back on his childhood as generally restless and unhappy due to his family's difficult economic status. One happy moment that he later recalled was when he was lifted in the air and kissed on the cheek by the Marquis de Lafayette during a celebration in Brooklyn on July 4, 1825.

At age eleven Whitman concluded formal schooling. He then sought employment for further income for his family; he was an office boy for two lawyers and later was an apprentice and printer's devil for the weekly Long Island newspaper the *Patriot*, edited by Samuel E. Clements. There, Whitman learned about the printing press and typesetting. He may have written "sentimental bits" of filler material for occasional issues. Clements aroused controversy when he and two friends attempted to dig up the corpse of Elias Hicks to create a plaster mold of his head. Clements left the *Patriot* shortly after, possibly as a result of the controversy.

Authorship

The following summer Whitman worked for another printer, Erastus Worthington, in Brooklyn. His family moved back to West Hills in the spring, but Whitman remained and took a job at the shop of Alden Spooner, editor of the leading Whig weekly newspaper the *Long-Island Star*. While at the *Star*, Whitman became a regular patron of the local library, joined a town debating society, began attending theater performances, and anonymously published some of his earliest poetry in the *New York Mirror*.

At age 16 in May 1835, Whitman left the *Star* and Brooklyn. He moved to New York City to work as a compositor though, in later years, Whitman could not remember where. He attempted to find further work but had difficulty in part due to a severe fire in the printing and publishing district and in part due to a general collapse in the economy leading up to the Panic of 1837. In May 1836, he rejoined his family, now living in Hempstead, Long Island. Whitman taught intermittently at various schools until the spring of 1838, though he was not satisfied as a teacher. After his teaching attempts, Whitman went back to Huntington, New York to found his own newspaper, the Long Islander. Whitman served as publisher, editor, pressman, and distributor and even provided home delivery. After ten months, he sold the publication to E. O. Crowell, whose first issue appeared on July 12, 1839. No copies of the *Long-Islander* published under Whitman survive.

By the summer of 1839, he found a job as a typesetter in Jamaica, Queens with the *Long Island Democrat,* edited by James J. Brenton. He left shortly thereafter, and made another attempt at teaching from the winter of 1840 to the spring of 1841, During this time, he published a series of ten editorials called "Sun-Down Papers—From the Desk of a Schoolmaster" in three newspapers between the winter of 1840 and July 1841. In these essays, he adopted a constructed persona, a technique he would employ throughout his career.

Whitman moved to New York City in May, initially working a low-level job at the *New World,* working under Park Benjamin, Sr. and Rufus Wilmot Griswold. He continued working for short periods of time for various newspapers; in 1842 he was editor of the *Aurora* and from 1846 to 1848 he was editor of the *Brooklyn Eagle.* He also contributed freelance fiction and poetry throughout the 1840s. Whitman lost his position at the *Brooklyn Eagle* in 1848 after siding with the free-soil "Barnburner" wing of the Democratic party against the newspaper's owner, Isaac Van Anden, who belonged to the conservative, or "Hunker", wing of the party. Whitman was a delegate to the 1848 founding convention of the Free Soil Party.

Leaves of Grass

Whitman claimed that after years of competing for "the usual rewards", he determined to become a poet. He first experimented with a variety of popular literary genres which appealed to the cultural tastes of the period. As early as 1850, he began writing what would become *Leaves of Grass,* a collection of poetry which he would continue editing and revising until his death. Whitman intended to write a distinctly American epic and used free verse with a cadence based on the Bible. At the end of June 1855, Whitman surprised his brothers with the already-printed first edition of *Leaves of Grass*. George "didn't think it worth reading".

Whitman paid for the publication of the first edition of *Leaves of Grass* himself and had it printed at a local print shop during their breaks from commercial jobs. A total of 795 copies were printed. No name is given as author; instead, facing the title page was an engraved portrait done by Samuel Hollyer, but in the body of the text he calls himself "Walt Whitman, an American, one of the roughs, a kosmos, disorderly, fleshly, and sensual, no sentimentalist, no stander above men or women or apart from them, no more modest than immodest".

The book received its strongest praise from Ralph Waldo Emerson, who wrote a flattering five page letter to Whitman and spoke highly of the book to friends. The first edition of *Leaves of Grass* was widely distributed and stirred up significant interest, in part due to Emerson's approval, but was occasionally criticized for the seemingly "obscene" nature of the poetry. Geologist John Peter Lesley wrote to Emerson, calling the book "trashy, profane & obscene" and the author "a pretentious ass". On July 11, 1855, a few days after *Leaves of Grass* was published, Whitman's father died at the age of 65.

In the months following the first edition of *Leaves of Grass,* critical responses began focusing more on the potentially offensive sexual themes. Though the second edition was already printed and bound, the publisher almost did not release it. In the end, the edition went to retail, with 20 additional poems, in August 1856. *Leaves of Grass* was revised and re-released in 1860 again in 1867, and several more times throughout the remainder of Whitman's life. Several well-known writers admired the work enough to visit Whitman, including Bronson Alcott and Henry David Thoreau.

During the first publications of *Leaves of Grass,* Whitman had financial difficulties and was forced to work as a journalist again, specifically with Brooklyn's *Daily Times* starting in May 1857. As an editor, he oversaw the paper's contents, contributed book reviews, and wrote editorials. He left the job in 1859, though it is unclear if he was fired or chose to leave. Whitman, who typically kept detailed notebooks and journals, left very little information about himself in the late 1850s.

Civil War Years

As the American Civil War was beginning, Whitman published his poem "Beat! Beat! Drums!" as a patriotic rally call for the North. Whitman's brother George had joined the Union army and began sending Whitman several vividly detailed letters of the battle front. On December 16, 1862, a listing of fallen and wounded soldiers in the *New York Tribune* included "First Lieutenant G. W. Whitmore", which Whitman worried was a reference to his brother George. He made his way south immediately to find him, though his wallet was stolen on the way. "Walking all day and night, unable to ride, trying to get information, trying to get access to big people", Whitman later wrote, he eventually found George alive, with only a superficial wound on his cheek. Whitman, profoundly affected by seeing the wounded soldiers and the heaps of their amputated limbs, left for Washington on December 28, 1862 with the intention of never returning to New York.

In Washington, D.C., Whitman's friend Charley Eldridge helped him obtain part-time work in the army paymaster's office, leaving time for Whitman to volunteer as a nurse in the army hospitals. He would write of this experience in "The Great Army of the Sick", published in a New York newspaper in 1863 and, 12 years later, in a book called *Memoranda during the War*. He then contacted Emerson, this time to ask for help in obtaining a government post. Another friend, John Trowbridge, passed on a letter of recommendation from Emerson to Salmon P. Chase, Secretary of the Treasury, hoping he would grant Whitman a position in that department. Chase, however, did not want to hire the author of such a disreputable book as *Leaves of Grass*.

The Whitman family had a difficult end to 1864. On September 30, 1864, Whitman's brother George was captured by Confederates in Virginia, another brother, Andrew Jackson, died of tuberculosis compounded by alcoholism on December 3. That month, Whitman committed his brother Jesse to the Kings County Lunatic Asylum. Whitman's spirits were raised, however, when he finally got a better-paying government post as a low-grade clerk in the Bureau of Indian Affairs in the Department of the Interior – thanks to his friend William Douglas O'Connor. O'Connor, a poet, daguerreotypist and an editor at the *Saturday Evening Post,* had written to William Tod Otto, Assistant Secretary of the Interior, on Whitman's behalf. Whitman began the new appointment on January 24, 1865, with a yearly salary of $1,200. A month later, on February 24, 1865, George was released from capture and granted a furlough because of his poor health. By May 1, Whitman received a promotion to a slightly higher clerkship and published *Drum-Taps.*

Effective June 30, 1865, however, Whitman was fired from his job. His dismissal came from the new Secretary of the Interior, former Iowa Senator James Harlan. Though Harlan dismissed several clerks who "were seldom at their respective desks", he may have fired Whitman on moral grounds after finding an 1860 edition of *Leaves of Grass.* O'Connor protested until J. Hubley Ashton had Whitman transferred to the Attorney General's office on July 1. O'Connor, though, was still upset and vindicated Whitman by publishing a biased and exaggerated biographical study, *The Good Gray Poet,* in January 1866. The fifty-cent pamphlet defended Whitman as a wholesome patriot, established the poet's nickname and increased his popularity. Also aiding in his popularity was the publication of "O Captain! My Captain!", a relatively conventional poem on the death of Abraham Lincoln, the only poem to appear in anthologies during Whitman's lifetime.

Part of Whitman's role at the Attorney General's office was interviewing former Confederate soldiers for Presidential pardons. "There are real characters among them", he later wrote, "and you know I have a fancy for anything out of the ordinary." In August 1866, he took a month off in order to prepare a new edition of *Leaves of Grass* which would not be published until 1867 after difficulty in finding a publisher. He hoped it would be its last edition. In February 1868 *Poems of Walt Whitman* was published in England thanks to the influence of William Michael Rossetti, with minor changes that Whitman reluctantly approved. The edition became popular in England, especially with endorsements from the highly respected writer Anne Gilchrist. Another edition of *Leaves of Grass* was issued in 1871, the same year it was mistakenly reported that its author died in a railroad accident. As Whitman's international fame increased, he remained at the attorney general's office until January 1872. He spent much of 1872 caring for his mother who was now nearly eighty and struggling with arthritis. He also traveled and was invited to Dartmouth College to give the commencement address on June 26, 1872.

Later Years

Early in 1873, Whitman suffered a paralytic stroke; his mother died in May the same year. Both events were difficult for Whitman and left him depressed. He moved to Camden, New Jersey to live with his brother George, paying room and board until he bought his own house on Mickle St. in 1884. Around this time, he began socializing with Mary Oakes Davis, the widow of a sea captain, who lived nearby. She moved in with Whitman on February 24, 1885 to serve as his housekeeper in exchange for free rent. She brought with her a cat, a dog, two turtledoves, a canary, and other assorted animals. During this time, Whitman produced further editions of *Leaves of Grass* in 1876, 1881, and 1889.

As the end of 1891 approached, he prepared a final edition of *Leaves of Grass,* an edition which has been nicknamed the "Deathbed Edition". He wrote, "L. of G. *at last complete*—after 33 y'rs of hackling at it, all times & moods of my life, fair weather & foul, all parts of the land, and peace & war, young & old". Preparing for death, Whitman commissioned a granite mausoleum shaped like a house for $4,000 and visited it often during construction. In the last week of his life, he was too weak to lift a knife or fork and wrote: "I suffer all the time: I have no relief, no escape: it is monotony — monotony — monotony — in pain."

Whitman died on March 26, 1892. An autopsy revealed his lungs had diminished to one-eighth their normal breathing capacity, a result of bronchial pneumonia, and that an egg-sized abscess on his chest had eroded one of his ribs. The cause of death was officially listed as "pleurisy of the left side, consumption of the right lung, general miliary tuberculosis and parenchymatous nephritis." A public viewing of his body was held at his Camden home; over one thousand people visited in three hours and Whitman's oak coffin was barely visible because of all the flowers and wreaths left for him. He was buried in his tomb at Harleigh Cemetery in Camden four days after his death. Another public ceremony was held at the cemetery, with friends giving speeches, live music, and refreshments. Whitman's friend, the orator Robert Ingersoll, delivered the eulogy. Later, the remains of Whitman's parents and two of his brothers and their families were moved to the mausoleum.

Whitman's work breaks the boundaries of poetic form and is generally prose-like. He also used unusual images and symbols in his poetry, including rotting leaves, tufts of straw, and debris. He also openly wrote about death and sexuality, including prostitution. He is often labeled as the father of free verse, though he did not invent it.

Whitman wrote in the preface to the 1855 edition of *Leaves of Grass*, "The proof of a poet is that his country absorbs him as affectionately as he has absorbed it." He believed there was a vital, symbiotic relationship between the poet and society. This connection was emphasized especially in "Song of Myself" by using an all-powerful first-person narration. As an American epic, it deviated from the historic use of an elevated hero and instead assumed the identity of the common people. *Leaves of Grass* also responded to the impact that recent urbanization in the United States had on the masses.

Whitman was a vocal proponent of temperance and in his youth rarely drank alcohol. He once claimed he did not taste "strong liquor" until he was thirty and occasionally argued for prohibition. One of his earliest long fiction works, the novel *Franklin Evans; or, The Inebriate,* first published November 23, 1842, is a temperance novel. Whitman wrote the novel at the height of popularity of the Washingtonian movement though the movement itself was plagued with contradictions, as was *Franklin Evans*. Years later Whitman claimed he was embarrassed by the book and called it a "damned rot". He dismissed it by saying he wrote the novel in three days solely for money while he was under the influence of alcohol himself. Even so, he wrote other pieces recommending temperance, including *The Madman* and a short story "Reuben's Last Wish". Later in life he was more liberal with alcohol, enjoying local wines and champagne.

Whitman was deeply influenced by deism. He denied any one faith was more important than another, and embraced all religions equally. In "Song of Myself", he gave an inventory of major religions and indicated he respected and accepted all of them – a sentiment he further emphasized in his poem "With Antecedents", affirming: "I adopt each theory, myth, god, and demi-god, / I see that the old accounts, bibles, genealogies, are true, without exception". In 1874, he was invited to write a poem about the Spiritualism movement, to which he responded, "It seems to me nearly altogether a poor, cheap, crude humbug." Whitman was a religious skeptic: though he accepted all churches, he believed in none.

Whitman was a proponent of the Shakespeare authorship question, refusing to believe in the historic attribution of the works to William Shakespeare of Stratford-upon-Avon. Whitman comments in his *November Boughs* (1888) regarding Shakespeare's historical plays:

> "Conceiv'd out of the fullest heat and pulse of European feudalism -personifying ill unparalleled ways the medieval aristocracy, its towering spirit of ruthless and gigantic caste, with its own peculiar air and arrogance (no mere imitation) -only one of the "wolfish earls" so plenteous in the plays themselves, or some born descendant and knower, might seem to be the true author of those amazing works -works in some respects greater than anything else in recorded literature."

Whitman opposed the extension of slavery in the United States and supported the Wilmot Proviso. At first he was opposed to abolitionism, believing the movement did more harm than good. In 1846, he wrote that the abolitionists had, in fact, slowed the advancement of their cause by their "ultraism and officiousness". His main concern was that their methods disrupted the democratic process, as did the refusal of the Southern states to put the interests of the nation as a whole above their own. In 1856, in his unpublished *The Eighteenth Presidency*, addressing the men of the South, he wrote "you are either to abolish slavery or it will abolish you". Whitman also subscribed to the widespread opinion that even free African-Americans should not vote and was concerned at the increasing number of African-Americans in the legislature.

Legacy and Influence

Walt Whitman has been claimed as America's first "poet of democracy", a title meant to reflect his ability to write in a singularly American character. A British friend of Walt Whitman, Mary Smith Whitall Costelloe, wrote: "You cannot really understand America without Walt Whitman, without *Leaves of Grass*... He has expressed that civilization, 'up to date,' as he would say, and no student of the philosophy of history can do without him." Modernist poet Ezra Pound called Whitman "America's poet... He *is* America." Andrew Carnegie called him "the great poet of America so far". Whitman considered himself a messiah-like figure in poetry. Others agreed: one of his admirers, William Sloane Kennedy, speculated that "people will be celebrating the birth of Walt Whitman as they are now the birth of Christ".

The literary critic, Harold Bloom wrote, as the introduction for the 150th anniversary of *Leaves of Grass*:

> If you are American, then Walt Whitman is your imaginative father and mother, even if, like myself, you have never composed a line of verse. You can nominate a fair number of literary works as candidates for the secular Scripture of the United States. They might include Melville's *Moby-Dick*, Twain's *Adventures of Huckleberry Finn*, and Emerson's two series of *Essays* and *The Conduct of Life*. None of those, not even Emerson's, are as central as the first edition of *Leaves of Grass*.

Whitman's vagabond lifestyle was adopted by the Beat movement and its leaders such as Allen Ginsberg and Jack Kerouac in the 1950s and 1960s as well as anti-war poets like Adrienne Rich and Gary Snyder. Whitman also influenced Bram Stoker, author of *Dracula*, and was the model for the character of Dracula. Stoker said in his notes that Dracula represented the quintessential male which, to Stoker, was Whitman, with whom he corresponded until Whitman's death.

The final stanza of the poem "The Wound-Dresser" by Walt Whitman has been engraved across the top of the massive granite walls encircling the 188-foot north entrance escalators descending to the underground trains at the DuPont Circle stop on the Washington, D.C. transit system. The installation was formally dedicated as a tribute to caregivers for those with HIV/Aids and other devastating illnesses at a ceremony on July 14, 2007.

13

Literary Life of Emily Dickinson

Emily Elizabeth Dickinson (December 10, 1830 – May 15, 1886) was an American poet. Born in Amherst, Massachusetts, to a successful family with strong community ties, she lived a mostly introverted and reclusive life. After she studied at the Amherst Academy for seven years in her youth, she spent a short time at Mount Holyoke Female Seminary before returning to her family's house in Amherst. Thought of as an eccentric by the locals, she became known for her penchant for white clothing and her reluctance to greet guests or, later in life, even leave her room. Most of her friendships were therefore carried out by correspondence.

Although Dickinson was a prolific private poet, fewer than a dozen of her nearly eighteen hundred poems were published during her lifetime. The work that was published during her lifetime was usually altered significantly by the publishers to fit the conventional poetic rules of the time. Dickinson's poems are unique for the era in which she wrote; they contain short lines, typically lack titles, and often use slant rhyme as well as unconventional capitalization and punctuation. Many of her poems deal with themes of death and immortality, two recurring topics in letters to her friends.

Although most of her acquaintances were probably aware of Dickinson's writing, it was not until after her death in 1886—when Lavinia, Emily's younger sister, discovered her cache of poems—that the breadth of Dickinson's work became apparent. Her first collection of poetry was published in 1890 by personal acquaintances Thomas Wentworth Higginson and Mabel Loomis Todd, both of whom heavily edited the content. A complete and mostly unaltered collection of her poetry became available for the first time in 1955 when *The Poems of Emily Dickinson* was published by scholar Thomas H. Johnson. Despite unfavorable reviews and skepticism of her literary prowess during the late 19th and early 20th century, critics now consider Dickinson to be a major American poet

Life

Emily Elizabeth Dickinson was born at the family's homestead in Amherst, Massachusetts, on December 10, 1830, into a prominent, but not opulent, family. Two hundred years earlier, the Dickinsons had arrived in the New World—in the Puritan Great Migration—where they prospered. Emily Dickinson's paternal grandfather, Samuel Dickinson, had almost single-handedly founded Amherst College. In 1813 he built the homestead, a large mansion on the town's Main Street, that became the focus of Dickinson family life for the better part of a century. Samuel Dickinson's eldest son, Edward, was treasurer of Amherst College for nearly forty years, served numerous terms as a State Legislator, and represented the Hampshire district in the United States Congress. On May 6, 1828, he married Emily Norcross from Monson. They had three children:

1) William Austin (1829–1895), known as Austin, Aust or Awe;
2) Emily Elizabeth; and
3) Lavinia Norcross (1833–1899), known as Lavinia or Vinnie.

By all accounts, young Emily was a well-behaved girl. On an extended visit to Monson when she was two, Emily's Aunt Lavinia described Emily as "perfectly well & contented—She is a very good child & but little trouble." Emily's aunt also noted the girl's affinity for music and her particular talent for the piano, which she called "the *moosic*".

Dickinson attended primary school in a two-story building on Pleasant Street. Her education was "ambitiously classical for a Victorian girl". Her father wanted his children well-educated and he followed their progress even while away on business. When Emily was seven, he wrote home, reminding his children to "keep school, and learn, so as to tell me, when I come home, how many new things you have learned". While Emily consistently described her father in a warm manner, her correspondence suggests that her mother was regularly cold and aloof. In a letter to a confidante, Emily wrote she "always ran Home to Awe [Austin] when a child, if anything befell me. He was an awful Mother, but I liked him better than none."

On September 7, 1840, Dickinson and her sister Lavinia started together at Amherst Academy, a former boys' school that had opened to female students just two years earlier. At about the same time, her father purchased a house on North Pleasant Street. Emily's brother Austin later described this large new home as the "mansion" over which he and Emily presided as "lord and lady" while their parents were absent. The house overlooked Amherst's burial ground, described by one local minister as treeless and "forbidding".

Dickinson spent seven years at the Academy, taking classes in English and classical literature, Latin, botany, geology, history, "mental philosophy," and arithmetic. She had a few terms off due to illness: the longest absence was in 1845–1846, when she was only enrolled for eleven weeks.

Dickinson was troubled from a young age by the "deepening menace" of death, especially the deaths of those who were close to her. When Sophia Holland, her second cousin and a close friend, grew ill from typhus and died in April, 1844, Emily was traumatized. Recalling the incident two years later, Emily wrote that "it seemed to me I should die too if I could not be permitted to watch over her or even look at her face." She became so melancholic that her parents sent her to stay with family in Boston to recover. With her health and spirits restored, she soon returned to Amherst Academy to continue her studies. During this period, she first met people who were to become lifelong friends and correspondents, such as Abiah Root, Abby Wood, Jane Humphrey, and Susan Huntington Gilbert (who later married Emily's brother Austin).

In 1845, a religious revival took place in Amherst, resulting in 46 confessions of faith among Dickinson's peers. Dickinson wrote to a friend the following year:

"I never enjoyed such perfect peace and happiness as the short time in which I felt I had found my savior." She went on to say that it was her "greatest pleasure to commune alone with the great God & to feel that he would listen to my prayers". The experience did not last: Dickinson never made a formal declaration of faith and attended services regularly for only a few years. After her church-going ended, about 1852, she wrote a poem opening: "Some keep the Sabbath going to Church – / I keep it, staying at Home".

During the last year of her stay at the Academy, Emily became friendly with Leonard Humphrey, its popular new young principal. After finishing her final term at the Academy on August 10, 1847, Dickinson began attending Mary Lyon's Mount Holyoke Female Seminary (which later became Mount Holyoke College) in South Hadley, about ten miles (16 km) from Amherst. She was at the seminary for only ten months. Although she liked the girls at Holyoke, Dickinson made no lasting friendships there. The explanations for her brief stay at Holyoke differ considerably: either she was in poor health, her father wanted to have her at home, she rebelled against the evangelical fervor present at the school, she disliked the discipline-minded teachers, or she was simply homesick. Whatever the specific reason for leaving Holyoke, her brother Austin appeared on March 25, 1848, to "bring [her] home at all events". Back in Amherst, Dickinson occupied her time with household activities. She took up baking for the family and enjoyed attending local events and activities in the budding college town.

Early Influences and Writing

When she was eighteen, Dickinson's family befriended

a young attorney by the name of Benjamin Franklin Newton. According to a letter written by Dickinson after Newton's death, he had been "with my Father two years, before going to Worcester – in pursuing his studies, and was much in our family." Although their relationship was probably not romantic, Newton was a formative influence and would become the second in a series of older men (after Humphrey) that Dickinson referred to, variously, as her tutor, preceptor or master.

Newton likely introduced her to the writings of William Wordsworth, and his gift to her of Ralph Waldo Emerson's first book of collected poems had a liberating effect. She wrote later that he, "whose name my Father's Law Student taught me, has touched the secret Spring". Newton held her in high regard, believing in and recognizing her as a poet. When he was dying of tuberculosis, he wrote to her, saying that he would like to live until she achieved the greatness he foresaw. Biographers believe that Dickinson's statement of 1862—"When a little Girl, I had a friend, who taught me Immortality – but venturing too near, himself – he never returned"—refers to Newton.

Dickinson was familiar not only with the Bible but also with contemporary popular literature. She was probably influenced by Lydia Maria Child's *Letters from New York*, another gift from Newton (after reading it, she enthused "This then is a book! And there are more of them!"). Her brother smuggled a copy of Henry Wadsworth Longfellow's *Kavanagh* into the house for her (because her father might disapprove) and a friend lent her Charlotte Brontë's *Jane Eyre* in late 1849. *Jane Eyre*'s influence cannot be measured, but when Dickinson acquired her first and only dog, a Newfoundland, she named him "Carlo" after the character St. John Rivers' dog. William Shakespeare was also a potent influence in her life. Referring to his plays, she wrote to one friend "Why clasp any hand but this?" and to another, "Why is any other book needed?"

Adulthood and Seclusion

In early 1850 Dickinson wrote that "Amherst is alive with fun this winter ... Oh, a very great town this is!" Her high spirits soon turned to melancholy after another death. The Amherst Academy principal, Leonard Humphrey, died suddenly of "brain congestion" at age 25. Two years after his death, she revealed to her friend Abiah Root the extent of her depression: "... some of my friends are gone, and some of my friends are sleeping – sleeping the churchyard sleep – the hour of evening is sad – it was once my study hour – my master has gone to rest, and the open leaf of the book, and the scholar at school *alone*, make the tears come, and I cannot brush them away; I would not if I could, for they are the only tribute I can pay the departed Humphrey".

During the 1850s, Emily's strongest and most affectionate relationship was with Susan Gilbert. Emily eventually sent her over three hundred letters, more than to any other correspondent, over the course of their friendship. Her missives typically dealt with demands for Sue's affection and the fear of unrequited admiration, but because Sue was often aloof and disagreeable, Emily was continually hurt by what was mostly a tempestuous friendship. Sue was nevertheless supportive of the poet, playing the role of "most beloved friend, influence, muse, and adviser whose editorial suggestions Dickinson sometimes followed, Susan played a primary role in Emily's creative processes." Sue married Austin in 1856 after a four-year courtship, although their marriage was not a happy one. Edward Dickinson built a house for him and Sue called the Evergreens, which stood on the west side of the Homestead.

Until 1855, Dickinson had not strayed far from Amherst. That spring, accompanied by her mother and sister, she took one of her longest and farthest trips away from home. First, they spent three weeks in Washington, where her father was representing Massachusetts in Congress. Then they went to Philadelphia for two weeks to visit family. In Philadelphia, she met Charles Wadsworth, a famous minister of the Arch Street Presbyterian Church, with whom she forged a strong friendship which lasted until his death in 1882. Despite only seeing him twice after 1855 (he moved to San Francisco in 1862), she variously referred to him as "my Philadelphia", "my Clergyman", "my dearest earthly friend" and "my Shepherd from 'Little Girl'hood".

From the mid-1850s, Emily's mother became effectively bedridden with various chronic illnesses until her death in 1882. Writing to a friend in summer 1858, Emily said that she would visit if she could leave "home, or mother. I do not go out at all, lest father will come and miss me, or miss some little act, which I might forget, should I run away – Mother is much as usual. I know not what to hope of her". As her mother continued to decline, Dickinson's domestic responsibilities weighed heavier upon her and she confined herself within the Homestead. Forty years later, Lavinia stated that because their mother was chronically ill, one of the daughters had to remain always with her. Emily took this role as her own, and "finding the life with her books and nature so congenial, continued to live it".

Withdrawing more and more from the outside world, Emily began in the summer of 1858 what would be her lasting legacy. Reviewing poems she had written previously, she began making clean copies of her work, assembling carefully pieced-together manuscript books. The forty fascicles she created from 1858 through 1865 eventually held nearly eight hundred poems. No one was aware of the existence of these books until after her death.

In the late 1850s, the Dickinsons befriended Samuel Bowles, the owner and editor-in-chief of the *Springfield Republican*, and his wife, Mary. They visited the Dickinsons regularly for years to come. During this time Emily sent him over three dozen letters and nearly fifty poems. Their friendship brought out some of her most intense writing and Bowles published a few of her poems in his journal. It was from 1858 to 1861 that Dickinson is believed to have written a trio of letters that have been called "The Master Letters". These three letters, drafted to an unknown man simply referred to as "Master", continue to be the subject of speculation and contention amongst scholars.

> Are you too deeply occupied to say if my Verse is alive? The Mind is so near itself – it cannot see, distinctly – and I have none to ask – Should you think it breathed – and had you the leisure to tell me, I should feel quick gratitude – If I make the mistake – that you dared to tell me – would give me sincerer honor – toward you – I enclose my name – asking you, if you please – Sir – to tell me what is true? That you will not betray me – it is needless to ask – since Honor is it's [sic] own pawn –

The letter was unsigned, but she had included her name on a card and enclosed it in an envelope, along with four of her poems. He praised her work but suggested that she delay publishing until she had written longer, being unaware that she had already appeared in print. She assured him that publishing was as foreign to her "as Firmament to Fin", but also proposed that "If fame belonged to me, I could not escape her".

Dickinson delighted in dramatic self-characterization and mystery in her letters to Higginson. She said of herself, "I am small, like the wren, and my hair is bold, like the chestnut bur, and my eyes like the sherry in the glass that the guest leaves." She stressed her solitary nature, stating that her only real companions were the hills, the sundown, and her dog, Carlo. She also mentioned that whereas her mother did not "care for Thought", her father bought her books, but begged her "not to read them – because he fears they joggle the Mind". Dickinson valued his advice, going from calling him "Mr. Higginson" to "Dear friend" as well as signing her letters, "Your Gnome" and "Your Scholar". His interest in her work certainly provided great moral support; many years later, Dickinson told Higginson that he had saved her life in 1862. They corresponded until her death.

In direct opposition to the immense productivity that she displayed in the early 1860s, Dickinson wrote fewer poems in 1866. Beset with personal loss as well as loss of domestic help, it is possible that Dickinson was too overcome to keep up her previous level of writing. Carlo died during this time after providing sixteen years of companionship; Dickinson never owned another dog. Although the household servant of nine years had married and left the Homestead that same year, it was not until 1869 that her family brought in a permanent household servant to replace the old one. Emily once again was responsible for chores, including the baking, at which she excelled.

Around this time, Dickinson's behavior began to change. She did not leave the Homestead unless it was absolutely necessary and as early as 1867, she began to talk to visitors from the other side of a door rather than speaking to them face to face. She acquired local notoriety; she was rarely seen, and when she was, she was usually clothed in white. Dickinson's one surviving article of clothing is a white cotton dress, possibly sewn circa 1878–1882. Few of the locals who exchanged messages with Dickinson during her last fifteen years ever saw her in person. Austin and his family began to protect Emily's privacy, deciding that she was not to be a subject of discussion with outsiders. Despite her physical seclusion, however, Dickinson was socially active and expressive through what makes up two-thirds of her surviving notes and letters. When visitors came to either the Homestead or the Evergreens, she would often leave or send over small gifts of poems or flowers. Dickinson also had a good rapport with the children in her life. Mattie Dickinson, the second child of Austin and Sue, later said that "Aunt Emily stood for *indulgence.*" MacGregor (Mac) Jenkins, the son of family friends who later wrote a short article in 1891 called "A Child's Recollection of Emily Dickinson", thought of her as always offering support to the neighborhood children.

When Higginson urged her to come to Boston in 1868 so that they could formally meet for the first time, she declined, writing: "Could it please your convenience to come so far as Amherst I should be very glad, but I do not cross my Father's ground to any House or town". It was not until he came to Amherst in 1870 that they met. Later he referred to her, in the most detailed and vivid physical account of her on record, as "a little plain woman with two smooth bands of reddish hair ... in a very plain & exquisitely clean white pique & a blue net worsted shawl." He also felt that he never was "with any one who drained my nerve power so much. Without touching her, she drew from me. I am glad not to live near her."

Posies and Poesies

Scholar Judith Farr notes that Dickinson, during her lifetime, "was known more widely as a gardener, perhaps, than as a poet". Dickinson studied botany from the age of nine and, along with her sister, tended the garden at Homestead. During her lifetime, she assembled a collection of pressed plants in a sixty-six page leather-bound herbarium. It contained 424 pressed flower specimens that she collected, classified, and labeled using the Linnaean system. The Homestead garden was well-known and admired locally in its time. It has not survived, and Dickinson kept no garden notebooks or plant lists, but a clear impression can be formed from the letters and recollections of friends and family. Her niece, Martha Dickinson Bianchi, remembered "carpets of lily-of-the-valley and pansies, platoons of sweetpeas, hyacinths, enough in May to give all the bees of summer dyspepsia. There were ribbons of peony hedges and drifts of daffodils in season, marigolds to distraction—a butterfly utopia". In particular, Dickinson cultivated scented exotic flowers, writing that she "could inhabit the Spice Isles merely by crossing the dining room to the conservatory, where the plants hang in baskets". Dickinson would often send her friends bunches of flowers with verses attached, but "they valued the posy more than the poetry".

Later Life

On June 16, 1874, while in Boston, Edward Dickinson suffered a stroke and died. When the simple funeral was held in the Homestead's entrance hall, Emily stayed in her room with the door cracked open. Neither did she attend the memorial service on June 28. She wrote to Higginson that her father's "Heart was pure and terrible and I think no other like it exists." A year later, on June 15, 1875, Emily's mother also suffered a stroke, which produced a partial lateral paralysis and impaired memory. Lamenting her mother's increasing physical as well as mental demands, Emily wrote that "Home is so far from Home".

Otis Phillips Lord, an elderly judge on the Massachusetts Supreme Judicial Court from Salem, in 1872 or 1873 became an acquaintance of Dickinson's. After the death of Lord's wife in 1877, his friendship with Dickinson probably became a late-life romance, though as their letters were destroyed, this is surmise. Dickinson found a kindred soul in Lord, especially in terms of shared literary interests; the few letters which survived contain multiple quotations of Shakespeare's work, including the plays *Othello, Antony and Cleopatra, Hamlet* and *King Lear*. In 1880 he gave her Cowden Clarke's *Complete Concordance to Shakespeare* (1877). Dickinson wrote that "While others go to Church, I go to mine, for are you not my Church, and have we not a Hymn that no one knows but us?" She referred to him as "My lovely Salem" and they wrote to each other religiously every Sunday. Dickinson looked forward to this day greatly; a surviving fragment of a letter written by her states that "Tuesday is a deeply depressed Day".

After being critically ill for several years, Judge Lord died in March 1884. Dickinson referred to him as "our latest Lost". Two years before this, on April 1, 1882, Dickinson's "Shepherd from 'Little Girl'hood", Charles Wadsworth, also had died after a long illness.

Decline and Death

Although she continued to write in her last years, Dickinson stopped editing and organizing her poems. She also exacted a promise from her sister Lavinia to burn her papers. Lavinia, who also never married, remained at the Homestead until her own death in 1899.

The 1880s were a difficult time for the remaining Dickinsons. Irreconcilably alienated from his wife, Austin fell in love in 1882 with Mabel Loomis Todd, an Amherst College faculty wife who had recently moved to the area. Todd never met Dickinson but was intrigued by her, referring to her as "a lady whom the people call the *Myth*". Austin distanced himself from his family as his affair continued and his wife became sick with grief Dickinson's mother died on November 14, 1882. Five weeks later, Dickinson wrote "We were never intimate ... while she was our Mother – but Mines in the same Ground meet by tunneling and when she became our Child, the Affection came." The next year, Austin and Sue's third and youngest child, Gilbert—Emily's favorite—died of typhoid fever.

As death succeeded death, Dickinson found her world upended. In the fall of 1884, she wrote that "The Dyings have been too deep for me, and before I could raise my Heart from one, another has come." That summer she had seen "a great darkness coming" and fainted while baking in the kitchen. She remained unconscious late into the night and weeks of ill health followed. On November 30, 1885, her feebleness and other symptoms were so worrying that Austin canceled a trip to Boston. She was confined to her bed for a few months, but managed to send a final burst of letters in the spring. What is thought to be her last letter was sent to her cousins, Louise and Frances Norcross, and simply read: "Little Cousins, Called Back. Emily". On May 15, 1886, after several days of worsening symptoms, Emily Dickinson died at the age of 55. Austin wrote in his diary that "the day was awful ... she ceased to breathe that terrible breathing just before the [afternoon] whistle sounded for six." Dickinson's chief physician gave the cause of death as Bright's disease and its duration as two and a half years.

Publications

Despite Dickinson's prolific writing, fewer than a dozen of her poems were published during her lifetime. After her younger sister Lavinia discovered the collection of nearly eighteen hundred poems, Dickinson's first volume was published four years after her death. Until the 1955 publication of Dickinson's *Complete Poems* by Thomas H. Johnson, her poetry was considerably edited and altered from their manuscript versions. Since 1890 Dickinson has remained continuously in print.

Contemporary

A few of Dickinson's poems appeared in Samuel Bowles' *Springfield Republican* between 1858 and 1868. They were published anonymously and heavily edited, with conventionalized punctuation and formal titles. The first poem, "Nobody knows this little rose", may have been published without Dickinson's permission. The *Republican* also published "A narrow Fellow in the Grass" as "The Snake"; "Safe in their Alabaster Chambers –" as "The Sleeping"; and "Blazing in the Gold and quenching in Purple" as "Sunset". The poem "I taste a liquor never brewed –" is an example of the edited versions; the last two lines in the first stanza were completely rewritten for the sake of conventional rhyme.

In 1864, several poems were altered and published in *Drum Beat,* to raise funds for medical care for Union soldiers in the war. Another appeared in April 1864 in the *Brooklyn Daily Union.*

In the 1870s, Higginson showed Dickinson's poems to Helen Hunt Jackson, who had coincidentally been at the Academy with Dickinson when they were girls. Jackson was deeply involved in the publishing world, and managed to convince Dickinson to publish her poem "Success is counted sweetest" anonymously in a volume called *A Masque of Poets.* The poem, however, was altered to agree with contemporary taste. It was the last poem published during Dickinson's lifetime.

Posthumous

After Dickinson's death, Lavinia Dickinson kept her promise and burned most of the poet's correspondence. Significantly though, Dickinson had left no instructions about the forty notebooks and loose sheets gathered in a locked chest. Lavinia recognized the poems' worth and became obsessed with seeing them published. She turned first to her brother's wife and then to Mabel Loomis Todd, her brother's mistress, for assistance. A feud ensued, with the manuscripts divided between the Todd and Dickinson houses, preventing complete publication of Dickinson's poetry for more than half a century.

The first volume of Dickinson's *Poems,* edited jointly by Mabel Loomis Todd and T. W. Higginson, appeared in November 1890. Although Todd claimed that only essential changes were made, the poems were extensively edited to match punctuation and capitalization to late 19th-century standards, with occasional rewordings to reduce Dickinson's obliquity. The first 115-poem volume was a critical and financial success, going through eleven printings in two years. *Poems: Second Series* followed in 1891, running to five editions by 1893; a third series appeared in 1896. One reviewer, in 1892, wrote: "The world will not rest satisfied till every scrap of her writings, letters as well as literature, has been published". Two years later, two volumes of Dickinson's letters, heavily edited, appeared. In parallel, Susan Dickinson placed a few of Dickinson's poems in literary magazines such as *Scribner's Magazine* and *The Independent.*

Between 1914 and 1929, Dickinson's niece, Martha Dickinson Bianchi, published a new series of collections, including many previously unpublished poems, with similarly normalized punctuation and capitalization. Other volumes edited by Todd and Bianchi followed through the 1930s, gradually making more previously unpublished poems available.

The first scholarly publication came in 1955 with a complete new three-volume set edited by Thomas H. Johnson. It formed the basis of all later Dickinson scholarship. For the first time, the poems were printed very nearly as Dickinson had left them in her manuscripts. They were untitled, only numbered in an approximate chronological sequence, strewn with dashes and irregularly capitalized, and often extremely elliptical in their language. Three years later, Johnson edited and published, along with Theodora Ward, a complete collection of Dickinson's letters.

Poetry

Dickinson's poems generally fall into three distinct periods, the works in each period having certain general characters in common.

1) *Pre-1861:* These are often conventional and sentimental in nature. Thomas H. Johnson, who later published *The Poems of Emily Dickinson,* was able to date only five of Dickinson's poems before 1858. Two of these are mock valentines done in an ornate and humorous style, and two others are conventional lyrics, one of which is about missing her brother Austin. The fifth poem, which begins "I have a Bird in spring", conveys her grief over the feared loss of friendship and was sent to her friend Sue Gilbert.

2) *1861–1865:* This was her most creative period—these poems are more vigorous and emotional. Johnson estimated that she composed 86 poems in 1861, 366 in 1862, 141 in 1863, and 174 in 1864. He also believed that this is when she fully developed her themes of life and death.

3) *Post-1866:* It is estimated that two-thirds of the entire body of her poetry was written before this year.

Structure and Syntax

The extensive use of dashes and unconventional capitalization in Dickinson's manuscripts, and the idiosyncratic vocabulary and imagery, combine to create a body of work that is "far more various in its styles and forms than is commonly supposed". She did not write in traditional iambic pentameter (a convention of English-speaking poetry for centuries), and did not even use a five-foot line. Her line lengths vary from four syllables or two feet to often eight syllables or four feet. Her frequent use of approximate or slant rhyme attracted attention since her work first appeared in print. Her poems typically begin with a declaration or definition in the first line ("The fact that Earth is Heaven"), which is followed by a metaphorical change of the original premise in the second line ("Whether Heaven is Heaven or not"). Dickinson's poems can easily be set to music because of the frequent use of rhyme and free verse. Written for the most part in common meter or ballad-meter, they can also be set to songs that use the same alternating lines of iambic tetrameter and iambic trimeter. (Familiar examples of such songs are *O Little Town of Bethlehem*, and *Amazing Grace*). Dickinson scholar Anthony Hecht finds resonances not only with songs but also with psalms and riddles, citing the following example: "Who is the East? / The Yellow Man / Who may be Purple if he can / That carries the Sun. / Who is the West? / The Purple Man / Who may be Yellow if He can / That lets Him out again."

Late 20th-century scholars are "deeply interested" by Dickinson's highly individual use of punctuation and lineation (line lengths and line breaks). Following the publication of one of the few poems that appeared in her lifetime – "A narrow Fellow in the Grass", published as "The Snake" in the *Republican* – Dickinson complained that the edited punctuation (an added comma and a full stop substitution for the original dash) altered the meaning of the entire poem.

As Farr points out, "snakes instantly notice you"; Dickinson's version captures the "breathless immediacy" of the encounter; and *The Republican*'s punctuation renders "her lines more commonplace". With the increasingly close focus on Dickinson's structures and syntax has come a growing appreciation that they are "aesthetically based". Although Johnson's landmark 1955 edition of poems was relatively unaltered from the original, later scholars critiqued it for deviating from the style and layout of Dickinson's manuscripts. Meaningful distinctions, these scholars assert, can be drawn from varying lengths and angles of dash, and differing arrangements of text on the page. Several volumes have attempted to render Dickinson's handwritten dashes using many typographic symbols of varying length and angle. R.W. Franklin's 1998 variorum edition of the poems provided alternate wordings to those chosen by Johnson, in a more limited editorial intervention. Franklin also used typeset dashes of varying length to approximate the manuscripts' dashes more closely.

Major Themes

Dickinson left no formal statement of her aesthetic intentions and, because of the variety of her themes, her work does not fit conveniently into any one genre.

She has been regarded, alongside Emerson (whose poems Dickinson admired), as a Transcendentalist. However, Farr disagrees with this analysis saying that Dickinson's "relentlessly measuring mind ... deflates the airy elevation of the Transcendental". Apart from the major themes discussed below, Dickinson's poetry frequently uses humor, puns, irony and satire.

1) *Flowers and gardens*: Farr notes that Dickinson's "poems and letters almost wholly concern flowers" and that allusions to gardens often refer to an "imaginative realm ... wherein flowers [are] often emblems for actions and emotions". She associates some flowers, like gentians and anemones, with youth and humility; others with prudence and insight. Her poems were often sent to friends with accompanying letters and nosegays. Farr notes that one of Dickinson's earlier poems, written about 1859, appears to "conflate her poetry itself with the posies": "My nosegays are for Captives – / Dim – long expectant eyes – / Fingers denied the plucking, / Patient till Paradise – / To such, if they sh'd whisper / Of morning and the moor – / They bear no other errand, / And I, no other prayer".

2) *The Master poems:* Dickinson left a large number of poems addressed to "Signor", "Sir" and "Master", who is characterized as Dickinson's "lover for all eternity". These confessional poems are often "searing in their self-inquiry" and "harrowing to the reader" and typically take their metaphors from texts and paintings of Dickinson's day. The Dickinson family themselves believed these poems were addressed to actual individuals but this view is frequently rejected by scholars. Farr, for

example, contends that the Master is an unattainable composite figure, "human, with specific characteristics, but godlike" and speculates that Master may be a "kind of Christian muse".

3) *Morbidity*: Dickinson's poems reflect her "early and lifelong fascination" with illness, dying and death. Perhaps surprisingly for a New England spinster, her poems allude to death by many methods: "crucifixion, drowning, hanging, suffocation, freezing, premature burial, shooting, stabbing and guillotinage". She reserved her sharpest insights into the "death blow aimed by God" and the "funeral in the brain", often reinforced by images of thirst and starvation. Dickinson scholar Vivian Pollak considers these references an autobiographical reflection of Dickinson's "thirsting-starving persona", an outward expression of her needy self-image as small, thin and frail. Dickinson's most psychologically complex poems explore the theme that the loss of hunger for life causes the death of self and place this at "the interface of murder and suicide".

4) *Gospel poems*: Throughout her life, Dickinson wrote poems reflecting a preoccupation with the teachings of Jesus Christ and, indeed, many are addressed to him. She stresses the Gospels' contemporary pertinence and recreates them, often with "wit and American colloquial language". Scholar Dorothy Oberhaus finds that the "salient feature uniting Christian poets ... is their reverential attention to the life of Jesus Christ" and contends that Dickinson's deep structures

place her in the "poetic tradition of Christian devotion" alongside Hopkins, Eliot and Auden. In a Nativity poem, Dickinson combines lightness and wit to revisit an ancient theme: "The Savior must have been / A docile Gentleman – / To come so far so cold a Day / For little Fellowmen / The Road to Bethlehem / Since He and I were Boys / Was leveled, but for that twould be / A rugged billion Miles –".

5) *The Undiscovered Continent:* Academic Suzanne Juhasz considers that Dickinson saw the mind and spirit as tangible visitable places and that for much of her life she lived within them. Often, this intensely private place is referred to as the "undiscovered continent" and the "landscape of the spirit" and embellished with nature imagery. At other times, the imagery is darker and forbidding—castles or prisons complete with corridors and rooms—to create a dwelling place of "oneself" where one resides with one's other selves. An example that brings together many of these ideas is: "Me from Myself – to banish – / Had I Art – / Impregnable my Fortress / Unto All Heart – / But since myself—assault Me – / How have I peace / Except by subjugating / Consciousness. / And since We're mutual Monarch / How this be / Except by Abdication – / Me – of Me?".

Reception

The surge of posthumous publication gave Dickinson's poetry its first public exposure. Backed by Higginson and with a favorable notice from William Dean Howells, an editor of *Harper's Magazine*, the poetry received mixed reviews after it was first published in 1890. Higginson himself stated in his preface to the first edition of Dickinson's published work that the poetry's quality "is that of extraordinary grasp and insight". Maurice Thompson, who was literary editor of *The Independent* for twelve years, noted in 1891 that her poetry had "a strange mixture of rare individuality and originality". Some critics hailed Dickinson's effort, but disapproved of her unusual non-traditional style. Andrew Lang, a British writer, dismissed Dickinson's work, stating that "if poetry is to exist at all, it really must have form and grammar, and must rhyme when it professes to rhyme. The wisdom of the ages and the nature of man insist on so much". Thomas Bailey Aldrich, a poet and novelist, equally dismissed Dickinson's poetic technique in *The Atlantic Monthly* in January 1892: "It is plain that Miss Dickinson possessed an extremely unconventional and grotesque fancy. She was deeply tinged by the mysticism of Blake, and strongly influenced by the mannerism of Emerson ... But the incoherence and formlessness of her — versicles are fatal ... an eccentric, dreamy, half-educated recluse in an out-of-the-way New England village (or anywhere else) cannot with impunity set at defiance the laws of gravitation and grammar".

Critical attention to Dickinson's poetry was meager from 1897 to the early 1920s. By the start of the 20th century, interest in her poetry became broader in scope and some critics began to consider Dickinson as essentially modern. Rather than seeing Dickinson's poetic styling as a result of lack of knowledge or skill, modern critics believed the irregularities were consciously artistic. In a 1915 essay, Elizabeth Shepley Sergeant called the poet's inspiration "daring" and named her "one of the rarest flowers the sterner New

England land ever bore". With the growing popularity of modernist poetry in the 1920s, Dickinson's failure to conform to 19th-century poetic form was no longer surprising nor distasteful to new generations of readers. Dickinson was suddenly referred to by various critics as a great woman poet, and a cult following began to form. R.P. Blackmur, in an attempt to focus and clarify the major claims for and against the poet's greatness, wrote in a landmark 1937 critical essay: "... she was a private poet who wrote as indefatigably as some women cook or knit. Her gift for words and the cultural predicament of her time drove her to poetry instead of antimacassars ... She came, as Mr. Tate says, at the right time for one kind of poetry: the poetry of sophisticated, eccentric vision."

The second wave of feminism created greater cultural sympathy for her as a female poet. In the first collection of critical essays on Dickinson from a female perspective, she is heralded as the greatest woman poet in the English language. Biographers and theorists of the past tended to separate Dickinson's roles as a woman and a poet. For example, George Whicher wrote in his 1952 book *This Was a Poet: A Critical Biography of Emily Dickinson*, "Perhaps as a poet [Dickinson] could find the fulfillment she had missed as a woman." Feminist criticism, on the other hand, declares that there is a necessary and powerful conjunction between Dickinson being a woman and a poet. Adrienne Rich theorized in "Vesuvius at Home: The Power of Emily Dickinson" (1976) that Dickinson's identity as a woman poet brought her power, making her "neither eccentric nor quaint; she was determined to survive, to use her powers, to practice necessary economics." Similarly, some scholars question the poet's sexuality, theorizing that the numerous letters and poems that were dedicated to Susan Gilbert Dickinson indicate a lesbian romance, and speculating about how this may have influenced her poetry. Critics such as John Cody, Lillian Faderman, Vivian R. Pollak, Paula Bennett, Judith Farr, Ellen Louise Hart, and Martha Nell Smith have argued that Susan was the central erotic relationship in Dickinson's life.

Legacy

Emily Dickinson is now considered a powerful and persistent figure in American culture. Although much of the early reception concentrated on Dickinson's eccentric and secluded nature, she has become widely acknowledged as an innovative, pre-modernist poet. As early as 1891, William Dean Howells wrote that "If nothing else had come out of our life but this strange poetry, we should feel that in the work of Emily Dickinson, America, or New England rather, had made a distinctive addition to the literature of the world, and could not be left out of any record of it." Twentieth-century critic Harold Bloom has placed her alongside Walt Whitman, Wallace Stevens, Robert Frost, T.S. Eliot, and Hart Crane as a major American poet.

Dickinson is taught in American literature and poetry classes in the United States from middle school to college. Her poetry is frequently anthologized and has been used as texts for art songs by composers such as Aaron Copland, Nick Peros, John Adams and Michael Tilson Thomas. Several schools have been established in her name; for example, two Emily Dickinson Elementary Schools exist in Bozeman, Montana, and Redmond, Washington. A few literary journals—including *The Emily Dickinson Journal*, the official publication of the Emily Dickinson International Society—have been founded to examine her work. An 8-cent commemorative stamp in honor of Dickinson was issued by the United States Postal Service on August 28, 1971 as the second stamp in the "American Poet" series.

The Amherst Jones Library's Special Collections department has an Emily Dickinson Collection consisting of approximately seven thousand items, including original manuscript poems and letters, family correspondence, scholarly articles and books, newspaper clippings, theses, plays, photographs and contemporary artwork and prints. The Archives and Special Collections at Amherst College has substantial holdings of Dickinson's manuscripts and letters as well as a lock of Dickinson's hair and the original of the only positively identified image of the poet. Dickinson's herbarium, which is now held in the Houghton Library at Harvard University, was published in 2006 as *Emily Dickinson's Herbarium* by Harvard University Press. In 1965, in recognition of Dickinson's growing stature as a poet, the Homestead was purchased by Amherst College. It opened to the public for tours, and also served as a faculty residence for many years. The Emily Dickinson Museum was created in 2003 when ownership of the Evergreens, which had been occupied by Dickinson family heirs until 1988, was transferred to the college.

14

Writings of Wallace Stevens

Wallace Stevens (October 2, 1879 – August 2, 1955) was an American Modernist poet. He was born in Reading, Pennsylvania, educated at Harvard and then New York Law School, and spent most of his life working as a lawyer for an insurance company in Connecticut.

His best-known poems include "Anecdote of the Jar," "Disillusionment of Ten O'Clock", "The Emperor of Ice Cream," "The Idea of Order at Key West," "Sunday Morning," "Thirteen Ways of Looking at a Blackbird."

Life and Career

The son of a prosperous lawyer, Stevens attended Harvard as a non-degree special student, after which he moved to New York City and briefly worked as a journalist. He then attended New York Law School, graduating in 1903. On a trip back to Reading in 1904 Stevens met Elsie Viola Kachel (1886-1963, aka Elsie Moll), a young woman who had worked as a saleswoman, milliner, and stenographer. After a long courtship, he married her in 1909 over the objections of his parents, who considered her lower-class. As *The New York Times* reported in an article in 2009, "Nobody from his family attended the wedding, and Stevens never again visited or spoke to his parents during his father's lifetime". A daughter, Holly, was born in 1924. She later edited her father's letters and a collection of his poems.

In 1913, the Stevenses rented a New York City apartment from sculptor Adolph A. Weinman, who made a bust of Elsie. Her striking profile was later used on Weinman's 1916-1945 Mercury dime design and possibly for the head of the Walking Liberty Half Dollar. In later years Elsie Stevens began to exhibit symptoms of mental illness and the marriage suffered as a result, but the Stevenses never divorced.

After working for several New York law firms from 1904 to 1907, he was hired on January 13, 1908, as a lawyer for the American Bonding Company. By 1914 he had become the vice-president of the New York office of the Equitable Surety Company of St. Louis, Missouri. When this job was abolished as a result of mergers in 1916, he joined the home office of Hartford Accident and Indemnity Company and left New York City to live in Hartford, where he would remain the rest of his life. By 1934, he had been named vice-president of the company. After he won the Pulitzer Prize in 1955, he was offered a faculty position at Harvard but declined since it would have required him to give up his vice-presidency of The Hartford.

From 1922 to 1940, Stevens made numerous visits to Key West, Florida, where he generally lodged at the Casa Marina, a hotel on the Atlantic Ocean. He first visited in January 1922, while on a business trip. "The place is a paradise," he wrote to Elsie, "midsummer weather, the sky brilliantly clear and intensely blue, the sea blue and green beyond what you have ever seen." The influence of Key West upon Stevens's poetry is evident in many of the poems published in his first two collections, *Harmonium* and *Ideas of Order*. In February 1935, Stevens encountered the poet Robert Frost at the Casa Marina. The two men argued, and Frost reported that Stevens had been drunk and acted inappropriately. The following year, Stevens allegedly assaulted Ernest Hemingway at a party at the Waddell Street home of a mutual acquaintance. Stevens broke his hand, apparently from hitting Hemingway's jaw, and was repeatedly knocked to the street by Hemingway. Stevens later apologized. In 1940, Stevens made his final trip to Key West. Frost was at the Casa Marina again, and again the two men argued.

In the 1930s and 1940s, he was welcomed as a member of the exclusive set centered on the artistic and literary devotees Barbara and Henry Church.

Stevens was baptized a Catholic in April 1955 by Fr. Arthur Hanley, chaplain of St. Francis Hospital in Hartford, Connecticut, where Stevens spent his last days suffering from stomach cancer. This purported deathbed conversion is disputed, particularly by Stevens's daughter, Holly. After a brief release from the hospital, Stevens was readmitted and died on August 2, 1955, at the age of 75. He is buried in Hartford's Cedar Hill Cemetery.

Later, when Stevens's daughter learned of Father Hanley's claim, she flatly denied it could have happened. While this flew utterly in the face of the facts as attested to not only by Father Hanley but also by others who attended Stevens's baptism, Holly Stevens's denial of her father's conversion dissuaded many scholars from taking it seriously or discussing it at any length. Although Holly sold her father's papers to Pasadena's Huntington Library in the 1970s, she still controlled their use until her death in 1992. She gave scholars the impression that they would have limited access to quote from Stevens's papers if they paid too much attention to his conversion. For this reason, it seems, Peter Brazeau, who wrote an oral biography of Stevens and interviewed Father Hanley at length, used only a small portion of the material he developed on Stevens's conversion. Brazeau's taped interviews with Father Hanley are now part of the Huntington Library collection.

Poetry

Stevens is a rare example of a poet whose main output came at a fairly advanced age. His first major publication was written at the age of thirty-five, although as an undergraduate at Harvard, Stevens had written poetry and exchanged sonnets with George Santayana, with whom he was close through much of his life. Many of his canonical works were written well after he turned fifty. According to the literary critic Harold Bloom, who called Stevens the "best and most representative" American poet of the time, no Western writer since Sophocles has had such a late flowering of artistic genius.

Stevens's first book of poetry, a volume of rococo inventiveness titled *Harmonium*, was published in 1923. He produced two more major books of poetry during the 1920s and 1930s and three more in the 1940s. He received the National Book Award in 1951 and 1955.

Imagination and Reality

Stevens, whose work was meditative and philosophical, is very much a poet of ideas. "The poem must resist the intelligence / Almost successfully " he wrote. Concerning the relation between consciousness and the world, in Stevens's work "imagination" is not equivalent to consciousness nor is "reality" equivalent to the world as it exists outside our minds. Reality is the product of the imagination as it shapes the world. Because it is constantly changing as we attempt to find imaginatively satisfying ways to perceive the world, reality is an activity, not a static object. We approach reality with a piecemeal understanding, putting together parts of the world in an attempt to make it seem coherent. To make sense of the world is to construct a worldview through an active exercise of the imagination. This is no dry, philosophical activity, but a passionate engagement in finding order and meaning

In his book *Opus Posthumous*, Stevens writes, "After one has abandoned a belief in god, poetry is that essence which takes its place as life's redemption." But as the poet attempts to find a fiction to replace the lost gods, he immediately encounters a problem: a direct knowledge of reality is not possible.

Stevens suggests that we live in the tension between the shapes we take as the world acts upon us and the ideas of order that our imagination imposes upon the world. The world influences us in our most normal activities: "The dress of a woman of Lhassa, / In its place, / Is an invisible element of that place / Made visible." Likewise, were we to place a jar on a hill in Tennessee, we would impose an order onto the landscape.

As Stevens says in his essay "Imagination as Value", "The truth seems to be that we live in concepts of the imagination before the reason has established them." The imagination is the mechanism by which we unconsciously conceptualize the normal patterns of life, while reason is the way we consciously conceptualize these patterns.

The jar is a striking example of an order that does not feel a part of the land, and so seems to violate the existing order: "It did not give of bird or bush, / Like nothing else in Tennessee". Contrast this to the feeling one gets while looking over the water where boats are anchored in darkness, with lanterns hanging on poles, "Arranging, deepening, enchanting night". When the imagination is available to reality and does not try to force itself, reality becomes like a bar of sand onto which the imagination naturally washes and recedes.

The imagination can only conceive of a world for a moment—a particular time, place and culture—and so must continually revise its conception to align with the changing world. And as these worldviews come and go, each person is pulled in his or her normal life between the influence the world has on imagination and the influence imagination has on the way we view the world.

For this reason, the best we can hope for is a well-conceived fiction, satisfying for the moment, but sure to lapse into obsolescence as new imaginings wash over the world.

Supreme Fiction

The imagination loses vitality as it ceases to adhere to what is real. When it adheres to the unreal and intensifies what is unreal, while its first effect may be extraordinary, that effect is the maximum effect that it will ever have.

Throughout his poetic career, Stevens was concerned with the question of what to think about the world now that our old notions of religion no longer suffice. His solution might be summarized by the notion of a "Supreme Fiction."

The saxophones squiggle because, as J. Hillis Miller says of Stevens in his book, *Poets of Reality*, the theme of universal fluctuation is a constant theme throughout Stevens poetry: "A great many of Stevens' poems show an object or group of objects in aimless oscillation or circling movement." In the end, reality remains.

The supreme fiction is that conceptualization of reality that seems to resonate in its rightness, so much so that it seems to have captured, if only for a moment, something actual and real.

In one of his last poems, "Final Soliloquy of the Interior Paramour", Stevens describes the experience of an idea which satisfies the imagination, "This is, therefore, the intensest rendezvous. / It is in that thought that we collect ourselves, / Out of all the indifferences, into one thing." This one thing is "a light, a power, the miraculous influence" wherein we can forget ourselves, sensing a comforting order, "A knowledge, that which arranged the rendezvous, / within its vital boundary, in the mind."

Stevens concludes that God is a human creation, but that feeling of rightness which for so long a time existed with the idea of God may be accessed again. This supreme fiction will be something equally central to our being, but contemporary to our lives, in a way that God can never again be. But with the right idea, we may again find the same sort of solace that we once found in divinity. "[Stevens] finds, too, a definite value in the complete contact with reality.

In this way, Stevens's poems adopt attitudes that are corollaries to those earlier spiritual longings that persist in the unconscious currents of the imagination. "The poem refreshes life so that we share, / For a moment, the first idea . . . It satisfies / Belief in an immaculate beginning / And sends us, winged by an unconscious will, / To an immaculate end." The "first idea" is that essential reality that stands before all others, that essential truth; but since all knowledge is contingent on its time and place, that supreme fiction will surely be transitory. This is the necessary angel of subjective reality—a reality that must always be qualified—and as such, always misses the mark to some degree—always contains elements of unreality.

Miller summarizes Stevens's position: "Though this dissolving of the self is in one way the end of everything, in another way it is the happy liberation. There are only two entities left now that the gods are dead: man and nature, subject and object. Nature is the physical world, visible, audible, tangible, present to all the senses, and man is consciousness, the nothing which receives nature and transforms it into something unreal . . . ."

Role of Poetry

Stevens often writes directly about poetry and its human function. The poet "tries by a peculiar speech to speak / The peculiar potency of the general, / To compound the imagination's Latin with / The lingua franca et jocundissima." Moreover, "The whole race is a poet that writes down / The eccentric propositions of its fate." In a manner reminiscent of Wordsworth, Stevens saw the poet as one with heightened powers, but one who like all ordinary people continually creates and discards cognitive depictions of the world, not in solitude but in solidarity with other men and women.

These cognitive depictions find their outlet and their best and final form as *words*; and thus Stevens can say, "It is a world of words to the end of it, / In which nothing solid is its solid self." In a poem called "Men Made out of Words," he says: "Life / Consists of propositions about life." Poetry is not *about* life, it *is* intimately a part of life. As Stevens wrote elsewhere, "The poem is the cry of its occasion, / Part of the res itself and not about it. / The poet speaks the poem as it is, // Not as it was." Modern poetry is "the poem of the mind in the act of finding / What will suffice."

> It has to be living, to learn the speech of the place.
> It has to face the men of the time and to meet
> The women of the time. It has to think about war
> And it has to find what will suffice. It has
> To construct a new stage. It has to be on that stage,
> And, like an insatiable actor, slowly and
> With meditation, speak words that in the ear,
> In the delicatest ear of the mind, repeat,
> Exactly, that which it wants to hear, at the sound
> Of which, an invisible audience listens,
> Not to the play, but to itself, expressed
> In an emotion as of two people, as of two
> Emotions becoming one.

His poem *An Ordinary Evening in New Haven* is a self-conscious digression about the creation of poetry.

> We keep coming back and coming back
> To the real: to the hotel instead of the hymns
> That fall upon it out of the wind. We seek
> The poem of pure reality, untouched
> By trope or deviation, straight to the word,
> Straight to the transfixing object, to the object
> At the exactest point at which it is itself,

Transfixing by being purely what it is
A view of New Haven, say, through the certain eye,
The eye made clear of uncertainty, with the sight
Of simple seeing, without reflection. We seek
Nothing beyond reality.

To create a stage is, for Stevens, a metaphor for the need of modern poetry to make its own new arena or realm in which it should be presented and in which it can be understood. Modern poetry is like "an insatiable actor" because it continually must be in "the act of finding what will suffice." Stevens puns on the meaning of "act." In one sense, poetry is an act, learning the speech, meeting the women, facing the men, etc. In another sense, it is a dramatic performance meant to be heard by an audience, as it speaks words that echo in the mind of the listener. The audience is "invisible" in the sense that a poet rarely meets his or her readers. The typical reader picks up a book of poems and reads a poem or two, and the author never sees this happening. The reading of poetry is often a conversation between strangers. In this poem the two people are the actor that is the poem and the audience that is the listener, and their emotions should become "one." The poet should find the words that will speak to the delicatest ear of its modern listeners, echoing what it wants to hear but cannot articulate for itself. The poet, in the act of the poem, finds the sufficing words and for the audience and they allow the listeners to hear what is in their ear, their mind. As a result, the emotions of speaking and listening, of poet as actor and listeners as audience, should become one.

Reputation and Influence

From the first, critics and fellow poets praised Stevens. Hart Crane wrote to a friend in 1919, after reading some of the poems that would make up *Harmonium*, "There is a man whose work makes most of the rest of us quail." In the 1930s, the critic Yvor Winters criticized Stevens as a decadent hedonist but acknowledged his great talent. Beginning in the 1940s, critics such as Randall Jarrell spoke of Stevens as one of the major living American poets, even if they did so (as Jarrell did) with certain reservations about Stevens's work. Stevens's work became even better known after his death. Harold Bloom, Helen Vendler, and Frank Kermode are among the critics who have cemented Stevens's position in the canon as a great poet. Many poets—James Merrill and Donald Justice most explicitly—have acknowledged Stevens as a major influence on their work, and his impact may also be seen in John Ashbery, Mark Strand, Jorie Graham, John Hollander, and others.

In 1977 David Hockney authored a book of etchings called "The Blue Guitar: Etchings By David Hockney Who Was Inspired By Wallace Stevens Who Was Inspired By Pablo Picasso". The book included the poetry of Wallace Stevens. The etchings were inspired by and were meant to represent the themes of Stevens's poem, "The Man With The Blue Guitar", which was inspired by a 1903 painting by Pablo Picasso titled "The Old Guitarist". It was published as a portfolio and as a book in spring 1997 by Petersburg Press.

15

Literary Life of Sylvia Plath

Known primarily for her poetry, Plath also wrote a semi-autobiographical novel, *The Bell Jar,* under the pseudonym Victoria Lucas. The book's protagonist, Esther Greenwood, is a bright, ambitious student at Smith College who begins to experience a mental breakdown while interning for a fashion magazine in New York. The plot parallels Plath's experience interning at *Mademoiselle* magazine and subsequent mental breakdown and suicide attempt.

Childhood

Plath was born during the Great Depression on October 27, 1932 in Jamaica Plain, Massachusetts, to Aurelia Schober Plath, a first-generation American of Austrian descent, and Otto Emile Plath, an immigrant from Grabow, Germany. Plath's father was a professor of biology and German at Boston University and author of a book about bumblebees. Plath's mother was approximately twenty-one years younger than her husband. She met him while earning her master's degree in teaching. Otto was alienated from his family because he chose not to become a Lutheran minister, as his grandparents wanted him to be. They went as far as taking his name out of the family Bible.

In April 1935, Plath's brother Warren was born. The family moved to Winthrop, Massachusetts in 1936 and Plath spent much of her childhood on Johnson Avenue. She was raised a Unitarian Christian and had mixed feelings toward religion throughout her life. Plath's mother, Aurelia, had grown up in Winthrop, and her maternal grandparents, the Schobers, had lived in a section of the town called Point Shirley, a location mentioned in Plath's poetry. At age eight when living in Winthrop, Plath published her first poem in the Boston Herald's children's section. In addition to writing, she also showed early promise as an artist, winning an award from The Scholastic Art & Writing Awards in 1947, for her paintings.

Otto Plath died on November 5, 1940, a week and a half after Plath's eighth birthday, of complications following the amputation of a foot due to diabetes. He had become ill shortly after a close friend died of lung cancer. Comparing the similarities between his friend's symptoms and his own, Otto became convinced he too was ill with lung cancer and did not seek treatment until his diabetes had progressed too far. Otto Plath is buried in Winthrop Cemetery, where his gravestone continues to attract readers of Plath's poem "Daddy." Visiting her father's grave prompted Plath to write the poem "Electra on Azalea Path." Subsequent to her husband's death, Aurelia Plath moved her children and her parents to 26 Elmwood Road, Wellesley, Massachusetts in 1942.

College Years

Plath attended Smith College, dating Yale senior Dick Norton during her junior year. Norton, upon whom the character of Buddy in *The Bell Jar* is based, contracted tuberculosis and was treated at the Ray

Brook Sanatorium near Saranac Lake. While visiting Norton, Plath broke her leg skiing, an incident that was fictionalized in the novel.

During the summer after her third year of college Plath was awarded a coveted position as guest editor at *Mademoiselle* magazine, during which she spent a month in New York City. The experience was not at all what she had hoped it would be, beginning within her a seemingly downward spiral in her outlook on herself and life in general. Many of the events that took place during that summer were later used as inspiration for her novel *The Bell Jar*. Following this experience Plath made her first medically documented suicide attempt by crawling under her house and taking an overdose of sleeping pills. Details of her attempts at suicide are chronicled in her book. After her suicide attempt, Plath was briefly committed to a mental institution where she received electroconvulsive therapy. Her stay at McLean Hospital was paid for by Olive Higgins Prouty, who had also funded the scholarship awarded to Plath to attend Smith. Prouty had successfully recovered from a mental breakdown herself. Plath seemed to make an acceptable recovery and graduated from Smith with honors in June 1955. She obtained a Fulbright scholarship to Newnham College, Cambridge where she continued actively writing poetry, occasionally publishing her work in the student newspaper *Varsity*. It was at a party given in Cambridge that she met the English poet Ted Hughes. After a tempestuous courtship, they were married on June 16, 1956 (Bloomsday) at St George the Martyr Holborn in the London Borough of Camden.

Personal Life and Poetry

Plath and Hughes spent from July 1957 to December

1959 living and working in the United States, where Plath taught at Smith College in Northampton, Massachusetts. The couple then moved to Boston where Plath audited seminars by Robert Lowell that were also attended by Anne Sexton. At this time Plath and Hughes met, for the first time, W. S. Merwin, who admired their work and was to remain a lifelong friend.

Upon learning Plath was pregnant the couple moved back to the United Kingdom. Plath and Hughes lived in London for a while on Chalcot Square near the Primrose Hill area of Regent's Park, and then settled in the small market town of North Tawton in Devon. In 1960, while in London, Plath published her first collection of poetry, *The Colossus*. In February 1961 she suffered a miscarriage. A number of her poems address this event.

Plath's marriage to Hughes was fraught with difficulties, particularly surrounding his affair with Assia Wevill, and the couple separated in late 1962. She returned to London with their children, Frieda and Nicholas, and rented a flat at 23 Fitzroy Road (only a few streets from the Chalcot Square flat) in a house where W.B. Yeats once lived. Plath was pleased by this fact and considered it a good omen.

End of Life

Plath took her own life after she completely sealed the rooms between herself and her sleeping children with "wet towels and cloths." Plath then placed her head in the oven while the gas was turned on. The next day an inquiry ruled that her death was a suicide.

It has been suggested Plath's suicide attempt was too precise and coincidental, and she had not intended to succeed in killing herself. Apparently, she had previously asked Mr. Thomas, her downstairs neighbor, what time he would be leaving; and a note had been placed that read "Call Dr. Horder" and listed his phone number. Therefore, it is argued Plath must have turned the gas on at a time when Mr. Thomas should have been waking and beginning his day. This theory maintains that the gas, for several hours, seeped through the floor and reached Mr. Thomas and another resident of the floor below. Also, an au pair was to arrive at nine o'clock that morning to help Plath with the care of her children. Upon arrival, the au pair could not get into the flat, but was eventually let in by painters, who had a key to the front door.

However, in the book *Giving Up: The Last Days of Sylvia Plath*, her best friend, Jillian Becker says "according to Mr. Goodchild—a police officer attached to the coroner's office . . . she had thrust her head far into the gas oven. 'She had really meant to die.'"

Plath's gravestone in Heptonstall churchyard bears the inscription "Even amidst fierce flames the golden lotus can be planted." The gravestone has been repeatedly vandalized by some of Plath's supporters who have chiseled the name "Hughes" off it. This practice intensified following the suicide in 1969 of Assia Wevill, the woman for whom Ted Hughes left Plath, which led to claims Hughes had been abusive toward Plath.

Journals

Plath began keeping a diary at age 11, and kept journals until her suicide. Her adult diaries, starting from her freshman year at Smith College in 1950, were first published in 1980 as *The Journals of Sylvia Plath,* edited by Frances McCullough. In 1982, when Smith College acquired Plath's remaining journals, Hughes sealed two of them until February 11, 2013, the fiftieth anniversary of Plath's death.

During the last years of his life, Hughes began working on a fuller publication of Plath's journals. In 1998, shortly before his death, he unsealed the two journals, and passed the project onto his children by Plath, Frieda and Nicholas, who passed it on to Karen V. Kukil. Kukil finished her editing in December 1999, and in 2000 Anchor Books published *The Unabridged Journals of Sylvia Plath*. According to the back cover, roughly two-thirds of the *Unabridged Journals* is newly released material. The American author Joyce Carol Oates hailed the publication as a "genuine literary event".

Hughes faced criticism for his role in handling the journals: he claims to have destroyed Plath's last journal, which contained entries from the winter of 1962 up to her death. In the foreword of the 1982 version, he writes, "I destroyed [the last of her journals] because I did not want her children to have to read it (in those days I regarded forgetfulness as an essential part of survival.

Poems

Plath has been criticized for her controversial allusions to the Holocaust, and is known for her uncanny use of metaphor. Her work has been compared to and associated with Anne Sexton, W.D. Snodgrass, and other confessional poets.

While the few critics who responded to Plath's first book, *The Colossus*, did so favorably, it has also been described as somewhat staid and conventional in comparison to the much more free-flowing imagery and intensity of her later work.

The poems in *Ariel* mark a departure from her earlier work into a more personal arena of poetry. It is a possibility Lowell's poetry—which is often labeled "confessional"—played a part in this shift. Indeed, in an interview before her death she listed Lowell's *Life Studies* as an influence. The impact of *Ariel* was dramatic, with its potentially autobiographical descriptions of mental illness in poems such as "Tulips", "Daddy" and "Lady Lazarus".

In 1982 Plath became the first poet to win a Pulitzer Prize posthumously for *The Collected Poems*. In 2006 a graduate student at Virginia Commonwealth University discovered a previously unpublished sonnet written by Plath entitled "Ennui". The poem, composed during Plath's early years at Smith College, is published in *Blackbird*, the online journal.

16

Writings of Ezra Pound

Ezra Weston Loomis Pound (October 30, 1885 - November 1, 1972) was an American expatriate poet, critic and intellectual who was a major figure of the Modernist movement in the first half of the 20th century. He is generally considered the poet most responsible for defining and promoting a modernist aesthetic in poetry. The critic Hugh Kenner said of Pound upon meeting him: "I suddenly knew that I was in the presence of the center of modernism."

In the early teens of the twentieth century, he opened a fruitful exchange of work and ideas between British and American writers, and was famous for the generosity with which he advanced the work of such major contemporaries as Robert Frost, William Carlos Williams, Marianne Moore, H. D., Ernest Hemingway, Wyndham Lewis, and especially T. S. Eliot. Pound also had a profound influence on the Irish writers W. B. Yeats and James Joyce.

His own significant contributions to poetry begin with his promotion of Imagism, a movement in poetry which derived its technique from classical Chinese and Japanese poetry—stressing clarity, precision, and economy of language, and forgoing traditional rhyme and meter in order to, in Pound's words, "compose in the sequence of the musical phrase, not in the sequence of the metronome." His later work, spanning nearly fifty years, focused on his epic poem *The Cantos*.

Early Life

Pound was born in Hailey, Idaho Territory, to Homer Loomis and Isabel Weston Pound. His grandfather was the Lieutenant Governor of Wisconsin, Thaddeus C. Pound; his mother was said to be related to the poet Henry Wadsworth Longfellow. When he was 18 months old, his family moved to the suburbs of Philadelphia. In 1901 at the age of 15, he entered the University of Pennsylvania, but after studying there for two years transferred to Hamilton College, where he received his Ph.B. in 1905. He then returned to Penn, completing an M.A. in Romance philology in 1906.

During his studies at Penn, he met and befriended William Carlos Williams and H.D. (Hilda Doolittle), to whom he became engaged for a short time. Afterward, Pound taught at Wabash College in Crawfordsville, Indiana, but when he allowed a stranded actress to spend the night in his room, the resulting scandal caused him to leave his teaching post after only four months, "all accusations", he later claimed, "having been ultimately refuted except that of being 'the Latin Quarter type'". He had been taken to Europe by relatives in 1898 and again to Europe and Morocco in 1902. In 1908 he moved to Europe, living first in Venice but eventually settling in London after spending a brief stint working as a tour guide in Gibraltar. Pound self-published *A Lume Spento*, his first published collection of short poems, while living in Venice.

London Years

Pound's early poetry was inspired by his reading of the pre-Raphaelites and other 19th-century poets, medieval Romance literature (especially Provençal) and the neo-Romantic and occult/mystical philosophy of that period. After he moved to London, the influence of Ford Madox Ford and T. E. Hulme encouraged him to cast off overtly archaic poetic language and forms and begin to remake himself as a poet. Pound believed that William Butler Yeats was the greatest living poet, and befriended him in England. He eventually became Yeats's secretary, and soon became mildly interested in Yeats's occult beliefs. During 1914 and 1915 Pound and Yeats lived together at Stone Cottage in Sussex, England, studying Japanese, especially Noh plays. They paid particular attention to the works of Ernest Fenollosa, an American professor in Japan whose work on Chinese characters fascinated Pound. Eventually, Pound used Fenollosa's work as a starting point for what he called the Ideogrammic Method. On April 20, 1914, Pound married Dorothy Shakespear, an artist and daughter of the novelist Olivia Shakespear, a former lover of Yeats.

In the years before the World War I, Pound was largely responsible for the appearance of Imagism, and coined the name of the movement Vorticism, which was led by his friend Wyndham Lewis, and which included the artists Edward Wadsworth, Jacob Epstein and Henri Gaudier-Brzeska. Pound contributed to Lewis' short-lived literary magazine *BLAST* whose two numbers appeared in 1914 and 1915. These two movements, Imagism and Vorticism, can be seen as central events in the birth of English-language modernism. They helped bring to notice the work of such poets and artists as James Joyce, Lewis, William Carlos Williams, H.D., Jacob Epstein, Richard Aldington, Marianne Moore, Rabindranath Tagore, Robert Frost, Rebecca West and Henri Gaudier-Brzeska. Later, Pound also edited his friend T. S. Eliot's *The Waste Land*, the poem that was to force the new poetic sensibility into public attention.

In 1915, Pound published *Cathay*, a small volume of poems that he described as "For the most part from the Chinese of Rihaku (Li Po), from the notes of the late Ernest Fenollosa, and the decipherings of the professors Mori and Ariga". The volume includes works such as *The River Merchant's Wife: A Letter* and *A Ballad of the Mulberry Road*. Unlike previous American translators of Chinese poetry, who tended to work with strict metrical and stanzaic patterns, Pound offered readers free verse translations celebrated for their ease of diction and conversationality. Many critics consider the poems in *Cathay* to be the most successful realization of Pound's Imagist poetics. Whether the poems are valuable as translations continues to be a source of controversy, although Arthur Waley found them to be beautiful paraphrases. Neither Pound nor Fenollosa spoke or read Chinese proficiently, and Pound has been criticized for omitting or adding sections to his poems which have no basis in the original texts, though many critics argue that the fidelity of *Cathay* to the original Chinese is beside the point. Hugh Kenner, in a chapter "The Invention of China" from *The Pound Era*, contends that *Cathay* should be read primarily as a work about World War I, not as an attempt at accurately translating ancient Eastern poems. The real achievement of the book, Kenner argues, is in how it combines meditations on violence and friendship with an effort to "rethink the nature of an English poem". These ostensible translations of ancient Eastern texts, Kenner argues, are actually experiments in English poetics and compelling elegies for a warring West.

The first World War had a profound effect on many writers and poets of that period. The Great War shattered Pound's belief in modern western civilization and he abandoned London soon after, but not before he published *Homage to Sextus Propertius* (1919) and *Hugh Selwyn Mauberley* (1920). If these poems together form a farewell to Pound's London career, *The Cantos,* which he began in 1915, pointed his way forward.

Life in Paris

In 1920, Pound moved to Paris, where he moved among a circle of artists, musicians, and writers who were revolutionizing the whole world of modern art. He was friends with notable figures such as Marcel Duchamp, Tristan Tzara, Fernand Léger and others of the Dada and Surrealist movements. He was also good friends with Basil Bunting and Ernest Hemingway, whom Pound asked to teach him to box. (Hemingway would later write, in *A Moveable Feast*: "I was never able to teach him to throw a left hook.") He continued working on *The Cantos,* writing the bulk of the "Malatesta Sequence", which introduced one of the major personas of the poem. The poem increasingly reflected his preoccupations with politics and economics. During this time, he also wrote critical prose and translations and composed two complete operas (with help from George Antheil) and several pieces for solo violin. In 1922 he met and became involved with Olga Rudge, a violinist. Together with Dorothy Shakespear, they formed an uneasy *ménage à trois* which was to last until the end of the poet's life.

Life in Italy

On 10 October 1924, Pound left Paris permanently and moved to Rapallo, Italy. Near neighbours were Max Beerbohm and his wife Florence Kahn. He and Dorothy stayed there briefly, moving on to Sicily, and then returning to settle in Rapallo in January 1925. In Italy he continued to be a creative catalyst. The young sculptor Heinz Henghes came to see Pound, arriving penniless. He was given lodging and marble to carve, and quickly learned to work in stone. The poet James Laughlin was also inspired at this time to start the publishing company New Directions which would become a vehicle for many new authors.

At this time Pound also organized an annual series of concerts in Rapallo, where a wide range of classical and contemporary music was performed. In particular this musical activity contributed to the 20th century revival of interest in Vivaldi, who had been neglected since his death. Pound also became alarmed at the importation taxes levied by the United States on what Pound believed to be works of art. In addition to lobbying the US Customs and the House of Representatives, Pound wrote an essay in 1928 entitled "Article 211", where he related a trial to the recent decision to categorise the Nassak Diamond as a work of art, and therefore let it into the United States without payment of an import duty.

In 1933, he had a personal audience with Italy's prime minister Benito Mussolini and presented him with a draft of XXX Cantos. Mussolini's response was: "How amusing." Later, Pound would be asked to make radio broadcasts from Rome. In a radio broadcast in June 1942 he would say "Every man of common sense, including the odd British MP, knows that every man of common sense prefers Fascism to Communism, from the moment that he learns a few concrete facts about both of them."

In 1939, on the eve of World War II, Pound made his first trip back home to the U.S. in many years. He considered moving back permanently, but in the end he chose to return to Italy. Pound also had personal reasons for staying in Italy. His elderly parents had retired to Italy to be with him, and were in poor health and would have difficulty making the trip back to America even under peacetime conditions. He also had an Italian-born daughter by his mistress Olga Rudge: Mary Rudge was a young woman in her late teens who had lived in Italy her whole life and who might have had difficulty relocating to America (even though she had American as well as Italian citizenship).

Pound remained in Italy, residing primarily in Rapallo, after the outbreak of World War II, which began more than two years before his native United States formally entered the war in December 1941 after Pearl Harbor. He made several radio broadcasts from Rome, for which he was paid a small sum, but he also continued to be involved in scholarly publishing. Pound wrote many newspaper pieces. He disapproved of American involvement in the war and tried to use his scant political contacts in Washington D.C. to prevent it. When Pound spoke on Italian radio, he gave a series of talks on political and cultural matters, art and patronage and economic theories. Pound believed that economics was the core issue for the cause of World War II. Specifically, his talks were largely about usury and the notion that representative democracy has been usurped by bankers' infiltration of governments through the existence of central banks, which made governments pay interest to private banks for the use of their own money. He maintained that the central bank's ability to create money out of thin air allowed banking interests to buy up American and British media outlets to sway opinion in favor of the war and the banks. Pound believed that economic freedom was a prerequisite for a free country. Inevitably, he touched on various sensitive political matters in his denunciations of the war. In addition, various comments of his were considered anti-semitic.

It is not clear if anyone in the United States ever actually heard Pound's radio broadcasts, since Italian radio's shortwave transmitters were weak and unreliable, though obviously his writings for Italian newspapers (as well as a number of pamphlets) were read in Italy. However, according to his biographer Humphrey Carpenter, the broadcasts were "a masterly performance". Carpenter wrote "Certainly there were Americans who, in 1941, would have agreed with virtually every word Ezra said at the microphone about the United States Government, the European conflict, and the power of the Jews." The broadcasts were monitored by the Foreign Broadcast Monitoring Service of the United States government, and transcripts, now stored in the Library of Congress, were made of them. Pound was indicted for treason by the United States government in 1943.

After Allied forces had landed in Sicily and began to overrun the southern part of Italy in July, 1943, Mussolini was dismissed by King Victor Emmanuel III and interned at the mountain resort of Gran Sasso. Two months later, Mussolini was freed by German troops and relocated to the north, where a Fascist Republic was established.

Pound also moved northwards On May 3, 1945, as Mussolini's puppet regime tumbled, Pound was arrested by partisans and taken (according to Hugh Kenner) "to their HQ in Chiavari, where he was soon released as possessing no interest." At his request, he was then brought to the U.S. command in Lavagna, whence he was driven to the C.I.C. in Genoa. On May 24 he was transferred from Genoa to a United States Army detention camp north of Pisa. He spent 25 days in an open cage before being given a tent, and appears to have suffered a nervous breakdown. He drafted the *Pisan Cantos* in the camp. This section of the work in progress marks a shift in Pound's work, being a meditation on his own and Europe's ruin and on his place in the natural world. The *Pisan Cantos* won the first Bollingen Prize from the Library of Congress in 1949.

St. Elizabeths

After the war, Pound was brought back to the United States to face charges of treason. The charges covered only his activities during the time when Italy was officially at war with the United States, i.e., the time before the Allies captured Rome and Mussolini fled to the North. Pound was not prosecuted for his activities on behalf of Mussolini's Salo Republic, evidently because the Republic's existence was never formally recognized by the United States. He was found incompetent to face trial by a special federal jury and sent to St. Elizabeths Hospital in Washington, D.C., where he remained for 12 years from 1946 to 1958. His insanity plea is still a matter of controversy, since in retrospect his activities and his writings during the war years do appear to be those of a sane person.

E. Fuller Torrey believed that Pound was given special treatment by colluding authorities, specifically Winfred Overholser, the superintendent of St. Elizabeths. According to Torrey, Overholser admired Pound's poetry and allowed him to live in a private room at the hospital, where he wrote books, received visits from literary figures and enjoyed conjugal relations with his wife. The reliability of Torrey's allegations has been questioned; other scholars have presented Overholser as behaving solely in a humane way to his famous patient, without allowing him special privileges. At St. Elizabeths, Pound continued working on *The Cantos* as well as translating the Confucian classics.

Pound was frequently visited by his protegé, a Library of Congress researcher named Eustace Mullins. Pound commissioned Mullins to write a book about the history of the Federal Reserve and to tell it like a detective story. Pound believed that the bankers in charge of the Federal Reserve and their associates in the Bank of England were responsible for getting the United States into both World Wars, in an effort to drive up government debt beyond sustainable levels (the national debt indeed rose astronomically because of the wars). He advocated an abandonment of the current system of money being created by private bankers. He favored government issued currency with no interest to pay, preventing the need for an income tax and national debt, much like the system used by the Pennsylvania Colony from 1723 to 1764. Pound argued that his views on money aligned with those of Thomas Jefferson, as well as with Benjamin Franklin's Colonial Scrip.

Pound was also befriended at St. Elizabeths by Hugh Kenner, whose *The Poetry of Ezra Pound* (1951) was highly influential in causing a reassessment of Pound's poetry. Other scholars began to edit the *Pound Newsletter*, which eventually led to the publication of the first guide to *The Cantos, Annotated Index to the Cantos of Ezra Pound* (1957). Pound had many friends and admirers among his fellow poets, like Elizabeth Bishop, who recorded her response to Pound's situation in the poem "Visits to St. Elizabeth's", and Robert Lowell, who visited and corresponded extensively with Pound. The artist Sheri Martinelli, meanwhile, is believed to have inspired the love poetry in Cantos XC–XCV. Both William Carlos Williams and Louis Zukofsky were among Pound's visitors, as was Guy Davenport, who subsequently wrote his Harvard dissertation on Pound's poetry (published as *Cities on Hills* in 1983).

Pound's other visitors included the Colonial French nonfigurative painter Rene Laubies, the first translator of the work of Pound into French (*Cantos et poèmes choisis / Ezra Pound*, Paris: P.J. Oswald, 1958. 77 pages). In his *Portraits et Aphorismes* (2001) Laubies writes that he did not remember having any "difficulties returning to visit Pound at the Asylum of St. Elisabeths." He asked Pound whether the surroundings obstructed him. "Not at all" Pound stated, "they are the only acceptable Americans." When Laubies told Pound that he was born in Saigon: "Ah, that's why! Only Europeans with a master key to the Suez Canal are worth something...." Charles Olson was a frequent visitor (Pound wrote in a note to his attorney that "Olson saved my life" by providing sane conversation). Olson eventually became disgusted with Pound's antisemitic statements and stopped his visits. Sinologist and budding Pound scholar Achilles Fang became an important correspondent on Chinese subjects, especially Confucius, during these years; he and Pound were to exchange 214 letters.

Rudd Fleming, a professor at the University of Maryland, visited Pound often. They collaborated on a translation of Sophocles' *Electra,* which was published by Princeton University Press in 1989. Fleming stated, when asked about Pound's antisemitism, that Pound considered it a mistake. A statement from Pound's foreword to a collection of his prose writings (written on July 4, 1972) would seem to support Fleming's assertion: "In sentences referring to groups or races 'they' should be used with great care. re USURY: I was out of focus, taking a symptom for a cause. The cause is AVARICE." Pound also declared in a 1967 interview with Allen Ginsberg, "The worst mistake I made was that stupid, suburban prejudice of anti-Semitism."

Pound was finally released after a concerted campaign by many of his fellow poets and artists, particularly Robert Frost and Archibald MacLeish. He was still considered incurably insane, but not dangerous to others. Following his release, Pound was asked his opinions on his home country. He famously quipped: "America is a lunatic asylum." Subsequently he returned to Italy (first to Castle Brunnenburg near Merano, in Bolzano-Bozen, then later to Rapallo and Venice). He remained in Italy until his death in 1972.

On his release, Pound returned to Italy continuing work on *The Cantos.* In 1972, two days after his 87th birthday, Pound died in Venice, where he is buried.

Pound and Music

Pound's *The Cantos* contains music and bears a title that could be translated as *The Songs*—although it never is. Pound's ear was tuned to the *motz et sons* of troubadour poetry where, as musicologist John Stevens has noted, "melody and poem existed in a state of the closest symbiosis, obeying the same laws and striving in their different media for the same sound-ideal - armonia."

In his essays, Pound wrote of rhythm as "the hardest quality of a man's style to counterfeit." He challenged young poets to train their ear with translation work to learn how the choice of words and the movement of the words combined. But having translated texts from 10 different languages into English, Pound found that translation did not always serve the poetry: "The grand bogies for young men who want really to learn strophe writing are Catullus and François Villon. I personally have been reduced to setting them to music as I cannot translate them." While he habitually wrote out verse rhythms as musical lines, Pound did not set his own poetry to music.

In 1919, when he was 34, Pound began charting his path as a novice composer, writing privately that he intended a revolt against the impressionistic music of Claude Debussy. An autodidact, Pound described his working method as "improving a system by refraining from obedience to all its present 'laws'..." With only a few formal lessons in music composition, Pound produced a small body of work, including a setting of Dante's sestina, "Al poco giorno", for violin. His most important output is the pair of operas: *Le Testament,* a setting of François Villon's long poem of that name, written in 1461; and *Cavalcanti,* a setting of 11 poems by Guido Cavalcanti (c. 1250–1300). Pound began composing the Villon with the help of Agnes Bedford, a London pianist and vocal coach. Though the work is notated in Bedford's hand, Pound scholar Robert Hughes has been able to determine that Pound was artistically responsible for the work's overall dramatic and acoustic design.

During his years in Paris (1921–1924), Pound formed close friendships with the American pianist and composer George Antheil, and Antheil's touring partner, the American concert violinist Olga Rudge. Pound championed Antheil's music and asked his help in devising a system of micro-rhythms that would more accurately render the vitalistic speech rhythms of Villon's Old French for *Le Testament*. The resulting collaboration of 1923 used irregular meters that were considerably more elaborate than Stravinsky's benchmarks of the period, *Le Sacre du Printemps* (1913) and *L'Histoire du Soldat* (1918). For example, "Heaulmiere", one of the opera's key arias, at a tempo of quarter note = M.M. 88, moves from 2/8 to 25/32 to 3/8 to 2/4 meter (bars 25–28), making it difficult for performers to hear the current bar of music and anticipate the upcoming bar. Rudge performed in the 1924 and 1926 Paris preview concerts of *Le Testament*, but insisted to Pound that the meter was impractical.

In *Le Testament* there is no predictability of manner; no comfort zone for singer or listener; no rests or breath marks. Though Pound stays within the hexatonic scale to evoke the feel of troubadour melodies, modern invention runs throughout, from the stream of unrelenting dissonance in the mother's prayer to the grand shape of the work's aesthetic arc over a period of almost an hour. The rhythm carries the emotion. The music admits the corporeal rhythms (the score calls for human bones to be used in the percussion part); scratches, hiccoughs, and counter-rhythms lurch against each other—an offense to courtly etiquette. With "melody against ground tone and forced against another melody", as Pound puts it, the work spawns a polyphony in polyrhythms that ignores traditional laws of harmony. It was a test of Pound's ideal of an "absolute" and "uncounterfeitable" rhythm conducted in the laboratory of someone obsessed with the relationship between words and music.

After hearing a concert performance of *Le Testament* in 1926, Virgil Thomson praised Pound's accomplishment. "The music was not quite a musician's music", he wrote, "though it may well be the finest poet's music since Thomas Campion. . . . Its sound has remained in my memory."

Robert Hughes has remarked that where *Le Testament* explores a Webernesque pointillistic orchestration and derives its vitality from complex rhythms, *Cavalcanti* (1931) thrives on extensions of melody. Based on the lyric love poetry of Guido Cavalcanti, the opera's numbers are characterized by a challenging bel canto, into which Pound incorporates a number of tongue-in-cheek references to Verdi and a musical motive that gestures to Stravinsky's neo-classicism. By this time his relationship with Antheil had considerably cooled, and Pound, in his gradual acquisition of technical self-sufficiency, was free to emulate certain aspects of Stravinsky. *Cavalcanti* demands attention to its varying cadences, to a recurring *leitmotif*, and to a symbolic use of octaves. The play of octaves creates a surrealist straining against the limits of established laws of composition, history, physiology, reason, and love.

17

Life and Works T.S. Eliot

Thomas Stearns Eliot (September 26, 1888–January 4, 1965) was an Anglo/American poet, playwright, and literary critic, arguably the most important English-language poet of the 20th century. His first notable publication, *The Love Song of J. Alfred Prufrock*, begun in February 1910 and published in Chicago in June 1915, is regarded as a masterpiece of the modernist movement. It was followed by some of the best-known poems in the English language, including *Gerontion* (1920), *The Waste Land* (1922), *The Hollow Men* (1925), *Ash Wednesday* (1930), *Old Possum's Book of Practical Cats* (1939), and *Four Quartets* (1945). He is also known for his seven plays, particularly *Murder in the Cathedral* (1935) and *The Cocktail Party* (1949). He was awarded the Nobel Prize in Literature and the Order of Merit in 1948.

Eliot was born in St. Louis, Missouri, and was educated at Harvard University. After graduating in 1909, he studied philosophy at the University of Paris for a year, then won a scholarship to Merton College, Oxford in 1914, becoming a British citizen when he was 39. "[M]y poetry has obviously more in common with my distinguished contemporaries in America than with anything written in my generation in

England," he said of his nationality and its role in his work. "It wouldn't be what it is, and I imagine it wouldn't be so good ... if I'd been born in England, and it wouldn't be what it is if I'd stayed in America. It's a combination of things. But in its sources, in its emotional springs, it comes from America."

Early Life

Eliot was born into the Eliot family, a bourgeois family, originally from New England, who had moved to St. Louis, Missouri. His father, Henry Ware Eliot (1843–1919), was a successful businessman, president and treasurer of the Hydraulic-Press Brick Company in St. Louis. His mother, Charlotte Champe Stearns (1843–1929), wrote poems and was a social worker. Eliot was the last of six surviving children; his parents were both 44 years old when he was born. His four sisters were between 11 and 19 years older than him; his brother was eight years older. Known to family and friends as Tom, he was the namesake of his maternal grandfather Thomas Stearns.

From 1898 to 1905, Eliot attended Smith Academy, where he studied Latin, Ancient Greek, French, and German. He began to write poetry when he was 14 under the influence of Edward Fitzgerald's *Rubaiyat of Omar Khayyam*, a translation of the poetry of Omar Khayyam, though he said the results were gloomy and despairing, and he destroyed them. The first poem that he showed anyone was written as a school exercise when he was 15, and was published in the *Smith Academy Record*, and later in *The Harvard Advocate*, Harvard University's student magazine.

After graduation, he attended Milton Academy in Massachusetts for a preparatory year, where he met

Scofield Thayer, who would later publish *The Waste Land*. He studied philosophy at Harvard from 1906 to 1909, earning his bachelor's degree after three years, instead of the usual four. Frank Kermode writes that the most important moment of Eliot's undergraduate career was in 1908, when he discovered Arthur Symons's *The Symbolist Movement in Poetry* (1899). This introduced him to Jules Laforgue, Arthur Rimbaud, and Paul Verlaine, and without Verlaine, Eliot wrote, he might never have heard of Tristan Corbière. He wrote that the book affected the course of his life. The *Harvard Advocate* published some of his poems, and he became lifelong friends with Conrad Aiken, the American novelist.

He worked as a philosophy assistant at Harvard from 1909–1910, then from 1910–1911, he lived in Paris, studying philosophy at the Sorbonne, where he attended lectures by Henri Bergson and read poetry with Alain-Fournier. From 1911–1914, he was back at Harvard studying Indian philosophy and Sanskrit. He was awarded a scholarship to Merton College, Oxford in 1914. He visited Marburg in Germany first, where he planned to take a summer program, but when the First World War broke out, he went to Oxford instead. There were so many American students at Merton at the time that the Junior Common Room proposed a motion "that this society abhors the Americanization of Oxford," defeated by two votes after Eliot reminded the students how much they owed American culture. But he didn't settle at Merton, and left after a year. He wrote to Conrad Aiken on New Year's Eve 1914: "I hate university towns and university people, who are the same everywhere, with pregnant wives, sprawling children, many books and hideous pictures on the walls ... Oxford is very pretty, but I don't like to be dead." By 1916, he had completed a PhD dissertion for Harvard on *Knowledge and Experience in the Philosophy of F. H. Bradley,* about F.H. Bradley but he failed to return for the *viva voce.*

Middle Years

In a letter to Aiken late in December 1914, Eliot, aged 26, wrote, "I am very dependent upon women (I mean female society)," and then added a complaint that he was still a virgin. Less than four months later, Thayer introduced Eliot to Vivienne Haigh-Wood, a Cambridge governess. They were married at Hampstead Register Office on June 26, 1915.

After a short, unaccompanied visit to his family in the United States, he returned to London and took several teaching jobs such as lecturing at Birkbeck College, University of London. The philosopher Bertrand Russell took an interest in Eliot's wife while the newlyweds stayed in his flat. Some scholars have suggested that she and Russell had an affair, but the allegations were never confirmed. In a private paper written in his sixties, Eliot confessed: "I came to persuade myself that I was in love with Vivienne simply because I wanted to burn my boats and commit myself to staying in England. And she persuaded herself (also under the influence of [Ezra] Pound) that she would save the poet by keeping him in England. To her, the marriage brought no happiness. To me, it brought the state of mind out of which came *The Waste Land.*" Their relationship was the subject of a 1984 play *Tom and Viv,* which in 1994 was made into a film.

After leaving Merton, Eliot worked as a schoolteacher, most notably at Highgate School, a private school in London, where he taught French and

Latin—his students included the young John Betjeman—and later at the Royal Grammar School, High Wycombe a state school in Buckinghamshire. To earn extra money, he wrote book reviews and lectured at evening extension courses. In 1917, he took a position at Lloyds Bank in London, working on foreign accounts. On a trip to Paris in August 1920, he met the writer James Joyce and artist Wyndham Lewis. Eliot said he found Joyce arrogant—Joyce doubted Eliot's ability as a poet at the time—but the two soon became friends, with Eliot's visiting Joyce whenever he was in Paris. In 1925, he left Lloyds to join the publishing firm Faber and Gwyer, later Faber and Faber, where he remained for the rest of his career, eventually becoming a director. Wyndham Lewis and Eliot became close friends, a friendship leading to Lewis's well-known painting of Eliot in 1938.

On June 29, 1927 Eliot converted to Anglicanism, and in November that year took British citizenship. He became a warden of his parish church, Saint Stephen's, Gloucester Road, London, and a life member of the Society of King Charles the Martyr.

By 1932, Eliot had been contemplating a separation from his wife for some time. When Harvard offered him the Charles Eliot Norton professorship for the 1932-1933 academic year, he accepted and left Vivienne in England. Upon his return, he arranged for a formal separation from her, avoiding all but one meeting with her between his leaving for America in 1932 and her death in 1947. Vivien was committed to the Northumberland House mental hospital, Stoke Newington, in 1938, and remained there until she died. Although Eliot was still her husband, he never visited her.

From 1946 to 1957, Eliot shared a flat with his friend John Davy Hayward, who gathered and archived Eliot's papers, styling himself "Keeper of the Eliot Archive". Hayward also collected Eliot's pre-Prufrock verse, commercially published after Eliot's death as *Poems Written in Early Youth.* When Eliot and Hayward separated their household in 1957, Hayward retained his collection of Eliot's papers, which he bequeathed to King's College, Cambridge in 1965.

Eliot's second marriage was happy. On January 10, 1957, he married Esme Valerie Fletcher, 37 years younger than him. In contrast to his first marriage, Eliot knew Fletcher well, as she had been his secretary at Faber and Faber since August 1949. They kept their wedding secret; the ceremony was held in a church at 6.15 a.m. with virtually no one in attendance other than his wife's parents. Since Eliot's death, Valerie has dedicated her time to preserving his legacy; she has edited and annotated *The Letters of T. S. Eliot* and a facsimile of the draft of *The Waste Land.*

In the early 1960s, by then in failing health, he served as an editorial consultant to the Wesleyan University Press, Connecticut, seeking out new poets in Europe for publication.

Later Years

Eliot died of emphysema in London on January 4, 1965. For many years he had had health problems caused by his heavy smoking, and had often been laid low with bronchitis or tachycardia. His body was cremated at Golders Green Crematorium. According to Eliot's wishes, the ashes were taken to St Michael's Church in East Coker, the village from which his ancestors had emigrated to America. There, a simple wall plaque commemorates him with a quotation from his poem "East Coker": "In my beginning is my end. In my end is my beginning." On the second anniversary of his death, he was commemorated by the installation of a large stone in the floor of Poets' Corner in London's Westminster Abbey. The stone is inscribed with his dates, his Order of Merit, and a quotation from his poem, "Little Gidding": "the communication / of the dead is tongued with fire beyond / the language of the living."

Poetry

For a poet of his stature, Eliot produced a relatively small amount of poetry. He was aware of this early in his career. He wrote to J.H. Woods, one of his former Harvard professors, that, "My reputation in London is built upon one small volume of verse, and is kept up by printing two or three more poems in a year. The only thing that matters is that these should be perfect in their kind, so that each should be an event."

Typically, Eliot first published his poems individually in periodicals or in small books or pamphlets, and then collected them in books. His first collection was *Prufrock and Other Observations* (1917). In 1920, he published more poems in *Ara Vos Prec* (London) and *Poems: 1920* (New York). These had the same poems (in a different order) except that "Ode" in the British edition was replaced with "Hysteria" in the American edition. In 1925, he collected *The Waste Land* and the poems in *Prufrock* and *Poems* into one volume and added *The Hollow Men* to form *Poems: 1909–1925*. From then on, he updated this work as *Collected Poems*. Exceptions are *Old Possum's Book of Practical Cats* (1939), a collection of light verse; *Poems Written in Early*

Youth, posthumously published in 1967 and consisting mainly of poems published 1907–1910 in *The Harvard Advocate*, and *Inventions of the March Hare: Poems 1909–1917*, material Eliot never intended to have published, which appeared posthumously in 1997.

Of his nationality and its role in his work Eliot said: "[M]y poetry has obviously more in common with my distinguished contemporaries in America than with anything written in my generation in England." He added: "It wouldn't be what it is, and I imagine it wouldn't be so good ... if I'd been born in England, and it wouldn't be what it is if I'd stayed in America. It's a combination of things. But in its sources, in its emotional springs, it comes from America."

In 1915 Ezra Pound, overseas editor of *Poetry* magazine, recommended to Harriet Monroe, the magazine's founder, that she publish "The Love Song of J. Alfred Prufrock". Although the character Prufrock seems to be middle-aged, Eliot wrote most of the poem when he was only 22. Its now-famous opening lines, comparing the evening sky to "a patient etherised upon a table," were considered shocking and offensive, especially at a time when Georgian Poetry was hailed for its derivations of the 19th century Romantic Poets. The poem follows the conscious experience of a man, Prufrock (relayed in the "stream of consciousness" form characteristic of the Modernists), lamenting his physical and intellectual inertia, the lost opportunities in his life and lack of spiritual progress, with the recurrent theme of carnal love unattained. Critical opinion is divided as to whether the narrator leaves his residence during the course of the narration. The locations described can be interpreted either as actual physical experiences, mental recollections, or even as symbolic images from the sub-conscious mind, as, for example, in the refrain "In the room the women come and go." The poem's structure was heavily influenced by Eliot's extensive reading of Dante Alighieri, in the Italian, and refers to a number of literary works, including *Hamlet* and those of the French Symbolists.

Its reception in London can be gauged from an unsigned review in *The Times Literary Supplement* on June 21, 1917: "The fact that these things occurred to the mind of Mr Eliot is surely of the very smallest importance to anyone, even to himself. They certainly have no relation to *poetry*..."

The Waste Land

In October 1922 Eliot published *The Waste Land* in *The Criterion*. It was composed during a period of personal difficulty for Eliot—his marriage was failing, and both he and Vivien were suffering from nervous disorders. The poem is often read as a representation of the disillusionment of the post-war generation. That year Eliot lived in Lausanne, Switzerland to take a treatment and to convalesce from a break-down. There he wrote the final section, "What the Thunder Said," which contains frequent references to mountains. The poem's original draft was submitted to Ezra Pound, who persuaded Eliot to shorten it very considerably. Before the poem's publication as a book in December 1922, Eliot distanced himself from its vision of despair. On November 15, 1922, he wrote to Richard Aldington, saying, "As for *The Waste Land*, that is a thing of the past so far as I am concerned and I am now feeling toward a new form and style." The poem is known for its obscure nature—its slippage between satire and prophecy; its abrupt changes of speaker, location, and time; its elegiac but intimidating summoning up of a vast and dissonant range of cultures and literatures. Despite this, it has become a touchstone of modern literature, a poetic counterpart to a novel published in the same year, James Joyce's *Ulysses*. Among its best-known phrases are "April is the cruellest month", "I will show you fear in a handful of dust"; and "Shantih shantih shantih," the Sanskrit word that ends the poem.

The Hollow Men

The Hollow Men appeared in 1925. For the critic Edmund Wilson, it marked "the nadir of the phase of despair and desolation given such effective expression in *The Waste Land.*" It is Eliot's major poem of the late twenties. Similar to other work, its themes are overlapping and fragmentary: post-war Europe under the Treaty of Versailles (which Eliot despised: compare *Gerontion*); the difficulty of hope and religious conversion; and Eliot's failed marriage.

Allen Tate perceived a shift in Eliot's method, writing that, "The mythologies disappear altogether in *The Hollow Men.*" This is a striking claim for a poem as indebted to Dante as anything else in Eliot's early work, to say little of the modern English mythology—the 'Old Guy [Fawkes]' of the Gunpowder Plot—or the colonial and agrarian mythos of Joseph Conrad and James George Frazer, which, at least for reasons of textual history, echo in *The Waste Land*. The "continuous parallel between contemporaneity and antiquity" that is so characteristic of his mythical method remained in fine form.

Ash Wednesday

Ash Wednesday is the first long poem written by Eliot after his 1927 conversion to Anglicanism. Published in 1930, it deals with the struggle that ensues when one who has lacked faith acquires it. Sometimes referred to as Eliot's "conversion poem," it is richly but ambiguously allusive, and deals with the aspiration to move from spiritual barrenness to hope for human salvation, inspired by Dante's *Purgatorio*. The style is different from the poetry that predates his conversion. *Ash Wednesday* and the poems that followed had a more casual, melodic, and contemplative method.

Many critics were particularly enthusiastic about it. Edwin Muir maintained that it is one of the most moving poems Eliot wrote, and perhaps the "most perfect," though it was not well-received by everyone. The poem's groundwork of orthodox Christianity discomfited many of the more secular *literati*.

Old Possum's Book of Practical Cats

In 1930, he published a book of light verse, *Old Possum's Book of Practical Cats*, "Old Possum" being Ezra Pound's nickname for him. This first edition had an illustration of the author on the cover. In 1954, the composer Alan Rawsthorne set six of the poems for speaker and orchestra, in a work entitled *Practical Cats*. After Eliot's death, it became the basis of the musical, *Cats*, by Andrew Lloyd Webber.

Four Quartets

Eliot regarded *Four Quartets* as his masterpiece, and it is the work that led to his being awarded the Nobel Prize in Literature. It consists of four long poems, each first published separately: *Burnt Norton* (1936), *East*

Coker (1940), *Dry Salvages* (1941) and *Little Gidding* (1942). Each has five sections. Although they resist easy characterisation, each begins with a rumination on the geographical location of its title, and each meditates on the nature of time in some important respect—theological, historical, physical—and its relation to the human condition. Each poem is associated with one of the four classical elements: air, earth, water, and fire.

Burnt Norton asks what it means to consider things that might have been. We see the shell of an abandoned house, and Eliot toys with the idea that all these merely possible realities are present together, invisible to us*East Coker* continues the examination of time and meaning, focusing in a famous passage on the nature of language and poetry. Out of darkness, Eliot offers a solution: "I said to my soul, be still, and wait without hope".

The Dry Salvages treats the element of water, via images of river and sea. It strives to contain opposites: "... the past and future/Are conquered, and reconciled".

Little Gidding (the element of fire) is the most anthologized of the Quartets. Eliot's experiences as an air raid warden in The Blitz power the poem, and he imagines meeting Dante during the German bombing. The beginning of the Quartets ("Houses .../Are removed, destroyed") had become a violent everyday experience; this creates an animation, where for the first time he talks of Love as the driving force behind all experience. From this background, the Quartets end with an affirmation of Julian of Norwich: "all shall be well and/All manner of thing shall be well".

The *Four Quartets* cannot be understood without reference to Christian thought, traditions, and history. Eliot draws upon the theology, art, symbolism and language of such figures as Dante, and mystics St. John of the Cross and Julian of Norwich. The "deeper communion" sought in *East Coker*, the "hints and whispers of children, the sickness that must grow worse in order to find healing," and the exploration which inevitably leads us home all point to the pilgrim's path along the road of sanctification.

Plays

With the important exception of his *magnum opus Four Quartets*, Eliot directed much of his creative energies after *Ash Wednesday* to writing plays in verse, mostly comedies or plays with redemptive endings. He was long a critic and admirer of Elizabethan and Jacobean verse drama; witness his allusions to Webster, Thomas Middleton, William Shakespeare and Thomas Kyd in *The Waste Land*. In a 1933 lecture he said: "Every poet would like, I fancy, to be able to think that he had some direct social utility. ... He would like to be something of a popular entertainer, and be able to think his own thoughts behind a tragic or a comic mask. He would like to convey the pleasures of poetry, not only to a larger audience, but to larger groups of people collectively; and the theatre is the best place in which to do it."

After *The Waste Land* (1922), he wrote that he was "now feeling toward a new form and style." One project he had in mind was writing a play in verse with a jazz tempo featuring Sweeney, a character who had appeared in a number of his poems. Eliot did not finish it. He did publish separately two pieces of what he had written. The two, *Fragment of a Prologue* (1926) and *Fragment of an Agon* (1927) were published together in 1932 as *Sweeney Agonistes*. Although Eliot noted that this was not intended to be a one-act play, it is sometimes performed as one.

A pageant play by Eliot called *The Rock* was performed in 1934 for the benefit for churches in the Diocese of London. Much of it was a collaborative effort; Eliot accepted credit only for the authorship of one scene and the choruses. George Bell, the Bishop of Chichester, had been instrumental in connecting Eliot with producer E. Martin Browne for the production of *The Rock*, and later asked Eliot to write another play for the Canterbury Festival in 1935. This one, *Murder in the Cathedral*, concerning the death of the martyr, Thomas Becket, was more under Eliot's control. After this, he worked on commercial plays for more general audiences: *The Family Reunion* (1939), *The Cocktail Party* (1949), *The Confidential Clerk*, (1953) and *The Elder Statesman* (1958). The Broadway production in New York of *The Cocktail Party* received the 1950 Tony Award for Best Play.

Literary Criticism

Eliot also made significant contributions to the field of literary criticism, strongly influencing the school of New Criticism. While somewhat self-deprecating and minimizing of his work—he once said his criticism was merely a "by-product" of his "private poetry-workshop"—Eliot is considered by some to be one of the greatest literary critics of the 20th century. The critic William Empson once said, "I do not know for certain how much of my own mind [Eliot] invented, let alone how much of it is a reaction against him or indeed a consequence of misreading him. He is a very penetrating influence, perhaps not unlike the east wind."

In his critical essay "Tradition and the Individual Talent," Eliot argues that art must be understood not in a vacuum, but in the context of previous pieces of art: "In a peculiar sense [an artist or poet] ... must inevitably be judged by the standards of the past." This essay was one of the most important works of the school of New Criticism. Specifically, it introduced the idea that the value of one work of art must be viewed in the context of all previous work, a "simultaneous order" or works. Also important to New Criticism was the idea—as articulated in Eliot's essay "Hamlet and His Problems"—of an "objective correlative," which posits a connection among the words of the text and events, states of mind, and experiences. This notion concedes that a poem means what it says, but suggests that there can be a non-subjective judgment based on different readers' different—but perhaps corollary—interpretations of a work.

More generally, New Critics took a cue from Eliot in regards to his "'classical' ideals and his religious thought; his attention to the poetry and drama of the early seventeenth century; his deprecation of the Romantics, especially Shelley; his proposition that good poems constitute 'not a turning loose of emotion but an escape from emotion'; and his insistence that 'poets...at present must be difficult'."

Eliot's essays were a major factor in the revival of interest in the metaphysical poets. Eliot particularly praised the metaphysical poets' ability to show experience as both psychological and sensual, while at the same time infusing this portrayal with—in Eliot's view—wit and uniqueness. Eliot's essay "The Metaphysical Poets," along with giving new significance and attention to metaphysical poetry, introduced his now well-known definition of "unified sensibility," which is considered by some to mean the same thing as the term "metaphysical."

His 1922 poem *The Waste Land*—which at the time of its publication, many critics believed to be a joke or hoax—also can be better understood in light of his work as a critic. He had argued that a poet must write "programmatic criticism"; that is, a poet should write to advance his own interests rather than to advance "historical scholarship". Viewed from Eliot's critical lens, *The Waste Land* likely shows his personal despair about World War I rather than an objective historical understanding of it.

In 1958, the Archbishop of Canterbury appointed Eliot to a commission that produced *The Revised Psalter* (1963). A harsh critic of Eliot's, C.S. Lewis, was also a member of the commission, where their antagonism turned into a friendship.

Responses Eliot's Writings

Eliot's poetry was first criticized as not being poetry at all. Many critics attacked his practice of widespread interweaving of quotations from other authors into his work. "Notes on the Waste Land," which follows the poem, gives the source of many of these, but not all. Eliot defended this as a necessary salvaging of tradition in an age of fragmentation, and completely integral to the work, adding richness through unexpected juxtaposition. Other critics have condemned the practice as showing a lack of originality, and for plagiarism. The prominent critic

F.W. Bateson published an essay called "T.S. Eliot: The Poetry of Pseudo-Learning". Eliot wrote in *The Sacred Wood*: "Immature poets imitate; mature poets steal; bad poets deface what they take, and good poets make it into something better, or at least something different."

Canadian academic Robert Ian Scott pointed out that the title of *The Waste Land* and some of the images had previously appeared in the work of a minor Kentucky poet, Madison Cawein (1865–1914). Bevis Hillier compared Cawein's lines "... come and go/ Around its ancient portico" with Eliot's "... come and go/talking of Michelangelo". (This line actually appears in Eliot's "The Love Song of J. Alfred Prufrock", and not in *The Waste Land.*) Cawein's "Waste Land" had appeared in the January 1913 issue of the Chicago magazine *Poetry* (which contained an article by Ezra Pound on London poets). But scholars are continually finding new sources for Eliot's *Waste Land,* often in odd places.

Many famous fellow writers and critics have paid tribute to Eliot. According to poet Ted Hughes, "Each year Eliot's presence reasserts itself at a deeper level, to an audience that is surprised to find itself more chastened, more astonished, more humble." Hugh Kenner commented, "He has been the most gifted and influential literary critic in English in the twentieth century." However, other writers have not supported this view. In one of his criticisms, Samuel Beckett suggests that Eliot's work belongs in what the reverse of "T. Eliot" spells.

C.S. Lewis thought Eliot's literary criticism "superficial and unscholarly". In a 1935 letter to a mutual friend of theirs, Paul Elmer More, Lewis wrote that he considered the work of Eliot to be "a very great evil." In a 1943 letter to Eliot, Lewis expressed both admiration along with antagonism toward his views when he wrote: "I hope the fact that I find myself often contradicting you in print gives no offence; it is a kind of tribute to you—whenever I fall foul of some widespread contemporary view about literature I always seem to find that you have expressed it most clearly. One aims at the officers first in meeting an attack!"

The depiction of Jews in some of Eliot's poems has led several critics to accuse him of anti-Semitism. *Gerontion* contains a depiction of a landlord referred to only as the "jew [who] squats on the window sill." Another much-quoted example is the poem, *Burbank with a Baedeker: Bleistein with a Cigar,* in which a character in the poem implicitly blames the Jews for the decline of Venice: "The rats are underneath the piles/ The Jew is underneath the lot." In *A Cooking Egg,* Eliot writes, "The red-eyed scavengers are creeping/ From Kentish Town and Golder's Green" (Golders Green is a largely Jewish suburb of London). On the other hand, commentators note that the publisher of *Gerontion* and *Burbank* was John Rodker, himself Jewish. Additionally, Eliot mailed a draft of *Gerontion* to his friend Sidney Schiff, also a Jew, for pre-publication editing and commentary. A third "anti-Semitic" poem, *Sweeney Among the Nightingales,* was published by Eliot's Jewish friend Leonard Woolf. None of these men considered the poems anti-Semitic.

Eliot wrote a letter to the *Daily Mail* in January 1932, congratulating the newspaper for a series of laudatory articles on the rise of Benito Mussolini, and in a series of lectures delivered at the University of Virginia in 1933, later published under the title *After*

Strange Gods: A Primer of Modern Heresy (1934), he said, regarding a homogeneity of culture, "What is still more important is unity of religious background, and reasons of race and religion combine to make any large number of free-thinking Jews undesirable." He later disavowed the book, and refused to allow any part of it to be reprinted. In *The Idea of a Christian Society* (1940) he writes, "totalitarianism can retain the terms 'freedom' and 'democracy' and give them its own meaning: and its right to them is not so easily disproved as minds inflamed by passion suppose."

One of the first protests against Eliot on the subject of anti-Semitism came in the form of a poem from the Anglo-Jewish writer and poet Emanuel Litvinoff, read out during an inaugural poetry reading for the Institute of Contemporary Arts in 1951, attended by Eliot. Only a few years after the Holocaust, Eliot had republished lines originally written in the 1920s about "money in furs" and the "protozoic slime" of Bleistein's "lustreless, protrusive eye" in his *Selected Poems* of 1948, angering Litvinoff. Litvinoff read out his poem, entitled "To T. S. Eliot," to a packed but silent room, ending with the lines, "Let your words/tread lightly on this earth of Europe/lest my people's bones protest".

18

Writings of Robert Frost

Robert Lee Frost (March 26, 1874 – January 29, 1963) was an American poet. He is highly regarded for his realistic depictions of rural life and his command of American colloquial speech. His work frequently employed settings from rural life in New England in the early twentieth century, using them to examine complex social and philosophical themes. A popular and often-quoted poet, Frost was honored frequently during his lifetime, receiving four Pulitzer Prizes for Poetry.

Early Years

Robert Frost was born in San Francisco, California to journalist William Prescott Frost, Jr., and Isabelle Moodie. His mother was of Scottish descent, and his father descended from Nicholas Frost of Tiverton, Devon, England, who had sailed to New Hampshire in 1634 on the *Wolfrana*

Frost's father was a teacher and later an editor of the *San Francisco Evening Bulletin* (which afterwords merged into the *San Francisco Examiner*), and an unsuccessful candidate for city tax collector. After his father's death on May 5, 1885, in due time the family moved across the country to Lawrence, Massachusetts under the patronage of (Robert's grandfather) William Frost, Sr., who was an overseer at a New England mill. Frost graduated from Lawrence High School in 1892. Frost's mother joined the Swedenborgian church and had him baptized in it, but he left it as an adult.

Despite his later association with rural life, Frost grew up in the city, and published his first poem in his high school's magazine. He attended Dartmouth College for two months, long enough to be accepted into the Theta Delta Chi fraternity. Frost returned home to teach and to work at various jobs including helping his mother teach her class of unruly boys, delivering newspapers, and working in a factory as a lightbulb filament changer. He did not enjoy these jobs at all, feeling his true calling as a poet.

Adult Years

In 1894 he sold his first poem, "My Butterfly: An Elegy" (published in the November 8, 1894 edition of the *New York Independent*) for fifteen dollars. Proud of this accomplishment he proposed marriage to Elinor Miriam White, but she demurred, wanting to finish college (at St. Lawrence University) before they married. Frost then went on an excursion to the Great Dismal Swamp in Virginia, and asked Elinor again upon his return. Having graduated she agreed, and they were married at Harvard University, where he attended liberal arts studies for two years.

He did well at Harvard, but left to support his growing family. Grandfather Frost had, shortly before his death, purchased a farm for the young couple in Derry, New Hampshire; and Robert worked the farm for nine years, while writing early in the mornings and producing many of the poems that would later become famous. Ultimately his farming proved unsuccessful and he returned to education as an English teacher, at Pinkerton Academy from 1906 to 1911, then at the New Hampshire Normal School (now Plymouth State University) in Plymouth, New Hampshire.

In 1912 Frost sailed with his family to Great Britain, living first in Glasgow before settling in Beaconsfield outside London. His first book of poetry, *A Boy's Will,* was published the next year. In England he made some important acquaintances, including Edward Thomas (a member of the group known as the Dymock Poets), T.E. Hulme, and Ezra Pound. Pound would become the first American to write a (favorable) review of Frost's work, though Frost later resented Pound's attempts to manipulate his American prosody. Surrounded by his peers, Frost wrote some of his best work while in England.

As World War I began, Frost returned to America in 1915. He bought a farm in Franconia, New Hampshire, where he launched a career of writing, teaching, and lecturing. This family homestead served as the Frosts' summer home until 1938, and is maintained today as 'The Frost Place', a museum and poetry conference site at Franconia. During the years 1916–20, 1923–24, and 1927–1938, Frost taught English at Amherst College, Massachusetts, notably encouraging his students to account for the sounds of the human voice in their writing.

For forty-two years, from 1921 to 1963, Frost spent almost every summer and fall teaching at the Bread Loaf School of English of Middlebury College, at the mountain campus at Ripton, Vermont. He is credited as a major influence upon the development of the school and its writing programs; the Bread Loaf Writers' Conference gained renown during Frost's time there. The college now owns and maintains his former Ripton farmstead as a national historic site near the Bread Loaf campus. In 1921 Frost accepted a fellowship teaching post at the University of Michigan, Ann Arbor, where he resided until 1927; while there he was awarded a lifetime appointment at the University as a Fellow in Letters. The Robert Frost Ann Arbor home is now situated at The Henry Ford Museum in Dearborn, Michigan. Frost returned to Amherst in 1927. In 1940 he bought a 5-acre plot in South Miami, Florida, naming it *Pencil Pines*; he spent his winters there for the rest of his life.

Harvard's 1965 alumni directory indicates Frost received an honorary degree there. Though he never graduated from college, Frost received over 40 honorary degrees, including ones from Princeton, Oxford and Cambridge universities; and he was the only person to receive two honorary degrees from Dartmouth College. During his lifetime the Robert Frost Middle School in Fairfax, Virginia, and the main library of Amherst College were named after him.

Frost was 86 when he spoke and performed a reading of his poetry at the inauguration of President John F. Kennedy on January 20, 1961. He died in Boston two years later, on January 29, 1963, of complications from prostate surgery. He was buried at the Old Bennington Cemetery in Bennington, Vermont. His epitaph quotes a line from one of his poems: "I had a lover's quarrel with the world."

Frost's poems are critiqued in the *Anthology of Modern American Poetry* (Oxford University Press) where it is mentioned that behind a sometimes charmingly familiar and rural façade, Frost's poetry frequently presents pessimistic and menacing undertones which often are either unrecognized or unanalyzed.

One of the original collections of Frost materials, to which he himself contributed, is found in the Special Collections department of the Jones Library in Amherst, Massachusetts. The collection consists of approximately twelve thousand items, including original manuscript poems and letters, correspondence, and photographs, as well as audio and visual recordings.

Personal Life

Robert Frost's personal life was plagued with grief and loss. His father died of tuberculosis in 1885, when Frost was 11, leaving the family with just $8. Frost's mother died of cancer in 1900. In 1920, Frost had to commit his younger sister, Jeanie, to a mental hospital, where she died nine years later. Mental illness apparently ran in Frost's family, as both he and his mother suffered from depression, and his daughter Irma was committed to a mental hospital in 1947. Frost's wife, Elinor, also experienced bouts of depression.

Elinor and Robert Frost had six children: son Elliot (1896–1904, died of cholera), daughter Lesley Frost Ballantine (1899–1983), son Carol (1902–1940, committed suicide), daughter Irma (1903–1967), daughter Marjorie (1905–1934, died as a result of puerperal fever after childbirth), and daughter Elinor Bettina (died three days after birth in 1907). Only Lesley and Irma outlived their father. Frost's wife, who had heart problems throughout her life, developed breast cancer in 1937, and died of heart failure in 1938.

Poems

At times bittersweet, sometimes ironic, or simply marveling at his surroundings, one can also see autobiographical details in Frost's works; he suffered devastating losses in his life including the untimely deaths of his sister, two of his children and his wife. He knew the soul's depths of psychic despair but was also capable of delighting in birch trees *'loaded with ice a sunny winter morning'*. While memorialising the rural landscape, vernacular, culture and people of New England in his traditional verse style, his poems also transcend the boundaries of time and place with metaphysical significance and modern exploration of human nature in all her beauty and contradictions. Though not without his critics, millions of readers the world over have found comfort and profound meaning in his poetry and he has influenced numerous other authors, poets, musicians, and playwrights into the 21st Century.

Robert Lee Frost (named after Southern General Robert E. Lee) was born on 26 March 1874 in San Francisco, California to Isabelle Moodie (1844-1900) teacher, and William Prescott Frost Jr. (1850-1885), teacher and journalist. San Francisco was a lively city full of citizens of Pioneering spirit, including Will who had ventured there from New Hampshire to seek his fortune as a journalist. He also started gambling and drinking, habits which left his family in dire financial straits when he died in 1885 after contracting tuberculosis. Honouring his last wishes to be buried in Lawrence, Massachusetts where he was born, Isabelle, Robert and his sister Jeanie Florence (1876-1929) made the long train journey across the country to the New England town. Isabelle took up teaching again to support her children.

With both parents as teachers, young Robert was early on exposed to the world of books and reading, studying such works as those by William Shakespeare and poets Robert Burns and William Wordsworth. He also formed a life-long love of nature, the great outdoors and rural countryside. After enrolling in Lawrence High School he was soon writing his own poems including "La Noche Triste" (1890) which was published in the school's paper. He excelled in many subjects including history, botany, Latin and Greek, and played football, graduating at the head of his class. In 1892 he entered Dartmouth, the Ivy League College in Hanover, New Hampshire, but soon became disenchanted with the atmosphere of campus life. He then took on a series of jobs including teaching and working in a mill, all the while continuing to write poetry.

Frost got his first break as a poet in 1894 when the New York magazine *Independent* published "My Butterfly: An Elegy" for a stipend of $15. A year later a wish he had had for some time came true; on 19 December 1895 he married Elinor Miriam White (1872-1938), his co-valedictorian and sweetheart from school. They had gone separate ways upon graduation to attend college, and while Frost had left early, Elinor wanted to wait until she was finished before getting married. They would have six children together; sons Elliott (b.1896-1900) and Carol (1902-1940) and daughters Lesley (b.1899), Irma (b.1903), Marjorie (b.1905-1934), and Elinor Bettina (1907-1907).

The newlyweds continued to teach, which Frost always enjoyed, but the demanding schedule interfered with his writing. In 1897 he entered Harvard University in Cambridge, Massachusetts, though illness caused him to leave in 1899 before finishing his degree. Despite that, it was one of many institutions that would award him an honorary degree later on. The next ten years, the 'Derry years', were trying times for Frost with a growing family to support. In 1900 they moved to a farm bought by his paternal grandfather in Derry, New Hampshire to try poultry farming. The same year his son Elliot died of cholera. Frost suffered greatly from grief and guilt, and compounding this was the loss of his mother to cancer the same year. In 1907 Elinor Bettina died just one day after birth. But the farm was a peaceful and secluded setting and Frost enjoyed farming, tending to his orchard trees, chickens and various other chores. This period inspired such poems as "The Mending Wall" (written in England in 1913) and "Hyla Brook" (1906). The house built in the typical New England clapboard style is now a restored State Historical Landmark.

But it was soon time for a change. In 1911 he sold the farm and the Frosts set sail for England. Elinor was enthusiastic about traveling, even with four children, and they moved into a cottage in Beaconsfield, just outside of London. Then finally it happened; after writing poetry and trying to get noticed by publishers for over twenty years, Frost's first collection of poetry *A Boy's Will* was published in England in 1913 by a small London printer, David Nutt. American publisher Henry Holt printed it in 1915. Frost's work was well-received and fellow poets Edward Thomas and Ezra Pound became friends, supporters, and helped promote his work. *North of Boston* (1914) followed. When World War I started the Frosts were back in New Hampshire, settling at their newly bought farm in Franconia in 1915. A year later Robert began teaching English at Amherst College. *Mountain Interval* was published in 1916 which contained many poems written at Franconia. He was also starting lecture tours for his ever-growing audience of avid readers.

In 1920, Frost bought 'Stone House' (now a museum) in South Shaftsbury, Vermont. There he wrote many of the poems contained in his fourth collection of poetry *New Hampshire* (1923) which won him the Pulitzer Prize for Poetry in 1923. It includes "Stopping By Woods On A Snowy Evening";

> The woods are lovely, dark and deep.
> But I have promises to keep,
> And miles to go before I sleep,
> And miles to go before I sleep.

While he also farmed on the idyllic property with its breathtaking views of mountains and valleys, another project Frost undertook was the founding of the Bread Loaf School of English at Middlebury College in Ripton, Vermont. After his son Carol married Lillian LaBatt (1905-1995) and his grandson Prescott arrived, he gave them Stone House to live in where Carol planted his thousand apple trees. Frost bought a second farm in Shaftsbury, "The Gulley". At the height of his career, his next collection of poems *West-running Brook* (1928) was published just one year before another great loss of a loved one hit him; his sister Jeanie died.

By now Frost was a popular speaker and had a demanding schedule of which Elinor, acting as his secretary, organised for him, so he spent a fair bit of time traveling, though still maintaining an impressive output of poetry. He was awarded the Pulitzer Prize for Poetry a second time in 1931 for his *Collected Poems* (1930), and also in 1937 for *A Further Range* (1936), and yet again in 1943 for his collection *A Witness Tree* (1942). All his children were married and he spent much time with them and his grandchildren, though it was not long before the heavy blows of loss struck again; his beloved daughter Marjorie died in 1934 after the birth of her first child, and in 1938 Elinor died of a heart attack. In 1940 Carol committed suicide.

Leaving the Stone House and The Gulley behind, in 1939 Frost bought the Homer Noble Farm in Ripton, Vermont for his summer residence, located near the Bread Loaf School. He occupied the cabin on the property *'Than smoke and mist who better could appraise, The kindred spirit of an inner haze?'* ("A Cabin in the Clearing") while his friends and colleagues the Morrisons stayed in the main house. *Collected Poems* (1939) was followed by *A Masque of Reason* (play, 1945), *Steeple Bush* (1947), *A Masque of Mercy* (play, 1947), *Complete Poems* (1949), and *In the Clearing* (1962). At the Inauguration of American President John F. Kennedy on 20 January 1961, Frost recited his poem "The Gift Outright" (1942).

Robert Frost died on the 29th of January 1963 in Boston, Massachusetts. *'Safe!, Now let the night be dark for all of me. Let the night be too dark for me to see, Into the future. Let what will be, be.'* ("Acceptance") He lies buried in the family plot in the Old Bennington Cemetery behind the Old First Congregational Church near Shaftsbury, Vermont. His gravestone reads 'I Had A Lover's Quarrel With The World'.

19

Writings of Edward Estlin Cummings

(October 14, 1894 – September 3, 1962), popularly known as E.E. Cummings, with the abbreviated form of his name often written by others in lowercase letters as e.e. cummings (in the style of his poems), was an American poet, painter, essayist, author, and playwright. His body of work encompasses approximately 2,900 poems, two autobiographical novels, four plays and several essays, as well as numerous drawings and paintings. He is remembered as a preeminent voice of 20th century poetry, as well as one of the most popular.

Cummings was born in Cambridge, Massachusetts, on October 14, 1894 to Edward and Rebecca Haswell Clarke Cummings. He was named after his father but his family called him by his middle name, Estlin. His father was a professor of sociology and political science at Harvard University and later a Unitarian minister. Cummings described his father as a hero and a person who could accomplish anything that he wanted to. Edward was well skilled and was always working or repairing things. He and his son were close, and Edward was one of Estlin's most ardent supporters.

His mother, Rebecca, never partook in stereotypically "womanly" things. She loved poetry and reading to her children. Raised in a well-educated family, Cummings was a very smart boy and his mother encouraged Estlin to write more and more poetry every day. His first poem came when he was only three: "Oh, the pretty birdie, O;/with his little toe, toe, toe!" His sister, Elizabeth, was born when he was six years old.

His boyhood home, the E.E. Cummings House, is listed on the National Register of Historic Places.

Education

In his youth, Estlin Cummings attended Cambridge Latin High School. Early stories and poems were published in the *Cambridge Review,* the school newspaper.

From 1911 to 1916, Cummings attended Harvard University, from which he received a B.A. degree in 1915 and a Master's degree for English and Classical Studies in 1916. While at Harvard, he befriended John Dos Passos, at one time rooming in Thayer Hall, named after the family of one of his Harvard acquaintances, Scofield Thayer, and not yet a freshman-only dormitory. Several of Cummings's poems were published in the *Harvard Monthly* as early as 1912. Cummings himself labored on the school newspaper alongside fellow Harvard Aesthetes Dos Passos and S. Foster Damon. In 1915, his poems were published in the *Harvard Advocate.*

From an early age, Cummings studied Greek and Latin. His affinity for each manifests in his later works, such as *XAIPE* (Greek: *Khaire!*, "Rejoice!"; a 1950 collection of poetry), *Anthropos* (Greek: "human"; the title of one of his plays), and "Puella Mea". In his final year at Harvard, Cummings was influenced by writers such as Gertrude Stein and Ezra Pound. He graduated *magna cum laude* in 1916, delivering a controversial commencement address entitled "The New Art". This speech gave him his first taste of notoriety, as he managed to give the false impression that the well-liked imagist poet, Amy Lowell, whom he himself admired, was "abnormal". For this, Cummings was chastised in the newspapers. In 1917, Cummings's first published poems appeared in a collection of poetry entitled *Eight Harvard Poets*.

Career

In 1917 Cummings enlisted in the Norton-Harjes Ambulance Corps, along with his college friend John Dos Passos. Due to an administrative mix-up, Cummings was not assigned to an ambulance unit for five weeks, during which time he stayed in Paris. He fell in love with the city, to which he would return throughout his life.

On September 21, 1917, just five months after his belated assignment, he and a friend, William Slater Brown, were arrested on suspicion of espionage. The two openly expressed anti-war views; Cummings spoke of his lack of hatred for the Germans. They were sent to a military detention camp, the *Depot de Triage,* in La Ferté-Macé, Orne, Normandy, where they languished for 3½ months. Cummings's experiences in the camp were later related in his novel, *The Enormous Room* about which F. Scott Fitzgerald opined, "Of all the work by young men who have sprung up since 1920 one book survives- *The Enormous Room* by e e cummings....Those few who cause books to live have not been able to endure the thought of its mortality." He was released from the detention camp on December 19, 1917, after much intervention from his politically connected father. Cummings returned to the United States on New Year's Day 1918. Later in 1918 he was drafted into the army. He served in the 12th Division at Camp Devens, Massachusetts, until November 1918.

Cummings returned to Paris in 1921 and remained there for two years before returning to New York. During the rest of the 1920s and 1930s he returned to Paris a number of times, and traveled throughout Europe, meeting, among others, Pablo Picasso. In 1931 Cummings traveled to the Soviet Union and recounted his experiences in *Eimi*, published two years later. During these years Cummings also traveled to Northern Africa and Mexico and worked as an essayist and portrait artist for *Vanity Fair* magazine.

Personal Life

In 1926, Cummings's father was killed in a car accident. Though severely injured, Cummings's mother survived. Cummings detailed the accident in the following passage from his *i: six nonlectures* series given at Harvard in 1952–1953:

> ... a locomotive cut the car in half, killing my father instantly. When two brakemen jumped from the halted train, they saw a woman standing -- dazed but erect -- beside a mangled machine; with blood spouting (as the older said to me) out of her head. One of her hands (the younger added) kept feeling her dress, as if trying to discover why it was wet. These men took my sixty-six year old mother by the arms and tried to lead her toward a nearby farmhouse; but she threw them off, strode straight to

> my father's body, and directed a group of scared spectators to cover him. When this had been done (and only then) she let them lead her away.

His father's death had a profound impact on Cummings and his work, who entered a new period in his artistic life. Cummings began to focus on more important aspects of life in his poetry. He began this new period by paying homage to his father's memory in the poem "my father moved through dooms of love".

Born into a Unitarian family, Cummings exhibited transcendental leanings his entire life. As he grew in maturity and age, Cummings moved more toward an "I, Thou" relationship with God. His journals are replete with references to "le bon Dieu" as well as prayers for inspiration in his poetry and artwork (such as "Bon Dieu! may I some day do something truly great. amen."). Cummings "also prayed for strength to be his essential self ('may I be I is the only prayer—not may I be great or good or beautiful or wise or strong'), and for relief of spirit in times of depression ('almighty God! I thank thee for my soul; & may I never die spiritually into a mere mind through disease of loneliness')."

Cummings was married three times, including a long common-law marriage.

Poetry

Despite Cummings's consanguinity with avant-garde styles, much of his work is quite traditional. Many of his poems are sonnets, albeit often with a modern twist, and he occasionally made use of the blues form and acrostics. Cummings's poetry often deals with themes of love and nature, as well as the relationship of the individual to the masses and to the world. His poems are also often rife with satire.

While his poetic forms and themes share an affinity with the romantic tradition, Cummings's work universally shows a particular idiosyncrasy of syntax, or way of arranging individual words into larger phrases and sentences. Many of his most striking poems do not involve any typographical or punctuation innovations at all, but purely syntactic ones.

As well as being influenced by notable modernists including Gertrude Stein and Ezra Pound, Cummings's early work drew upon the imagist experiments of Amy Lowell. Later, his visits to Paris exposed him to Dada and surrealism, which in turn permeated his work. Cummings also liked to incorporate imagery of nature and death into much of his poetry.

While some of his poetry is free verse (with no concern for rhyme or meter), many have a recognizable sonnet structure of 14 lines, with an intricate rhyme scheme. A number of his poems feature a typographically exuberant style, with words, parts of words, or punctuation symbols scattered across the page, often making little sense until read aloud, at which point the meaning and emotion become clear. Cummings, who was also a painter, understood the importance of presentation, and used typography to "paint a picture" with some of his poems.

Readers sometimes experience a jarring, incomprehensible effect with Cummings's work, as the poems do not act in accordance with the conventional combinatorial rules that generate typical English sentences. (For example, "why must itself..." or "they sowed their isn't...''). His readings of Stein in the early part of the century probably served as a springboard to this aspect of his artistic development (in the same way that Robert Walser's work acted as a springboard for Franz Kafka). In some respects, Cummings's work is more stylistically continuous with Stein's than with any other poet or writer.

In addition, a number of Cummings's poems feature, in part or in whole, intentional misspellings, and several incorporate phonetic spellings intended to represent particular dialects. Cummings also made use of inventive formations of compound words, as in "in Just-", which features words such as "mud-luscious" "puddle-wonderful", and "eddieandbill." This poem is part of a sequence of poems entitled *Chansons Innocentes*; it has many references comparing the "balloonman" to Pan, the mythical creature that is half-goat and half-man.

Many of Cummings's poems are satirical and address social issues, but have an equal or even stronger bias toward romanticism: time and again his poems celebrate love, sex, and the season of rebirth.

Cummings's talent extended to children's books, novels, and painting. A notable example of his versatility is an introduction he wrote for a collection of the comic strip *Krazy Kat*. Examples of Cummings's unorthodox typographical style can be seen in his poem "the sky was candy luminous...". His books still sell great.

Plays

During his lifetime, Cummings published four plays: *HIM* (1927), *Anthropos: or, the Future of Art* (1930), *Tom: A Ballet* (1935), and *Santa Claus: A Morality* (1946).

1) *HIM*: A three-act play, was first produced in 1928 by the Provincetown Players in New York City. The production was directed by James Light. The play's main characters are "Him", a playwright, and "Me", his girlfriend. Cummings said of the unorthodox play:

   > Relax and give the play a chance to strut its stuff—relax, stop wondering what it is all 'about'—like many strange and familiar things, Life included, this play isn't 'about,' *it simply is. . . . Don't try to enjoy* it, let it try to enjoy you. Don't try to understand it, let it try to understand you."

2) *Anthropos, or the Future of Art* is a short, one-act play that Cummings contributed to the anthology *Whither, Whither or After Sex, What? A Symposium to End Symposium.* The play consists of dialogue between Man, the main character, and three "infrahumans", or inferior beings. The word *anthropos* is the Greek word for "man", in the sense of "mankind".

3) *Tom: A Ballet* is a ballet based on *Uncle Tom's Cabin.* The ballet is detailed in a "synopsis" as well as descriptions of four "episodes", which were published by Cummings in 1935. It has never been performed. More information about the play as well as an illustration can be found at this webpage from the E. E. Cummings Society.

4) *Santa Claus: A Morality* was probably Cummings's most successful play. It is an allegorical Christmas fantasy presented in one act of five scenes. The play was inspired by his daughter Nancy, with whom he was reunited in 1946. It was first published in the Harvard College magazine the *Wake.* The play's main characters are Santa Claus,

his family (Woman and Child), Death, and Mob. At the outset of the play, Santa Claus's family has disintegrated due to their lust for knowledge (Science). After a series of events, however, Santa Claus's faith in love and his rejection of the materialism and disappointment he associates with Science are reaffirmed, and he is reunited with Woman and Child.

Final Years and Death

In 1952, his alma mater, Harvard, awarded Cummings an honorary seat as a guest professor. The Charles Eliot Norton Lectures he gave in 1952 and 1955 were later collected as *i: six nonlectures*.

Cummings spent the last decade of his life traveling, fulfilling speaking engagements, and spending time at his summer home, Joy Farm, in Silver Lake, New Hampshire.

He died on September 3, 1962, at the age of 67 in North Conway, New Hampshire of a stroke. His cremated remains were buried in Lot 748 Althaea Path, in Section 6, Forest Hills Cemetery and Crematory in Boston. In 1969, his third wife, Marion Morehouse Cummings, died and was buried in an adjoining plot.

20

Literary Life of Margaret Fuller

Sarah Margaret Fuller Ossoli, more commonly known as Margaret Fuller, (May 23, 1810 – July 19, 1850) was a journalist, critic and women's rights activist associated with the American transcendental movement. She was the first full-time female book reviewer in journalism. Her book *Woman in the Nineteenth Century* is considered the first major feminist work in the United States.

Born Sarah Margaret Fuller in an area of Cambridge, Massachusetts, she was given a substantial early education by her father, Timothy Fuller. She later had more formal schooling and became a teacher before, in 1839, she began overseeing what she called "conversations": discussions among women meant to compensate for their lack of access to higher education. She became the first editor of the transcendental publication *The Dial* in 1840 before joining the staff of the *New York Tribune* under Horace Greeley in 1844. By the time she was in her 30s, Fuller had earned a reputation as the best-read person in New England, male or female, and became the first woman allowed to use the library at Harvard College. Her seminal work, *Woman in the Nineteenth Century*, was published in 1845. A year later, she was sent to Europe for the

Tribune as its first female correspondent. She soon became involved with the revolution in Italy and allied herself with Giuseppe Mazzini. She also met Giovanni Ossoli, with whom she had a child. All three members of the family died in a shipwreck off Fire Island, New York, traveling back to the United States in 1850. Fuller's body was never recovered.

Fuller was an advocate of women's rights and, in particular, women's education and the right to employment. She also encouraged many other reforms in society, including prison reform and the emancipation of slaves in the United States. Many other advocates for women's rights and feminism, including Susan B. Anthony, cite Fuller as a source of inspiration. Many of her contemporaries, however, were not supportive, including her former friend Harriet Martineau, who said that Fuller was a talker rather than an activist. Shortly after Fuller's death her importance faded; the editors who prepared her letters to be published, believing her fame would be short-lived, were not concerned about accuracy and censored or altered much of her words before publication.

Early Life

Sarah Margaret Fuller was born May 23, 1810, in Cambridgeport, Massachusetts, the first child of Timothy Fuller and Margaret Crane Fuller. She was named after her paternal grandmother and her mother; by the age of nine, however, she dropped "Sarah" and insisted on being called "Margaret". The Margaret Fuller House, in which she was born, is still standing. Her father taught Fuller to read and write at the age of three and a half, shortly after the couple's second daughter, Julia Adelaide, had died at the age of fourteen months. He offered her an education as rigorous as any boy's at the time and forbade her from reading the typical feminine fare such as etiquette books and sentimental novels. He incorporated Latin into his teaching shortly after the birth of the couple's son, Eugene, in May 1815, and soon she was translating simple passages from Virgil. During the day, young Margaret spent time with her mother, who taught her household chores and sewing. In 1817, her brother William Henry Fuller was born and her father was elected as a representative in the United States Congress. For the next eight years, he would spend four to six months of the year in Washington, D.C. At the age of 10, Fuller wrote a cryptic note which her father saved: "On the 23rd of May, 1810, was born one foredoomed to sorrow and pain, and like others to have misfortunes".

In 1824, Fuller was sent to the School for Young Ladies in Groton at the advice of aunts and uncles, though she resisted the idea at first. While she was in Groton, Timothy Fuller, in order to help John Quincy Adams with his presidential campaign in 1824, did not run for re-election; he had hoped Adams would return the favor with some kind of government appointment. On June 17, 1825, Fuller was in attendance at the ceremony when the American Revolutionary War hero Marquis de Lafayette laid the cornerstone of the Bunker Hill Monument 50 years after the battle. Fuller left the Groton school and returned home at the age of 16 after having studied there for two years. At home, she studied the classics and trained herself in several modern languages and various examples of world literature. By this time, she realized she did not fit in with other young women her age. She wrote, "I have felt that I was not born to the common womanly lot".

Eliza Farrar, wife of Harvard professor John Farrar and author of *The Young Lady's Friend* (1836), attempted to train her in feminine etiquette until the age of 20, though Farrar was never wholly successful.

Early Career

Fuller was an avid reader; by the time she was in her 30s, she had earned a reputation as the best-read person, male or female, in New England. She used her knowledge to give private lessons based on the teaching style of Elizabeth Palmer Peabody. Fuller hoped to earn her living through journalism and translation; her first published work, a response to historian George Bancroft, appeared in November 1834 in the *North American Review*. When she was 23, her father's law practice failed and he moved the family to a farm in Groton. On February 20, 1835, both Frederick Henry Hedge and James Freeman Clarke requested written contributions from her to publish in their respective periodicals. Clarke helped her publish her first literary review in the *Western Messenger* in June: criticisms of recent biographies on George Crabbe and Hannah More. In the fall of that year, she suffered a terrible migraine with a fever that lasted nine days; Fuller would often be plagued with headaches throughout her life. While she was still recovering, her father died of cholera on October 2, 1835. She was deeply affected by his death: "My father's image follows me constantly", she wrote. She vowed to step in as the head of the family and take care of her newly widowed mother and her younger siblings. Her father had not left a will, and two of her uncles gained control of his property and finances, later assessed at \$18,098.15, and forced the family to rely on them for support. Humiliated by the way her uncles were treating the family, Fuller wrote that she regretted being "of the softer sex, and never more than now".

Around this time, Fuller had hoped to prepare a biography of Johann Wolfgang von Goethe, but felt that she could work on it only if she traveled to Europe. Her father's death and her sudden responsibility over her family caused her to abandon this idea. In 1836, Fuller was given a job teaching at Bronson Alcott's Temple School in Boston, where she remained for a year. She then accepted an invitation to teach at the Greene Street School in Providence, Rhode Island, in April 1837 with the unusually high salary of $1,000 per year. Her family sold the Groton farm and Fuller moved with them to Jamaica Plain, Massachusetts. On November 6, 1839, Fuller held the first of her "conversations", discussions among local women who met in the Boston home of the Peabodys. Fuller intended these meetings to compensate for the lack of education for women with discussions and debates which focused on subjects including the fine arts, history, mythology, literature, and nature. Serving as the "nucleus of conversation", Fuller also intended to answer the "great questions" facing women: "What were we born to do? How shall we do it? which so few ever propose to themselves 'till their best years are gone by". A number of significant figures in the women's rights movement attended these "conversations", including Sophia Dana Ripley, Caroline Sturgis, and Maria White Lowell.

The Dial

In October 1839, Ralph Waldo Emerson was seeking an editor for his transcendental journal *The Dial* and, after several had declined the role, he offered it to Fuller, referring to her as "my vivacious friend". Emerson had first met Fuller in Cambridge in 1835; of that meeting, he admitted "she made me laugh more than I liked". The next summer, Fuller spent two weeks at Emerson's home in Concord where their friendship grew. Fuller accepted Emerson's offer to edit *The Dial* on October 20, 1839, though she did not begin work until the first week of 1840. She edited the journal for the first two years of its existence from 1840 to 1842, though her promised annual salary of $200 was never paid. Because of her role, she was soon recognized as one of the most important figures of the transcendental movement and was invited to George Ripley's Brook Farm communal experiment. She never officially joined the community but was a frequent visitor, often spending New Year's Eve there. In the summer of 1843, she traveled to Chicago, Milwaukee, Niagara Falls and Buffalo, New York; while there, she interacted with several Native Americans, including members of the Ottawa tribe and the Chippewa tribe. She reported her experiences in a book called *Summer on the Lakes,* which she completed writing on her 34th birthday in 1844; critic Evert Augustus Duyckinck called it "the only genuine book, I can think of, this season". She had used the library at Harvard College for further background information on the Great Lakes region, making her the first woman allowed to use Harvard's library.

One of Fuller's most important works, "The Great Lawsuit", was written in serial form for *The Dial.* She originally intended to name the work "The Great Lawsuit: Man *versus* Men, Woman *versus* Women"; when it was expanded and published independently in 1845, it was instead named *Woman in the Nineteenth Century.* After completing it, she wrote to a friend: "I had put a good deal of my true self in it, as if, I suppose I went away now, the measure of my footprint would be left on earth." The work discussed the role that women played in the American democracy and Fuller's opinion on possibilities for improvement. It has since become one of the major documents in American feminism and is considered the first of its kind in the United States.

New York Tribune

Fuller left *The Dial* in 1844 in part because of ill health but also because of her disappointment with the publication's dwindling subscription list. She moved to New York that autumn and joined Horace Greeley's *New York Tribune* as literary critic, becoming the first full-time book reviewer in journalism and, by 1846, was the publication's first female editor. Her first article, a review of a collection of essays by Emerson, was printed in the December 1, 1844, issue. At this time, the *Tribune* had some 50,000 subscribers and Fuller earned $500 a year for her work. In addition to American books, she reviewed foreign literature, concerts, lectures, and art exhibits. During her four years with the publication, she published more than 250 columns, most signed with a "*" as a byline. In these columns, Fuller discussed topics ranging from art and literature to political and social issues such as the plight of slaves and women's rights. She also published poetry; her poems, styled after the work of Emerson, do not have the same intellectual vigor as her criticism.

Around this time, she was also involved in a scandal involving fellow literary critic Edgar Allan Poe, who had been carrying on a public flirtation with the married poet Frances Sargent Osgood. At the same time, another poet, Elizabeth F. Ellet, became enamored of Poe and jealous of Osgood and suggested the relationship between Poe and Osgood was more than just innocent flirtation. Osgood then sent Fuller and Anne Lynch Botta to Poe's cottage on her behalf to request that he return the personal letters she had sent him. Angered by their interference, Poe called them "Busy-bodies". A public scandal erupted and continued until Osgood's estranged husband Samuel Stillman Osgood stepped in and threatened to sue Ellet.

Assignment in Europe

Fuller was sent to Europe in 1846 by the *New York Tribune,* specifically England and Italy, as its first female foreign correspondent. She traveled from Boston to Liverpool in August on the *Cambria,* a vessel that used both sail and steam to make the journey in ten days and sixteen hours. Over the next four years she provided thirty-seven reports from overseas. She interviewed many prominent writers including George Sand and Thomas Carlyle—whom she found disappointing because of his reactionary politics, among other things. George Sand had previously been an idol of hers, but Fuller was disappointed when Sand chose not to run for the French National Assembly, saying that women were not ready to vote or to hold political office. Fuller was also given a letter of introduction from Cornelius Mathews for Elizabeth Barrett; the two women did not meet, as Barrett had just eloped with Robert Browning.

In the spring of 1846, she met Giuseppe Mazzini in England, who had been in exile from Italy since

1837. Fuller also met the Italian revolutionary Giovanni Angelo Ossoli, a marquis who had been disinherited by his family because of his support for Mazzini. Fuller and Ossoli moved in together in Florence, Italy, likely before they were married, if they ever were. Fuller originally did not support marrying him, in part because of their different religions; she was Protestant and he was Roman Catholic.

Emerson speculated that the couple was "married perhaps in Oct. Nov. or Dec" of 1847, though he did not explain his reasoning. Biographers have speculated that the couple married on April 4, 1848, to celebrate the anniversary of their first meeting. By the time the couple moved to Florence, they were referred to as husband and wife, though it is unclear if any formal ceremony took place. It seems certain that at the time their child was born, they were not married. By New Year's Day 1848, she suspected that she was pregnant but kept it from Ossoli for several weeks. Their child, Angelo Eugene Philip Ossoli, was born in early September 1848; they nicknamed him Angelino.

The couple was very secretive about their relationship but, after Angelino suffered an unnamed illness, they became closer. Fuller finally informed her mother about Ossoli and Angelino in August 1849. The letter explained that she had kept silent so as not to upset her "but it has become necessary, on account of the child, for us to live publicly and permanently together." Her mother's response makes it clear that she was aware that a legal marriage had not taken place. Even so, she was happy for her daughter, writing: "I send my first kiss with my fervent blessing to my grandson." Modern biographers are still unclear if Fuller and Ossoli ever married.

The couple supported Giuseppe Mazzini's revolution for the establishment of a Roman Republic in 1849—Ossoli fought in the struggle while Fuller volunteered at a supporting hospital. After generations of rule by several parties, few of which were Italian, Italy had been left without an official central government with various pieces of the country overseen by different weak governments, including one under the control of the Papacy. When Pope Pius IX was appointed in 1846, he made small steps towards the establishment of a central Italian democratic government, though revolutionaries like Mazzini did not trust the Pope's efforts. The political unrest was enough that the Pope disguised himself and escaped on November 24, 1848. A Roman republic with a representative government was established in February 1849, only to be destroyed by an invasion from France a few months later. Because Fuller and Ossoli were aligned with the revolution, when Pope Pius IX returned to Rome in 1850, they had to flee Italy and decided to move to the United States. She intended to use her experience to write a book about the history of the Roman Republic, a work she may have begun as early as 1847, hoping to find an American publisher after a British one rejected it. She believed the work would be her most important, referring to it in a March 1849 letter to her brother Richard as, "something good which may survive my troubled existence."

Death

In the beginning of the year 1850, Fuller wrote to a friend: "It has long seemed that in the year 1850 I should stand on some important plateau in the ascent of life... I feel however no marked and important change as yet." Also that year, Fuller wrote: "I am absurdly fearful and various omens have combined to give me a dark feeling... It seems to me that my future upon earth will soon close... I have a vague expectation of some crisis—I know not what". A few days after writing this, Fuller, Ossoli, and their child began a five-week return voyage to the United States aboard the ship *Elizabeth*. The ship was an American merchant freighter carrying cargo that included mostly marble from Carrara as well as a statue of John C. Calhoun sculpted by Hiram Powers. After a short delay due to rain, the *Elizabeth* set sail on May 17. At sea, the ship's captain, Seth Hasty, died of smallpox. The child, Angelino, contracted the disease as well, though he recovered.

Possibly because of the inexperienced first mate, now serving as captain, the ship slammed into a sandbar less than 100 yards from Fire Island, New York, on July 19, 1850, around 3:30 a.m. Many of the other passengers and crew members abandoned ship. The first mate, Mr. Bangs, urged Fuller and Ossoli to try to save themselves and their child as he himself jumped overboard, later claiming he believed Fuller had wanted to be left behind to die. On the beach, people arrived with carts hoping to take advantage if any cargo washed to shore; none made any effort to rescue the crew or passengers of the *Elizabeth*, though they were only 50 yards from shore. Ossoli and Fuller, along with their child, were some of the last on the ship; most others had attempted to swim to shore. Eventually, Ossoli was thrown overboard by a massive wave and, after the wave had passed, a crewman who witnessed the event said Fuller could not be seen.

Henry David Thoreau traveled to New York, at the urging of Emerson, to search the shore but neither

Fuller's body nor that of her husband were ever recovered; only Angelino had washed ashore. Few of their possessions were found other than some of the child's clothes and a few letters. Fuller's manuscript on the history of the Roman Republic was also lost. A memorial to Fuller was erected on the beach at Fire Island in 1901 through the efforts of Julia Ward Howe. A cenotaph to Fuller and Ossoli, under which Angelino is buried, is in Mount Auburn Cemetery, Cambridge, Massachusetts. The inscription reads, in part:

> By birth a child of New England
> By adoption a citizen of Rome
> By genius belonging to the world

Within a week after her death, Horace Greeley suggested to Emerson that a biography of Fuller, to be called *Margaret and Her Friends*, be prepared quickly "before the interest excited by her sad decease has passed away". Many of her writings were soon collected together by her brother Arthur as *At Home and Abroad* (1856) and *Life Without and Life Within* (1858). He also edited a new version of *Woman in the Nineteenth Century* in 1855. In February 1852, *The Memoirs of Margaret Fuller Ossoli* was published, edited by Emerson, James Freeman Clarke, and William Henry Channing, though much of the work was censored or reworded. It particularly left out details about her love affair with Ossoli and an earlier relationship with a man named James Nathan. The three editors, believing the public interest in Fuller would be short-lived and that she would not survive as a historical figure, were not concerned about accuracy. Even so, for a time, it was the best-selling biography of the decade and went through thirteen editions before the end of the century. The book focused on her personality rather than her work and, as a result, detractors of the book ignored her status as a critic and instead criticized her personal life and her "unwomanly" arrogance.

Beliefs

Fuller was an early proponent of feminism and especially believed in providing education to women. Once equal educational rights were afforded women, she believed, women could push for equal political rights as well. She advocated that women seek any employment they wish, rather than catering to the stereotypical "feminine" roles of the time, such as teaching. She once said, "If you ask me what office women should fill, I reply—any... let them be sea captains if you will. I do not doubt that there are women well fitted for such an office". She had great confidence in all women but doubted that a woman would produce a lasting work of art or literature in her time and disliked the popular female poets of her time. Fuller also warned women to be careful about marriage and not to become dependent on their husbands. As she wrote, "I wish woman to live, *first* for God's sake. Then she will not make an imperfect man for her god, and thus sink to idolatry. Then she will not take what is not fit for her from a sense of weakness and poverty". By 1832, she had made a personal commitment to stay single. Fuller also questioned a definitive line between male and female: "There is no wholly masculine man... no purely feminine" but that both were present in any individual. She suggested also that within a female were two parts: the intellectual side (which she called the Minerva) and the "lyrical" or "Femality" side (the Muse). She admired the work of Emanuel Swedenborg, who believed men and women shared "an angelic ministry", as she wrote, as well as Charles Fourier, who placed "Woman on an entire equality with Man". Unlike several contemporary women writers, including "Mrs. Sigourney" and "Mrs. Stowe", she was familiarly referred to in a less formal manner as "Margaret".

Fuller also advocated reform at all levels of society, including prison. In October 1844, she visited Sing Sing and interviewed the women prisoners, even staying overnight in the facility. Sing Sing was developing a more humane system for its women inmates, many of whom were prostitutes. Fuller was also concerned about the homeless and those living in dire poverty, especially in New York. She also admitted that, though she was raised to believe "that the Indian obstinately refused to be civilized", her travels in the American West made her realize that the white man unfairly treated the Native Americans; she considered Native Americans an important part of American heritage. She also supported the rights of African-Americans, referring to "this cancer of slavery", and suggested that those who were interested in the Abolition movement follow the same reasoning when considering the rights of women: "As the friend of the Negro assumes that one man cannot by right hold another in bondage, so should the Friend of Woman assume that Man cannot by right lay even well-meant restrictions on Woman." She suggested that those who spoke against the emancipation of slaves were similar to those who did not support the emancipation of Italy.

Fuller agreed with the transcendental concern for the psychological well-being of the individual, though she was never comfortable being labeled a transcendentalist. Even so, she wrote, if being labeled a transcendentalist means "that I have an active mind frequently busy with large topics I hope it is so". She criticized people like Emerson, however, for focusing too much on individual improvement and not enough on social reform. Like other members of the so-called Transcendental Club, she rebelled against the past and believed in the possibility of change. However, unlike others in the movement, her rebellion was not based on religion.

Legacy and Criticism

Margaret Fuller was especially known in her time for her personality and, in particular, for being overly self-confident and having a bad temper. This personality was the inspiration for the character Hester Prynne in Nathaniel Hawthorne's novel *The Scarlet Letter*, specifically her radical thinking about "the whole race of womanhood". She may also be the basis for the character Zenobia in another of Hawthorne's works, *The Blithedale Romance*. Hawthorne and his then-fiancée Sophia had first met Fuller in October 1839.

She was also an inspiration to poet Walt Whitman, who believed in her call for the forging of a new national identity and a truly American literature. Elizabeth Barrett Browning was also a strong admirer, but believed that Fuller's unconventional views were unappreciated in the United States and, therefore, she was better off dead. She also said that Fuller's history of the Roman Republic would have been her greatest work: "The work she was preparing upon Italy would probably have been more equal to her faculty than anything previously produced by her pen (her other writings being curiously inferior to the impressions her conversation gave you)". An 1860 essay collection, *Historical Pictures Retouched,* by Caroline Healey Dall, called Fuller's *Woman in the Nineteenth Century* "doubtless the most brilliant, complete, and scholarly statement ever made on the subject". Despite his personal issues with Fuller, the typically harsh literary critic Edgar Allan Poe wrote of the work as "a book which few women in the country could have written, and no woman in the country would have published, with the exception of Miss Fuller", noting its "independence" and "unmitigated radicalism". Thoreau also thought highly of the book, suggesting that its strength came in part from Fuller's conversational ability. As he called it, it was "rich extempore writing, talking with pen in hand".

Another admirer of Fuller was Susan B. Anthony, a pioneer of women's rights, who wrote that Fuller "possessed more influence on the thought of American women than any woman previous to her time". Fuller's work may have partially inspired the Seneca Falls Convention in 1848. Anthony, along with Elizabeth Cady Stanton and Matilda Joslyn Gage wrote in their *History of Woman Suffrage* that Fuller "was the precursor of the Women's Rights agitation" who "possessed more influence upon the thoughts of America, than any woman previous to her time". Modern scholars have suggested *Woman in the Nineteenth Century* was the first major women's rights work since Mary Wollstonecraft's *A Vindication of the Rights of Woman* (1792), though an early comparison between the two women came from George Eliot in 1855. It is unclear if Fuller was familiar with Wollstonecraft's works; in her childhood, her father prevented her from reading them. In 1995, Fuller was inducted into the National Women's Hall of Fame.

Fuller, however, was not without her critics. A one-time friend, the English writer Harriet Martineau, was one of her harshest detractors after Fuller's death. Martineau said that Fuller was a talker rather than an activist, that she had "shallow conceits" and often "looked down upon persons who acted instead of talking finely... and despised those who, like myself, could not adopt her scale of valuation". The influential editor Rufus Wilmot Griswold, who believed she went against his notion of feminine modesty, referred to *Woman in the Nineteenth Century* as "an eloquent expression of her discontent at having been created female". New York writer Charles Frederick Briggs said that she was "wasting the time of her readers", especially because she was an unmarried woman and therefore could not "truly represent the female character". English writer and critic Matthew Arnold scoffed at Fuller's conversations as well, saying, "My G–d, what rot did she and the other female dogs of Boston talk about Greek mythology!" Nathaniel Hawthorne, who had previously been a supporter of Fuller, was critical of her after *Woman of the Nineteenth Century* was published:

> The impression it left was disagreeable. I did not like the tone of it—& did not agree with her at all about the change in woman's outward circumstances... Neither do I believe in such a character of man as she gives. It is altogether too ignoble... I think Margaret speaks of many things that should not be spoken of.

Fuller had angered fellow poet and critic James Russell Lowell when she reviewed his work, calling him "absolutely wanting in the true spirit and tone of poesy... his verse is stereotyped, his thought sounds no depth; and posterity will not remember him." In response, Lowell took revenge in his satirical *A Fable for Critics,* first published in October 1848. At first, he considered excluding her entirely but ultimately gave her what was called the "most wholly negative characterization" in the work. Referring to her as Miranda, Lowell wrote that she stole old ideas and presented them as her own, she was genuine only in her spite and "when acting as censor, she privately blows a censer of vanity 'neath her own nose".

Shortly after Fuller's death, her importance faded. Her obituary in the newspaper she had once edited, the *Daily Tribune,* said that her works had a few great sentiments, "but as a whole they must commend themselves mainly by their vigor of thought and habitual fearlessness rather than freedom of utterance". As biographer Abby Slater wrote, "Margaret had been demoted from a position of importance in her own right to one in which her only importance was in the company she kept". Years later, Hawthorne's son Julian wrote, "The majority of readers will, I think, not be inconsolable that poor Margaret Fuller has at last taken her place with the numberless other dismal frauds who fill the limbo of human pretension and failure." In the 20th century, American writer Elizabeth Hardwick, former wife of Robert Lowell, wrote an essay called "The Genius of Margaret Fuller" (1986). She compared her own move from Boston to New York to Fuller's, saying that Boston was not a good place for intellectuals, despite the assumption that it was the best place for intellectuals.

21

Writings of Ernest Hemingway

Ernest Miller Hemingway (July 21, 1899 – July 2, 1961) was an American writer and journalist. During his lifetime he wrote and had published seven novels; six collections of short stories; and two works of non-fiction. Since his death three novels, four collections of short stories, and three non-fiction autobiographical works have been published. Hemingway received the Nobel Prize in Literature in 1954 for his novella *The Old Man and the Sea.*

Hemingway was born and raised in Oak Park, Illinois. After high school he worked as a reporter but within months he left for the Italian front to be an ambulance driver in World War I. He was seriously injured and returned home within the year. He married his first wife Hadley Richardson in 1922 and moved to Paris, where he worked as a foreign correspondent. During this time Hemingway met, and was influenced by, writers and artists of the 1920s expatriate community known as the "Lost Generation". In 1924 Hemingway wrote his first novel, *The Sun Also Rises.*

In the late 1920s, Hemingway divorced Hadley, married his second wife Pauline Pfeiffer, and moved to

Key West, Florida. In 1937 Hemingway went to Spain as a war correspondent to cover the Spanish Civil War. After the war he divorced Pauline, married his third wife Martha Gellhorn, wrote *For Whom the Bell Tolls,* and moved to Cuba. Hemingway covered World War II in Europe and he was present at Operation Overlord. Later he was in Paris during the liberation of Paris. After the war, he divorced again, married his fourth wife Mary Welsh Hemingway, and wrote *Across the River and Into the Trees.* In the summer of 1961, Hemingway committed suicide.

Hemingway produced most of his work between the mid 1920s and the mid 1950s, though a number of unfinished works were published posthumously. Hemingway's distinctive writing style is characterized by economy and understatement, and had a significant influence on the development of twentieth-century fiction writing. His protagonists are typically stoical men who exhibit an ideal described as "grace under pressure." Many of his works are now considered classics of American literature. During his lifetime, Hemingway's popularity peaked after the publication of *The Old Man and the Sea.* His impact on American literature has been considerable. For example, J.D. Salinger admired Hemingway's style and methods of writing.

Early Life

Ernest Miller Hemingway was born on July 21, 1899 in Oak Park, Illinois, a suburb of Chicago. Hemingway was the first son and the second child born to Clarence Edmonds "Doc Ed" Hemingway—a country doctor, and Grace Hall Hemingway. The Hemingways lived in a six-bedroom Victorian house built by Hemingway's maternal grandfather, Ernest Miller Hall, an English immigrant and Civil War veteran who lived with the family. Hemingway was named after his grandfather, although he disliked his name, and "associated it with the naive, even foolish hero of Oscar Wilde's play *The Importance of Being Earnest*".

Hemingway's mother, who wanted to be an opera singer, earned money with voice and music lessons. She was domineering and narrowly religious, mirroring the strict Protestant ethic of Oak Park. The town, according to Hemingway, had "wide lawns and narrow minds". Her insistence that he learn the cello became a "source of conflict", but he later admitted the music lessons were useful to his writing as in the "contrapunctal structure of *For Whom the Bell Tolls* ". The family owned a summer home called *Windemere* on Walloon Lake, near Petoskey, Michigan where they spent the summers. Hemingway learned to hunt, fish, and camp in the woods and lakes of Northern Michigan. His early experiences with nature instilled a passion for outdoor adventure, living in remote or isolated areas, hunting and fishing, and became permanent interests.

Hemingway attended Oak Park and River Forest High School from 1913 until 1917. There he was involved with sports: boxing, track, water polo, and football. He showed talent in English classes and was on the debate team. He wrote and edited the "Trapeze" and "Tabula" (the school's newspaper and yearbook), where he imitated the language of sportswriters, and sometimes used the pen name Ring Lardner, Jr., a nod to his literary hero Ring Lardner of the Chicago Tribune who used the byline "Line O'Type". After high school, Hemingway was hired as a cub reporter at *The Kansas City Star*, and like Mark Twain, Stephen Crane, Theodore Dreiser and Sinclair Lewis he worked as a journalist prior to becoming a novelist. Although he worked at the newspaper for only six months—from October 17, 1917 to April 30, 1918—he relied on the *Star*'s style guide as a foundation for his writing: "Use short sentences. Use short first paragraphs. Use vigorous English. Be positive, not negative."

Hemingway volunteered to become an ambulance driver for the Red Cross in Italy early in 1918. He left New York in May, and arrived in Paris as the city was under bombardment from German artillery. By June he was stationed at the Italian Front. On July 8 he was seriously wounded by mortar fire as he ran an errand to the canteen. Despite his wounds, Hemingway carried an Italian soldier to safety, for which he was honored with the Italian Silver Medal of Bravery. Still only eighteen, Hemingway said of the incident: "When you go to war as a boy you have a great illusion of immortality. Other people get killed; not you....Then when you are badly wounded the first time you lose that illusion and you know it can happen to you." He had shrapnel wounds to both legs, had an operation at a distribution center, spent five days at a field hospital, and was transferred to the Red Cross hospital in Milan for recuperation. He spent six months in the hospital where he met and fell in love with Agnes von Kurowsky, a Red Cross nurse seven years older than he. Agnes and Hemingway planned to marry; however, she became engaged to an Italian officer in March 1919. Biographer Jeffrey Meyers claims Hemingway was devastated by Agnes' rejection, and in future relationships he followed a pattern of abandoning a wife before she abandoned him.

Toronto, Chicago and Paris

Hemingway returned home in early 1919, and spent the following summer in Michigan, fishing and camping with high school friends. The summer became the genesis for his Nick Adams' story "Big Two-Hearted River". He then moved to Toronto and began writing for the *Toronto Star Weekly* where he worked as a freelancer, staff writer, and foreign correspondent. In the fall of 1920, after having spent the summer in Michigan, he moved to Chicago for a short period while still filing stories for the *Toronto Star*. He also worked as associate editor of the monthly journal *Co-operative Commonwealth*. Hemingway met Hadley Richardson in Chicago. She was eight years older than he (and one year older than Agnes). They married on September 3, 1921; in November he became foreign correspondent for the *Toronto Star* and the couple left for Paris.

Sherwood Anderson gave Hemingway letters of introduction to Gertrude Stein and other writers he had recently met in Paris. Stein, who became Hemingway's mentor for a period, and introduced him to the "Parisian Modern Movement" in the Montparnasse Quarter, referred to the expatriate artists as the "Lost Generation". The group included writers and artists such "Ezra Pound, Gertrude Stein, Sylvia Beach, James Joyce, Max Eastman, Lincoln Steffens and Wyndham Lewis [and] the painters Miro and Picasso." Eventually Hemingway withdrew from Stein's influence and their relationship deteriorated to a literary quarrel that spanned decades. Hemingway and Ezra Pound forged a friendship; and Pound mentored the young writer in whom he recognized a natural talent. They met in February 1922, toured Italy together in 1923, and lived on the same street in 1924.Sylvia Beach, who published James Joyce's *Ulysses*, owned the bookshop Shakespeare and Company that was a popular gathering place for writers, where Hemingway met Joyce in March 1922. The two writers frequently embarked on "alcoholic sprees."

Hemingway covered the Greco-Turkish War for the *Toronto Star*, where he witnessed the burning of Smyrna. He also wrote travel pieces such as "Tuna Fishing in Spain", "Trout Fishing All Across Europe: Spain Has the Best, Then Germany", and he wrote about bullfighting—"Pamplona in July; World's Series of Bull Fighting a Mad, Whirling Carnival". In December 1922 Hemingway was devastated when Hadley lost a suitcase filled with his manuscripts at the Gare de Lyons as she was travelling from Paris to Geneva to meet him. When Hadley became pregnant in 1923 they returned to Toronto where their son John Hadley Nicanor was born on October 10, 1923. They returned to Paris at the beginning of the new year in 1924, and Hemingway decided to stop writing for the *Toronto Star*, recreate the lost stories, and begin writing for publication. Also in 1924 Hemingway assisted Ford Madox Ford in editing *The Transatlantic Review*. Ford published works by Pound, John Dos Passos, and Gertrude Stein, as well as some of Hemingway's early stories such as "Indian Camp". When Hemingway's first collection of short stories, "In Our Time" was published in 1925, the dust jacket included comments from Ford. Six months earlier, Hemingway had met F. Scott Fitzgerald, and they began a friendship of "admiration and hostility."

In the summer of 1925, Hemingway and Hadley went on their annual trip to Pamplona to the Festival of San Fermín accompanied by a group of American and British ex-patriates. The events of the trip inspired Hemingway's first novel, *The Sun Also Rises*. He finished the first draft in two months. During the next six months he revised the manuscript as his marriage to Hadley began to disintegrate. Scribner's published *The Sun Also Rises* in October 1926. Hemingway divorced Hadley in January 1927, and in May married Pauline Pfeiffer. Pfeiffer wrote for *Vanity Fair* and worked for *Vogue* in Paris. Hemingway converted to Catholicism to marry Pauline. *Men Without Women*, a collection of short stories, containing *The Killers*, was published in October 1927. By the end of the year Pauline was pregnant, and on the recommendation of Dos Passos, Hemingway and Pauline moved to Key West. After his departure from Paris, Hemingway "never again lived in a big city."

Key West and the Caribbean

Hemingway's second son Patrick was born in Kansas City on June 28, 1928. Pauline's labor was difficult and she had a Caesarean. For a time they lived with Pauline's parents at the Pfeiffer House in Piggott, Arkansas, where Hemingway worked on *A Farewell to Arms*. After Patrick's birth Hemingway travelled to Wyoming, Massachusetts and New York. That December, Hemingway's father shot himself with his own father's (Hemingway's grandfather's) American Civil War pistol, having suffered ill health, depression and financial difficulties.

Hemingway continued to travel extensively, returning to France and Spain in the summer of 1929 to gather material for *Death in the Afternoon*. *A Farewell to Arms* was published in September of that year.

Hemingway spent winters in Key West, and summers in Wyoming where he found "the most beautiful country he had seen in the American West" and where the hunting included deer, elk, and grizzly bear. His third son, Gregory, was born on November 12, 1931. Also In 1931, Pauline's uncle bought the couple a house. In a converted den on the second floor of the "carriage house" Hemingway had a space to work. While in Key West he also spent time fishing the waters around the Dry Tortugas with his longtime friend Waldo Peirce, and at Sloppy Joe's.

In 1933, Hemingway and Pauline travelled to Africa for ten weeks. The trip provided material for *Green Hills of Africa,* and the short stories "The Snows of Kilimanjaro" and "The Short Happy Life of Francis Macomber". He visited Mombasa, Nairobi, and Machakos in Kenya, then Tanganyika on safari, where he hunted in the Serengeti, around Lake Manyara and west and southeast of the present-day Tarangire National Park. He contracted amoebic dysentery causing a prolapsed intestine and he was evacuated to Nairobi by plane, an experience reflected in "The Snows of Kilimanjaro". On this trip Hemingway's guide was Philip Hope Percival, who had guided Theodore Roosevelt on his 1909 safari. Hemingway began writing *Green Hills of Africa* as soon as he returned, which was published in 1935.

Back in Key West, Hemingway bought a boat in 1934, named it the "Pilar", and began sailing the Caribbean. In 1935 he discovered Bimini where he spent considerable time. During this period he also worked on *To Have and Have Not,* published in 1937 when he was in Spain, and the only novel he wrote during the 1930s.

Spanish Civil War and World War II

In 1937 Hemingway reported on the Spanish Civil War for the North American Newspaper Alliance (NANA). He arrived in France in March, and in Spain ten days later with Dutch filmmaker Joris Ivens. Ivens was filming *The Spanish Earth* working with John Dos Passos as screen writer. However, Dos Passos wanted to leave because his friend Jose Robles had been arrested (and was later executed), so he passed the screen-writing work over to Hemingway. At that time Dos Passos changed his opinion of the republicans, causing a rift between himself and Hemingway who spread a rumor that Dos Passos was a coward when he left Spain. Journalist Martha Gellhorn, whom Hemingway had met in Key West in 1936, joined him in Spain. Hemingway and Gellhorn continued their relationship during the war, until Hemingway divorced Pauline in 1940. Pauline, a devout Catholic, sided with the pro-Catholic nationalists; whereas Hemingway supported the republicans. Hemingway wrote *The Fifth Column*, his only piece of drama, during the bombardment of Madrid in 1937. His involvement with the republicans and the International Brigade may have gone so far as teaching young Spaniards how to use rifles. In 1938, after having returned home to Key West for a few months, Hemingway returned to Spain and was present at the Battle of the Ebro, the last republican stand. With fellow British and American journalists, Hemingway rowed the group across the river, some of the last to leave the battle. A later letter to XI International Brigade's commander Hans Kahle gives the impression, as if he had seen the war as an exciting adventure.

Hemingway and Martha Gellhorn moved to Cuba in 1939, and in 1940 bought the "Finca Vigia" which they had been renting. A few months later Hemingway divorced Pauline and married Martha. During that period he wrote *For Whom the Bell Tolls,* which he began in March 1939, finished in July 1940, and which was published in October 1940. As he wrote *For Whom the Bell Tolls* he travelled from Cuba to Wyoming to Sun Valley, Idaho. He also changed the location of his homes, as he had after his split with Hadley, moving his primary summer residence to Ketchum, Idaho, just outside of the newly built resort Sun Valley, having already moved his winter residence from Key West to Cuba. In January 1941, Martha was sent to China on assignment for Collier's magazine, and Hemingway accompanied her. Although Hemingway wrote dispatches for PM, he had little affinity for China.

When he returned to Cuba, after the beginning of World War II, Hemingway refitted the Pilar to hunt down German submarines. From June to December 1944, he was in Europe, and was present at the D-Day landing. He then attached himself to "the 22nd Regiment commanded by Col. Charles "Buck" Lanaham as it drove toward Paris", and he also had a small band of village militia in Rambouillet outside of Paris. Of Hemingway's exploits, a war historian remarks: " 'Hemingway got into considerable trouble playing infantry captain to a group of Resistance people that he gathered because a correspondent is not supposed to lead troops, even if he does it well.' " On August 25 he was present at the liberation of Paris, though the assertion that he was first in the city, or that he liberated the Ritz is considered part of the Hemingway legend. While in Paris he attended a reunion hosted by Sylvia Beach and also made up his long feud with Gertrude Stein. Hemingway was present at heavy fighting in the Hürtgenwald at the end 1944.

When Hemingway arrived in Europe, he met Time correspondent Mary Welsh in London. During the war his marriage to Martha disintegrated and the last time he saw her was in March 1945 as he was preparing to return to Cuba. In 1947 Hemingway was awarded a Bronze Star for his bravery during World War II. His valor for having been " 'under fire in combat areas in order to obtain an accurate picture of conditions,' " was recognized, with the commendation that " 'Through his talent of expression, Mr. Hemingway enabled readers to obtain a vivid picture of the difficulties and triumphs of the front-line soldier and his organization in combat.' "

Life in Cuba

Hemingway married Mary Welsh in March 1946, and five months later she suffered an ectopic pregnancy. Hemingway and Mary suffered a series of accidents after the war: in 1945 Hemingway had a car accident and injured his knee, and over the next five years Mary suffered a number of broken bones. In 1947 his sons Patrick and Gregory had a car accident and Gregory suffered a serious illness as a consequence. Also the 1940s was a decade when many of Hemingway's friends died. In 1939 Yeats and Ford Madox Ford died; in 1940 Scott Fitzgerald died; in 1941 Sherwood Anderson and James Joyce died; in 1946 Gertrude Stein died; and the following year in 1947, Max Perkins, Hemingway's long time editor and friend, died.

Hemingway began to suffer from ill health: headaches, high blood pressure, weight problems, depression, and eventually diabetes, although he was also working on the manuscript of *The Garden of Eden*. In 1948 Hemingway and Mary travelled to Europe, and in Italy he visited the site of his World War I accident. Soon thereafter he began work on *Across the River and Into the Woods*, which he worked on through 1949 and published it in 1950. In 1951 he completed the draft of *Old Man and the Sea* in eight weeks and considered it "the best I can write ever for all of my life." *The Old Man and the Sea* won the Pulitzer Prize in May 1952, a month before he left for his second trip to Africa. In Africa he was seriously injured in two successive plane crashes: he sprained his right shoulder, arm, and left leg; had a concussion; temporarily lost vision in his left eye and the hearing in his left ear; suffered paralysis of the spine; had a crushed vertebra, ruptured liver, spleen and kidney; and sustained first degree burns on his face, arms, and leg. Some American newspapers published his obituary, believing he had been killed. A month later he was again badly injured in a bushfire accident, which left him with second degree burns on his legs, front torso, lips, left hand and right forearm.

In October 1954, Hemingway received the Nobel Prize. Because he was in pain as a result of the African accidents, and had recently returned home to Cuba after a an absence of almost a full year, Hemingway chose not to travel to Stockholm to accept the prize in person. Instead he sent a speech to be read in which he defines the writer's life: "Writing, at its best, is a lonely life. Organizations for writers palliate the writer's loneliness but I doubt if they improve his writing. He grows in public stature as he sheds his loneliness and often his work deteriorates. For he does his work alone and if he is a good enough writer he must face eternity, or the lack of it, each day."

During the mid-1950s, Hemingway was often ill and he was bedridden from late 1956 to early 1957. The Finca Vigia became crowded with guests and tourists. He became disaffected with life in Cuba and considered a permanent move to Idaho. In 1959 he bought a home, overlooking the Big Wood River, outside of Ketchum and left Cuba, although he apparently remained on easy terms with the Castro government, going so far as telling the *New York Times* he was "delighted" with Castro's overthrow of Havana. However, the Hemingway account "The Shot" is used by Cabrera Infante and others as evidence of conflict between Hemingway and Fidel Castro dating back to 1948 and the killing of "Manolo" Castro, a friend of Hemingway. In 1960, he left Cuba and Finca Vigía for the last time. The Cuban government claims that after her husband's death, Mary Welsh Hemingway deeded the home to the Cuban government, which made it into a museum devoted to the author. In fact, the house was appropriated after the Bay of Pigs invasion, complete with Hemingway's collection of "four to six thousand books". The Hemingways lost their home, and were forced to leave art and manuscripts in a bank vault in Havana.

Idaho and Suicide

In 1957 he began *A Moveable Feast,* which he worked on in Cuba and Idaho from 1957 to 1960. In 1959, his passion for bullfighting was renewed when he spent the summer in Spain for a series of bullfight articles he was to write for Life Magazine. The following winter the manuscript grew to 63,000 words—*Life* only wanted 10,000 words and he asked his friend A.E Hotchner for help organizing the manuscript. Although Hemingway's mental deterioration was noticeable, he travelled to Spain to gather photographs for the manuscript. Alone in Spain, without Mary, Hemingway's mental state disintegrated rapidly. *Life* published the first installment in September 1960 to good reviews. Hemingway left Spain, travelled straight to Idaho, and in November he entered the Mayo Clinic in Minnesota. He was registered as George Saviers, the name of his physician from Sun Valley. He had been receiving treatment for high blood pressure and liver problems, and he may have believed he was going to be treated for hypertension. Also, Hemingway suffered paranoia, believing he was being watched by the FBI. In fact, the FBI had opened a file on him during WWII when he used the Pilar to patrol the waters off Cuba, and J. Edgar Hoover had an agent in Havana watching Hemingway during the 1950s. The FBI knew Hemingway was at the Mayo, as an agent documented in a letter written in January, 1961. Hemingway suffered real problems as well: his eyesight was failing; his health was poor; and his home and possessions had been lost in Cuba (spring, 1961).

In the spring of 1961, three months after his initial treatment at the Mayo with a series of ECT treatment, Hemingway attempted suicide. Mary convinced Saviers to an immediate hospitalization at the Sun Valley hospital, and from there he was returned to the Mayo for more shock treatments. He was released in late June and arrived home in Ketchum on June 30. On the morning of July 2, 1961, he committed suicide by shooting himself with his shotgun. Arriving at 7:40

a.m., Dr. Scott Earle certified the death. Because foul play was ruled out an inquest was not required under Idaho state law.

Other members of Hemingway's immediate family also committed suicide, including his father Clarence Hemingway; his sister Ursula; his brother Leicester; and his granddaughter Margaux Hemingway. During his last years, Hemingway's behavior was similar to his father's before he committed suicide. Hemingway's father may had the genetic disease haemochromatosis in which the inability to metabolize iron culminates in mental and physical deterioration. Medical records, available in 1991, in fact confirm that Hemingway's haemochromatosis had been diagnosed early in 1961. Additionally, Hemingway had been a heavy drinker for most of his life.

Notable Works

During his Paris years, in addition to filing stories for the *Toronto Star*, Hemingway published short stories in various journals; the Parisian edition of the short story collection *in our time* (1924); the *Three Stories and Ten Poems* (1924); and the revised and renamed American edition of *In Our Time* (1925). Hemingway wrote the satire *The Torrents of Spring* in an effort to break his contract with his publisher Boni and Liveright. According to the contract Boni and Liveright were to publish Hemingway's next three books, one of which was to be a novel, with the proviso that if a newly submitted work were to be rejected the contract would be terminated. Written in ten days, *The Torrents of Spring* was a satirical treatment of pretentious writers. Hemingway submitted the manuscript early in

December 1925, and it was rejected by the end of the month. In January Max Perkins at Scribner's agreed to publish *The Torrents of Spring* in addition to Hemingway's future work.

The Sun Also Rises (1926), was Hemingway's first novel. Written in 1925 and published in 1926, *The Sun Also Rises* (initially named *Fiesta*) was an autobiographical novel that epitomized the post-war expatriate generation for future generations. In *The Sun Also Rises,* Hemingway melds Paris to Spain; vividly depicts the running of the bulls in Pamplona; presents the symmetry of bullfighting as a place to face death; and blends the frenzy of the fiesta with the tranquility of the Spanish landscape. The novel is generally considered Hemingway's best work. *The Sun Also Rises* was adapted to film in 1957.

Men Without Women (1927) was Hemingway's second collection of short stories. The volume consists of fourteen stories, ten of which had been previously published in magazines. The story subjects include bullfighting, infidelity, divorce and death. "The Killers", "Hills Like White Elephants" and "In Another Country" are considered to be among Hemingway's best work.

Published in 1929, *A Farewell to Arms,* on the surface, is about the tragic romance between an American soldier Frederic Henry, and Catherine Barkley, a British nurse. The novel is autobiographical and the plot inspired by his earlier relationship with Agnes von Kurowsky in Milan; Catherine's parturition mirrors Pauline's difficult labour with Patrick. Below the surface, the novel is about World War I and individual tragedy within the larger picture of greater tragedy. The novel portrays the cynicism of soldiers, the displacement of populations. Hemingway's stature as an American writer was secured with the publication of *A Farewell to Arms. A Farewell to Arms* was adapted to film in 1932 and again in 1957.

Death in the Afternoon, a book about bullfighting, was published in 1932. Hemingway became an aficionado of the sport after seeing the Pamplona fiesta in the 1920s, fictionalized in *The Sun Also Rises.* In *Death in the Afternoon,* Hemingway explores the metaphysics of bullfighting—the ritualized, almost religious practice—that he considered analgous to the writer's search for meaning and the essence of life. In bullfighting, he found the elemental nature of life and death. In his writings on Spain, he was influenced by the Spanish master Pío Baroja. When Hemingway won the Nobel Prize, he traveled to see Baroja, then on his death bed, specifically to tell him he thought Baroja deserved the prize more than he. Baroja agreed and something of the usual Hemingway tiff with another writer ensued despite his original good intentions.

Green Hills of Africa (1935) initially appeared in serialization in Scribner's magazine, and was published in 1935. An autobiographical journal of his 1933 trip to Africa, Hemingway presents the subject of big game hunting in a non-fiction form in *Green Hills of Africa.*

To Have and Have Not (1937) is Hemingway's only novel set in the United States. Written sporadically between 1935 and 1937, and revised as he travelled back and forth from the Spanish Civil War, *To Have and Have Not* is a novel about Key West and Cuba. The novel also addresses social commentary of the 1930s, and received mixed critical reception. *To Have or Have Not* was adapted to film in 1944, starring Humphrey Bogart and Lauren Bacall.

The Fifth Column and the First Forty-Nine Stories was published in 1938, with Hemingway's only play *The Fifth Column* and 49 short stories. Hemingway's intention was, as he openly stated in his foreword, to write more. Many of the stories of the collection exist in other collections, including *In Our Time, Men Without Women, Winner Take Nothing,* and *The Snows of Kilimanjaro.* Some of the collection's important stories include "Old Man at the Bridge", "On The Quai at Smyrna", "Hills Like White Elephants", "One Reader Writes", "The Killers" and "A Clean, Well-Lighted Place". While these stories are rather short, the book also includes some longer stories, among them "The Snows of Kilimanjaro" and "The Short Happy Life of Francis Macomber".

Hemingway wrote *For Whom the Bell Tolls* in Cuba, Key West, and Sun Valley, Idaho in 1939. In Cuba, he lived in the Hotel Ambos-Mundos where he worked on the manuscript. The novel was finished in July 1940, and published in October. The novel is based on his experiences during the Spanish Civil War, with an American protagonist named Robert Jordan who fights with Spanish soldiers for the republicans. The novel has three types of characters: those who are purely fictional; those based on real people but fictionalized; and those who were actual figures in the war. Set in Andalusia, in the town of Ronda, the action takes place during four days and three nights. *For Whom the Bell Tolls* became a Book-of-the-month choice, sold half a million copies within months, was nominated for a Pulitzer Prize, and became a literary triumph for Hemingway. In 1944, the novel was adapted to film, starring Gary Cooper and Ingrid Bergman.

Across the River and into the Trees (1950) is set in post-World War II Venice. Initially serialized in *Cosmopolitan Magazine,* the novel was criticized for being an unsuitable autobiography; and for presenting the protagonist, Cantwell, as a bitter soldier. For the first time Hemingway received bad reviews for a novel, to which he responded in an interview with the *New York Times*: " 'Sure they can say anything about nothing happening in *Across the River,* all that happens is the defense of the lower Piave, the breakthrough in Normandy, the taking of Paris...plus a man who loves a girl and dies' ". Generally the novel is considered better than the critical reviews he received upon publication.

Written in 1951, and published in 1952, *The Old Man and the Sea* is the final work published during Hemingway's lifetime. The book was featured in Life Magazine on September 1, 1952, and five million copies of the magazine were sold in two days. *The Old Man and the Sea* also became a Book-of-the Month selection, and made Hemingway a celebrity. The novella received the Pulitzer Prize in May, 1952, and contributed to his receiving the Nobel Prize in Literature in 1954. Upon receiving the latter he noted that Carl Sandburg or Isak Dinesen were both worthy of winning; but he expressed happiness and claimed to " 'need the dough' ". The success of *The Old Man and the Sea* made Hemingway an international celebrity. *The Old Man and the Sea* is taught at schools around the world and continues to earn foreign royalties.

Hemingway began *The Garden of Eden* in 1946 and wrote 800 pages. The novel was published posthumously in a much-abridged form in 1986. Early in 1950 he started work on a "sea trilogy", to consist of three sections: "The Sea When Young" (set in Bimini); "The Sea When Absent" (set in Havana); and "The Sea in Being". The latter was published in 1952 as *The Old Man and the Sea*.He also wrote an unpublished "Sea-Chase" story which his wife and editor combined with the stories about the islands, renamed *Islands in the Stream* and published in 1970.

Posthumous Works

In 1956 Hemingway found a trunk left in the basement of the Ritz Hotel in Paris. The trunk contained notebooks he filled during the years he lived in Paris. He had the notebooks transcribed, and during the period he worked on *A Dangerous Summer* he finished the Paris manuscript also. Scribner's published *A Moveable Feast* in 1964 after Hemingway's death. A rewritten edition of the novel has been published in late 2009, with revisions made by Hemingway's grandson. The restorations are based on a " 'typed manuscript with original notations in Hemingway's hand - the last draft of the book that he ever worked on' " and are apparently closer to the final version intended by Hemingway.

Published in 1970, *Islands in the Stream* is largely autobiographical. Hemingway began work on the novel in 1946 and kept it in a bank vault during the last years of his life. In a note forwarding *Islands in the Stream,* Mary Hemingway indicated that she worked with Charles Scribner, Jr. on "preparing this book for publication from Ernest's original manuscript." She also stated that "beyond the routine chores of correcting spelling and punctuation, we made some cuts in the manuscript, I feel that Ernest would surely have made them himself. The book is all Ernest's. We have added nothing to it." The novel is his seventh novel, and he conceived it as a trilogy about the sea, using the working title "The Sea Book".

The Nick Adams Stories was published in 1972. A full compilation of Hemingway's short stories was published as *The Complete Short Stories Of Ernest Hemingway*, was published in 1987. As well, in 1969 *The Fifth Column and Four Stories of the Spanish Civil War* was published. It contains Hemingway's only full length play, *The Fifth Column*, which was previously published along with the *First Forty-Nine Stories* in 1938, along with four unpublished works about Hemingway's experiences during the Spanish Civil War.

Although not published until 1985, Hemingway worked on the draft of the *The Dangerous Summer*. during 1959. He finished the manuscript (which grew beyond the original scope) in the spring of 1960 and sent it to *Life* for serialization. The first installment was published in September, 1960. The initial project was to write about the matadors Ordonez and his brother-in-law Dominguin and their "mano a mano duel between two matadors".

Early in 1946 Hemingway began work on *Garden of Eden* and had written eight hundred pages by the following summer. For fifteen years he continued to work on the novel which remained uncompleted. It was published in 1986, consisting of 30 chapters and 70,000 words. The publisher's "note" admits that cuts were made to the novel, and according to biographers, Hemingway had achieved 48 chapters and 200,000 words. Scribner's removed a as much as two thirds of the extant manuscript and one long subplot.

True at First Light was published in 1999. The book is a presented as a "fictional memoir" and was edited by Hemingway's second son, Patrick Hemingway. Six years later the work was republished a second time as *Under Kilimanjaro*. The work is based on a partially written manuscript, and is about Hemingway's second trip to Africa. *Under Kilimanjaro* was edited by Robert W. Lewis and Robert E. Fleming who state: "this book deserves as complete and faithful a publication as possible without editorial distortion, speculation, or textually unsupported attempts at improvement."

Also published posthumously were several collections of his work as a journalist. These contain his columns and articles for Esquire Magazine, The North American Newspaper Alliance, and the Toronto *Star*; they include *Byline: Ernest Hemingway* edited by William White, and *Hemingway: The Wild Years* edited by Gene Z. Hanrahan. In 2006, a collection of miscellenea such as "statements, prefaces, blurbs", written by Hemingway was edited by Matthew J. Bruccoli.

Hemingway was a prolific correspondent and, in 1981, many of his letters were published by Scribner's in *Ernest Hemingway Selected Letters* edited by Carlos Baker. Although Hemingway wrote to his executors in 1958 asking that his letters not be published, Mary Hemingway made the decision to publish the letters in 1979. Further letters were published in a book of his correspondence with his editor Max Perkins, *The Only Thing that Counts* in 1996.

Writing Style

Reviewing Hemingway's first novel in 1926, the *New York Times* wrote: "No amount of analysis can convey the quality of *The Sun Also Rises*. It is a truly gripping story, told in a lean, hard, athletic narrative prose that puts more literary English to shame". *The Sun Also Rises* is written in the spare, tightly written prose for which Hemingway is famous, a style which has influenced countless crime and pulp fiction novels. It is a style which some critics consider Hemingway's greatest contribution to literature. But the simplicity is deceptive. Hemingway uses polysyndeton to convey both a timeless immediacy and a Biblical grandeur. Hemingway's polysyndetonic sentence—or, in later works, his use of subordinate clauses—uses conjunctions to juxtapose startling visions and images; the critic Jackson Benson has compared them to haikus. Many of Hemingway's acolytes misinterpreted his lead and frowned upon all expression of emotion; Saul Bellow satirized this style as "Do you have emotions? Strangle them." Hemingway, however, was not trying to eliminate emotion but to portray it more scientifically.

Hemingway thought it would be easy, and pointless, to describe emotions; he sculpted his bright and finely chiseled collages of images in order to grasp "the real thing, the sequence of motion and fact which made the emotion and which would be as valid in a year or in ten years or, with luck and if you stated it purely enough, always". This use of an image as an objective correlative is characteristic of Ezra Pound, T.S. Eliot, James Joyce, and of course Proust compares Hemingway's and Proust's use of memory to find the objective correlative. Hemingway's letters refer to Proust's *Remembrance of Things Past* several times over the years, and indicate he might have read the massive book at least twice and is also part of the Japanese poetic canon. Hemingway's writing style, in other words, is not artless but poetic.

Bibliography

Alpana Sharma. *New Immigrant Literatures in the United States: A Sourcebook to Our Multicultural Literary Heritage*. Knippling Westport, Connecticut: Greenwood, 1996.

Andrews, W., Foster, F., and Harris, T. (Editors).*The Oxford Companion to African American Literature*. Oxford, 1997.

Baym, Nina, ed. *The Norton Anthology of American Literature*. New York: W.W. Norton & Company, 2007.

Brodhead, R. "An Anatomy of Multiculturalism". *Yale Alumni Magazine*, April 1994. Excerpted here.

Campbell, Donna M. "The Early American Novel: Introductory Notes." *Literary Movements*. 14 July 2008. 1 March 2010.

Davis, Gwenn. *Drama by women to 1900: a bibliography of American and British writers*. London: Mansell, 1992.

Davis, M., Graham, M., and Pineault-Burke, S. (Editors). *Teaching African American Literature: Theory and Practice*. Routledge, 1998.

Emmanuel S. Nelson, *Asian American Novelists: A Bio-Bibliographical Critical Sourcebook*. Westport, Connecticut: Greenwood Press, 2000.

Gates, H. *The Trials of Phillis Wheatley: America's First Black Poet and Her Encounters With the Founding Fathers* Basic Civitas Books, 2003

Gilyard, K., and Wardi, A. *African American Literature*. Penguin, 2004.

Groden, M., and Krieswirth, M. (Editors). "African-American Theory and Criticism" from the *Johns Hopkins Guide to Literary Theory and Criticism*

Grossman, J. "Historical Research and Narrative of Chicago and the Great Migration".

Gura, Philip F. *American Transcendentalism: A History*. New York: Hill and Wang, 2007: 7–8.

Hamilton, Kristie. "An Assault on the Will: Republican Virtue and the City in Hannah Webster Foster's "The Coquette." *Early American Literature*.24.2: (1989) 135-151.

Jay, G. *American Literature and the Culture Wars*. Cornell University Press, 1997. Excerpted here.

John Callahan, Ph.D., *In the African-American Grain: Call and Response in Twentieth-Century Black Fiction*, University of Illinois Press, reprint ed., 2001.

Kimball, Roger, Existentialism, Semiotics and Iced Tea, Review of Conversations with Walker Percy, New York Times, August 4, 1985, Accessed September 24, 2006

Lowney, J. "Haiti and Black Transnationalism: Remapping the Migrant Geography of Home to Harlem" *African American Review*, Fall, 2000.

McKay, N., and Gates, H. (Editors). *The Norton Anthology of African American Literature, Second Edition*. W. W. Norton & Company, 2004.

Mitchem, S. "No Longer Nailed to the Floor". *Cross Currents*, spring, 2003.

Nishikawa, K. "African American Critical Theory." *The Greenwood Encyclopedia of Multiethnic American Literature*. Ed. Emmanuel S. Nelson. 5 vols. Westport, CT: Greenwood Press, 2005. 36-41.

Nishikawa, K. "Crime and Mystery Fiction." *The Greenwood Encyclopedia of African American Literature*. Ed. Hans Ostrom and J. David Macey, Jr. 5 vols. Westport, CT: Greenwood Press, 2005. 360-67.

Rutherford, Mildred. *American Authors*.Atlanta: The Franklin Printing and Publishing Co., 1902.

Schweitzer, Ivy. "Review: *Early American Literature*. 23.2: (1988) 221-225. "JSTOR." Web. 1 March 2010.

Wilmeth, Don B. *American and English popular entertainment: a guide to information sources*. Detroit, MI: Gale Research Co., c1980.

Index